Where was Rebecca Shot?

━━━━

Curiosities, Puzzles,
and Conundrums in
Modern Fiction

━━━━

John Sutherland

Weidenfeld & Nicolson

Also by John Sutherland

Thackeray at Work

Victorian Novelists and Publishers

Fictions and the Fiction Industry

Bestsellers

Offensive Literature

The Longman Companion to Victorian Fiction

Mrs Humphry Ward: Eminent Victorian,
Pre-eminent Edwardian

Sir Walter Scott

Victorian Novelists, Publishers, and Readers

Is Heathcliff a Murderer?

Can Jane Eyre be Happy?

First published in Great Britain in 1998
by Weidenfeld & Nicolson

1998 John Sutherland

The moral right of John Sutherland to be identified as the
author of this work has been asserted in accordance with
the Copyright, Designs and Patents Act of 1988

A CIP catalogue record for this book is available from the British Library.

ISBN 0 297 84146 7

Printed in Great Britain by Butler & Tanner Ltd,
Frome and London

Weidenfeld & Nicolson
The Orion Publishing Group Ltd
Orion House
5 Upper Saint Martin's Lane
London, WC2H 9EA

Contents

The Joy of Puzzles

> In reading one should notice and fondle details. There is
> nothing wrong about the moonshine of generalization when
> it comes *after* the saucy trifles of the book have been lovingly
> collected.
>
> (Vladimir Nabokov, introducing his course on the novel
> to students at Cornell University in the 1950s)[1]

Marianne Moore's formulation—about poetry giving us real
toads in imaginary gardens—can be reversed for fiction.
Novels, that is, give us imaginary toads (Heathcliffs) in
real gardens (Yorkshire). This book is an investigation into
the clash of toad/garden categories: the collision of fictional
with real worlds and the enjoyable (I hope) puzzlement such
collisions create.

I became interested in such puzzles in two way: annotating
Victorian fiction (mainly for the World's Classics series)[2]
and reviewing contemporary fiction (mainly for the *London
Review of Books*). I recall as significant being given to
review for the *LRB* a collection of stories by William Boyd
(a writer I admire) called *On the Yankee Station* (1981).
Boyd's title story was set on an American aircraft carrier
on active service in the South China Sea, off Vietnam.
The plot revolved around a practice called 'fragging'—the
assassination of unpopular officers by disgruntled enlisted
men.[3] In the story a spectacularly disgruntled seaman
'frags' a pilot-officer by jamming the steam catapult used
for assisted take-off. Lieutenant Larry Pfizer's Crusader
plane, without the necessary acceleration, plunges into the
sea, loaded with napalm, killing its luckless occupant (and
sparing innumerable Vietnamese innocents from an even
more horrible death than drowning). The seaman carries out
his sabotage by means of a beer can full of sand, strategically
placed in the carrier's deck machinery. There are many such

empty cans around—the *Chester B.* is a bibulous and not
particularly tidy vessel.

The problem is, the US Navy, unlike its British counterpart, is (one is told) 'dry' when at sea. American seamen
and their officers have neither access to alcohol nor the cans
it comes in. I wrote to Mr Boyd, and received a courteous
reply indicating (as I recall) that he had not been aware of
the fact. But neither would most of his readers be aware
of it. It remains a small puzzle, of no importance in itself,
but teasing if one dwells on it. The object in question cannot
easily be changed (to a Coke can, for instance), because surly
drunkenness figures centrally in the narrative. Good order
and morale, one concludes, had so deteriorated during that
unhappy war that US Navy regulations were routinely and
openly flouted. No wonder the Americans lost.

What doesn't particularly interest me are banal lapses of
vraisemblance, what film buffs call 'bloopers' and literary
critics *Scheinprobleme*. The all-action film *Die Hard II* (1990),
for example, is set in Chicago's O'Hare airport 'snowed in' at
Christmas. The hero, Bruce Willis (in one of his rare intervals
from blowing away bad guys), is shown making a call on a
Pac-Bell public phone in the airport concourse. Such phones
are restricted, of course, to the Western States. The blunder
was noted by many American film-goers, who good-naturedly
saw it as no more improbable than Willis's blowing up (as he
does in the last scene) a jumbo-jet with a Zippo cigarette
lighter. It's not a movie in which the canons of realism have
strict authority.

A (literally) titanic blooper was noticed by a reader of
the *Spectator*, Mr Norman Cleland, in the correspondence
columns of the magazine (7 February 1998):

Sir: Yesterday I saw the *Titanic* film. Twice during the *Titanic*'s
approach to the looming iceberg, ship's officers refer to steering
'starboard', yet the helm is turned to port. The ship undeniably
turns to port, and the iceberg scrapes the right side.

What's going on here?

What's going on, of course, is that most film audiences don't know as much about navigation as the hawk-eyed Mr Cleland.

Bloopers of this kind can be found frequently enough in prose fiction. John Braine, at the sad end of his career, brought out a novel called *One and Last Love* (1981). Braine's personal life was going badly, he was drinking heavily, his health was poor (he was to die of a burst stomach ulcer, in 1986), and his reputation had sunk disastrously from the high point of *Room at the Top* (1962).

One and Last Love begins with a bedroom scene:

We're lying in bed in a flat off Monkman Street, off Shaftesbury Avenue, at four o'clock on a June afternoon. The bed is king-sized, with a white padded headboard and matching white bedside cupboards, with a pink-shaded bedside lamp on each. (p. 10)

Four pages later, during the same scene, we are given the following description of the same Monkman Street love nest:

The room is lofty for its size. It's large enough comfortably to accommodate the king-sized bed, the large mahogany wardrobe, two mahogany bedside tables, and a mahogany dressing table. The bed is modern, the rest of the furniture was, I think, bought new when the first tenant moved in . . . I like the room as it is, want nothing to change. (pp. 14–15)

Something has changed—the bedside tables.

This lapse in continuity is of no importance except as an index of Braine's professional deterioration and the total indifference of his publisher, Eyre Methuen, who clearly did not even cursorily bother to edit the novel (ironically, it is dedicated to 'Geoffrey Strachan: best of editors'). John Braine, one assumes, was a lost cause.

Bloopers are of little interest beyond the transient and rather discreditable pleasure of catching authors out. Careless writing is, in itself, less reprehensible than the much more common vice of careless reading. Nor am I interested in the licence which romantic fiction has traditionally allowed itself. In Jackie Collins's *American Star* (1993, the first bodice-ripper, as I believe, to have carried a 'safe-sex' warning) the heroine is said to have visited, from her Beverly Hills hotel, Disneyland, Magic Mountain and the Universal Studios theme park in the same day. Since these pleasure resorts lie at distances of up to fifty miles in different points of the compass from each other, and require travel on crowded freeways, the exploit—if true—would merit a listing in the *Guinness Book of Records*. But, of course, one accepts it in the same forgiving spirit as the stud-hero's amazingly priapic sexual exploits.

Much more interesting are the issues raised wittily by Julian Barnes in Chapter 6 of *Flaubert's Parrot*. Barnes (through his narrator, Geoffrey Braithwaite) makes the point that the only reliable critics of the novel are the novelists themselves. Trust the tale, the teller, but never the outsider who presumes to tell you (and sometimes even the teller) what the tale 'really means'.

Chapter 6 ('Emma Bovary's Eyes') opens, scathingly:

Let me tell you why I hate critics. Not for the normal reasons: that they're failed creators (they usually aren't; they may be failed critics, but that's another matter); or that they're by nature carping, jealous and vain (they usually aren't; if anything, they might better be accused of over-generosity, of upgrading the second-rate so that their own fine discriminations thereby appear the rarer). No, the reason I hate critics—well, some of the time—is that they write sentences like this:

> Flaubert does not build up his characters, as did Balzac,
> by objective, external description; in fact, so careless is
> he of their outward appearance that on one occasion he
> gives Emma [Bovary] brown eyes (14); on another deep
> black eyes (15) ; and on another blue eyes (16).

This precise and disheartening indictment was drawn up by the late Dr Enid Starkie, Reader Emeritus in French Literature at the University of Oxford, and Flaubert's most exhaustive British biographer. The numbers in her text refer to footnotes in which she spears the novelist with chapter and verse. (p. 74)[4]

Barnes–Braithwaite goes on to spear the luckless Dr

Starkie with *ad feminam* adversions on her physical appearance and professional expertise ('she had an atrocious French accent . . . Naturally this didn't affect her competence to teach at the University of Oxford'). More importantly, he establishes that the fluid hue of Emma's eyes is both well observed by Flaubert and a fine (intended) artistic effect. Barnes–Braithwaite's clinching piece of evidence (having, on the way, demolished much of the dead lady-critic's evidence) is a contemporary description of the woman on whom Emma Bovary was based: 'her eyes, of uncertain colour, green, grey, or blue, according to the light, had a pleading expression, which never left them' (p. 81).

Barnes–Braithwaite's anathema against 'critics' should be engraved in brass over the entrance to every university English department in the country. But the point one would make is that this wonderfully corrective outburst, which will enhance every reader's appreciation of Flaubert's genius, was stimulated by a 'real world' objection, a 'puzzle'—what colour(s) is (are) Emma's eyes? Rotten critic she may have been, Dr Starkie was the occasion of good criticism in her novelist opponent. So too I hope the following essays will stimulate or—failing that—amuse.

One of the advantages of writing about contemporary literature is that the authors are still around to make their opinions known. At the risk of finding myself at the sharp end of Mr Barnes's spear, I have asked him and others, where relevant, for comments on various puzzles. I have gathered their reactions in the last chapter in the volume: 'The Authors (and Other Experts) Respond'. In addition to these experts and authors, I should like to thank Guilland Sutherland, Jane Dietrich, Kasia Boddy, Phil Horne, René Weis, and Henry Woudhuysen.

What is Lionel Croy's 'Unspeakable' Crime?

Written in James's 'late' style, *The Wings of the Dove* artfully omits to tell us many things. Two pools of opacity obscure the early and later parts of the narrative. What, exactly, is Lionel Croy's 'unspeakable' offence? and what is the fatal disease that kills the radiant young American heiress, Milly Theale?[1] Interrogating these enigmas may seem as pointless as peering into the background of a Whistler nocturne. None the less most readers (and, after 1997, many film-goers), being only human, will be curious about what James, so deliberately, seems not to want to say. It is with Lionel Croy's enigmatic offence (crime? misdemeanour? misfortune?) that I am concerned here.

The something which has ruined Mr Croy's life and blighted the lives of his dependants features in the opening chapter in which Kate offers live-in companionship to her disgraced and recently widowed parent. Mr Croy has fallen in the world. He now lives by himself in seedy rooms in seedy Chirk Street. His health may not be good. He has just been to the chemist's shop (the 'beastly fellow at the corner'—why 'beastly'?) for an obscure prescription. Even after his fall, Mr Croy contrives to cut a 'wonderful' figure in his daughter's eyes:

He looked exactly as much as usual—all pink and silver as to skin and hair, all straightness and starch as to figure and dress; the man in the world least connected with anything unpleasant. He was so particularly the English gentleman. (p. 22)[2]

The English gentleman has, however, dabbled in things

unpleasant and, as we apprehend, 'ungentlemanly'. Perhaps even something 'un-English'. But his appearance is unblemished. James is at pains to stress that Mr Croy is, above all, a 'plausible' wrongdoer:

His plausibility had been the heaviest of her [Kate's] mother's crosses; inevitably so much more present to the world than whatever it was that was horrid—thank God they didn't really know!—that he had done. (p. 24)

Kate knows, but the world ('they') doesn't. Or does that 'they' mean Mrs Croy and her daughters don't really know? James's idiom is slippery.

The young lady's suitor, Merton Densher, poses Kate some circumspect questions about Mr Croy (it is odd that after a year's courtship the young man knows so little of his potential father-in-law). 'What was it, to speak plainly, that Mr Croy had originally done?' Merton asks. 'I don't know, and I don't want to,' replies Kate, 'plainly' but uninformatively. Whatever it was that made her father 'impossible' happened 'years' ago, she adds, 'when I was about fifteen' (p. 58). Kate is now twenty-five. Mr Croy left home, and reduced family circumstances led to Kate's eventually being boarded with her aunt (Mrs Lowder, we assume, has paid for the fashionable mourning clothes the young lady is wearing). The domestic *ménage* of the Croy ladies has—since Mr Croy's downfall—been straitened but not disastrously so. In various 'weak and expensive' attempts at 'economy', following the catastrophe of her husband's disgrace, Mrs Croy has retreated with her daughters to 'Dresden, to Florence, to Biarritz' (p. 74). These are not the resorts of the wholly impoverished. Reduced in circumstances the Croys may be, but Kate never for a moment thinks of work—that would be disgrace indeed.

Whatever it was that Mr Croy did cost him most of his bank balance. After her mother's death, Kate and her widowed elder sister Marian (mother of four) have been left £200-a-year apiece. This presumably arises out of the profit from the sale of the lease of the house in Lexham Gardens and the family furniture. At 5 per cent annual yield, this would represent an invested sum of £8,000. Kate, who is in self-sacrificial mood, has donated half of her little £200 fortune to her needier sister. She evidently calculates that she and her father can scrape by on whatever he has plus the remaining £100.

Merton politely objects that Kate's information is so 'vague' that he may jump to wrong conclusions: 'What has he done, if no one can name it?' Kate falls back on her customary riddles:

'He has done everything.'
  'Oh—everything! Everything's nothing.'
  'Well then,' said Kate, 'he has done some particular thing. It's known—only, thank God, not to us. But it has been the end of him.' (p. 59)

Merton goes on to inquire: 'Doesn't he belong to some club?'—can't he, that is, find something to do with himself other than impose on his daughter? He used to belong to many clubs, Kate replies, 'gravely'. He has dropped them? Merton asks: 'They've dropped *him*. Of that I'm sure,' she says. This is the only 'hard' piece of evidence one has as to Mr Croy's offence, and the reader clings on to it, like a drowning man to a plank.

To summarise. Mr Croy was once a man of substance and some position in London society. His profession—if he had a profession—is unknown to us; but he follows it no longer. Ten years ago he did 'something' in consequence of which he has been blackballed for life throughout the length and breadth of the West End. Kate claims not to know what 'vile' and 'odious' 'particular thing' her father has done. Neither, apparently, does the world 'know'. It did not get into the papers—otherwise the Fleet Street journalist Merton would not need to inquire on the subject. He would have picked it up from office gossip. Mr Croy has manifestly not been to prison nor, apparently, fallen foul of the police. Otherwise, we may be sure, he would not be living under his own name in the West End of London but skulking with disreputable *émigrés* like Sebastian Melmoth in Boulogne or Paris (if his funds ran to it) where a gentleman's 'unspeakable' tastes might be indulged without hindrance.

Film-makers have less licence for background cover-up than the elderly Henry James. In the 1997 screen version of *The Wings of the Dove*, the scriptwriters filled in James's teasing blank by building on the 'beastly' chemist. They made Mr Croy into an opium addict—a frequenter of low 'dens', with pig-tailed Chinese and other dazed degenerates puffing in the background. There is a historical plausibility in this narrative hypothesis.[3] Around the turn of the century the British authorities were beginning to take 'the opium problem' seriously. Public concern led to the International Opium Commission in 1909 and the Hague Convention on control of the drug in 1912. It is interesting, in view of the drug subplot, that the film-makers should have decided to bring forward the period of James's action from 1900 to 1910. Intentionally or unintentionally it makes the opium business historically plausible.

Opium use was still non-criminal at the time James was writing, but was increasingly frowned on. Being drunk in a London club was acceptable if not indulged in too often or too outrageously. Being visibly fuddled with opium— or introducing younger members to the 'vice' would be something else, and might conceivably lead to the universal blackballing Mr Croy has suffered.

Opium addiction would also fit the episode at the very end of the narrative when, like the bad penny he is, Lionel Croy turns up on his daughter Marian's doorstep at Christmas. He needs money ('that, of course, always', p. 412) and is later described as mysteriously indisposed—in bed, but 'not ill'. He is 'in a state which made it impossible not to take him in . . . in terror . . . of somebody—of something' (p. 426). Broke and suffering the pangs of withdrawal, we may deduce— particularly if we have seen the film. Opium fills the hole in James's narrative, but not entirely snugly. Lionel Croy is, when one weighs up all the facts, an unlikely drug fiend. And, surely, if so disposed he would, at this period, have been able to indulge his habit discreetly. Nor would cure be out of the question.

One group of contemporary critics feels quite able to 'name' Mr Croy's unnamable offence. The leading queer theorist of the 1990s, Eve Kosovsky Sedgwick, in her quaintly titled essay 'Is the Rectum Straight? Identification and Identity in *The Wings of the Dove*' (1994), 'outs' Lionel Croy. According to Sedgwick ('the queen of gay studies') Kate's father is self-evidently bent: 'an unspeakable of the Oscar Wilde sort', as E. M. Forster has his hero, Maurice, describe himself.

'Lionel Croy's homosexuality', as Sedgwick tells us, 'is spelled out in a simple code with deep historical roots: the code of *illum crimen horribile quod non nominandum est,* of "the crime not to be named among Christian men" and "the love that dare not speak its name." The code is, in short, that of naming something "unspeakable" as a way of denoting (without describing) male same-sex activity.'[4] If they followed Sedgwick, the film-makers should have shown Mr Croy in a hot bedroom clinch with a rent boy.[5]

Sedgwick's line is challenged by a less doctrinaire critic, Philip Horne. According to Horne, Sedgwick's reading of *The Wings of the Dove* (and other crucial texts, such as 'The Beast in the Jungle') depends on a false syllogism:

1. James writes about the unnamable.
2. Homosexuality has often been spoken of as unnamable.
3. James *therefore* means homosexuality when he refers to something unnamable. [6]

As Horne points out:

Readers of James are familiar with the late Jamesian practice of abstaining from specification of significant facts, names and events, creating epistemological abysses round which one warily treads— gaps one may imagine filling in a multiplicity of ways, temptations to the over-confident guesser: in *The Ambassadors* what the Newsomes manufacture in Woollett [speculation has ranged from condoms to

chamber-pots]; in 'The Turn of the Screw' what Miles says at school
that is so bad; in 'The Figure in the Carpet', especially, what is the
clue to the works of Hugh Vereker. Mysteries of reference are James's
stock in trade. (p. 119)

Is there a way out of this stalemate? One can begin with
the historical context. *The Wings of the Dove* is, we gather,
set in the present day. There are no direct references to
events such as the Boer War or Queen Victoria's funeral.
The prominence of the London underground, where Merton
and Kate first become acquainted, suggests modernity (even
though, as Claire Tomalin points out to me, the Metropolitan
Line opened as early as 1864). The narrative *feels* modern,
and most readers, I think, will assume a setting around 1900,
when James wrote the work.

Mr Croy's offence—which took place in Kate's mid-teens—
would therefore have been committed in the late 1880s or
early 1890s. Whatever else, this decade was anything but
tolerant of flagrant homosexuality. If he were indeed an
'unspeakable of the Oscar Wilde kind', Croy would have fallen
foul of the metropolitan police as did Wilde in the mid-1890s.
There had been for some time a crackdown on homosexual
vice, implementing the 1885 Labouchere amendment to the
Criminal Law Act. The Cleveland Street Scandal of 1889, for
example, drove Lord Arthur Somerset out of England because
of alleged offences with telegraph boys at a male brothel.

As Richard Ellmann notes in his life of Oscar Wilde,
'English society tolerated homosexuality only so long as one
was not caught at it.'[7] Lionel Croy has evidently been 'caught'
at whatever he was doing. His offence is known about in
all the London clubs—who have collectively blackballed him.
The fact that it is known among his own set but not to the
world or his (all-female) family argues against some plainly
felonious sexual offence.

Buggery, carnal knowledge of an under-age prostitute girl
(one of the 'maiden tribute of Babylon'), or some Parnell-style
divorce scandal might well be 'unnamable' among the Croy

ladies. But at this period (and at most periods) such offences would lead to newspaper publicity, punitive retribution and extreme ostracization, of a kind which Mr Croy seems *not* to have suffered. He has, we recall, been quietly 'dropped' by his clubs, not drummed out or expelled.

There is a category of offence which might well lead to the kind of blackballing which Mr Croy suffered—cheating at cards (Mr Croy's 'plausibility' suggests something of the card-sharp) or passing bad (or forged) IOUs. This could also lead to the kind of professional downfall which he has evidently undergone over the previous ten years—assuming that he was in a line of work (such as the stock exchange, the bar, or politics) where a 'good name' and 'contacts' counted.

These things are, given James's inscrutability, ultimately subjective. Not to play Horne's 'over-confident guesser', the evidence seems to weigh equally against the 'drug fiend' or 'straight rectum' hypotheses. My feeling is that Mr Croy is more likely to have been caught with an ace up his sleeve than with his trousers down or an opium pipe in his mouth.

Joseph Conrad · *Heart of Darkness*

═══

'L'horreur! l'horreur!'

═══

Among the most famous lines from twentieth-century fiction
are the anonymous boy's blunt announcement: 'Mistah
Kurtz—he dead' (p. 86). Almost as famous are Kurtz's last
words: 'The horror! The horror!' (p. 85). But why isn't it:
M'sieur Kurtz, il mort!, and *L'horreur, l'horreur*?[1]

Every student's edition of *Heart of Darkness* informs us
that the novel was directly inspired by Conrad's trip to the
Belgian Congo in 1890 and the ruthless exploitation of the
region by the Belgian authorities which he witnessed there.
The critic Patrick Brantlinger summarises the facts of the
case in his monograph on literature and imperialism, *Rule of
Darkness*:

> Conrad was appalled by the 'high-sounding rhetoric' used to mask
> the 'sordid ambitions' of King Leopold II of Belgium, Conrad's
> ultimate employer during his six months in the Congo in 1890.
> *Heart of Darkness* expresses not only what Conrad saw and partially
> recorded in his 'Congo Diary' but also the revelations of atrocities
> which began appearing in the British press as early as 1888 and
> reached a climax twenty years later, in 1908, when the mounting
> scandal forced the Belgian government to take control of Leopold's
> private domain. During that period the population of the Congo was
> decimated, perhaps halved; as many as six million persons may have
> been uprooted, tortured, and murdered through the forced labor
> system used to extract ivory and what reformers called 'red rubber'
> from the 'heart of darkness'.[2]

Although Conrad never says so, no one who has thought
about the matter doubts that the company Charles Marlow
works for is (under thin disguise) the Société Anonyme-Belge
pour le Commerce du Haut-Congo. Kurtz is, of course, a
French-speaking employee of the *Société*. Although Charlie

Marlow is archetypally English, the 'sepulchral city' is Brussels, and the 'Intended' (Kurtz's fiancée) is manifestly Belgian. We assume Marlow is bilingual. Is the novel?

Critics of *Heart of Darkness* are confronted with (but rarely face) the puzzling fact that a Belgian *agent*, all members of his company and his native servants speak in various dialects of idiomatic English. Criticism typically finesses the problem by latching on to the pregnant description of Kurtz's miscegenated origins:

Mind, I am not trying to excuse or even explain—I am trying to account to myself for—for—Mr. Kurtz—for the shade of Mr. Kurtz. This initiated wraith from the back of Nowhere honoured me with its amazing confidence before it vanished altogether. This was because it could speak English to me. The original Kurtz had been educated partly in England, and—as he was good enough to say himself—his sympathies were in the right place. His mother was half-English, his father was half-French. All Europe contributed to the making of Kurtz . . . (p. 65)

The insight that 'All Europe went into his making' sanctions slipping into discussion of European (as opposed to any singly national) 'imperialism'. Correspondingly, a vaguely identified lingua franca (English) is in order. Kurtz, we deduce, incarnates *all* European exploitation of Africa in the late nineteenth century. Britain, France, Germany, Belgium—all the colonial powers are tarred with the same brush. This runs counter, however, to a clear Conradian line of apology in the novel: namely that British imperialism (as embodied in admirable figures like Marlow, or elsewhere Lord Jim) is to be firmly discriminated from rapacious, commercially ruthless, Belgian imperialism. Conrad, as the biographers inform us, was not anti-colonialism: he was anti-Belgian colonialism.

When, therefore, Kurtz croaks his famous last words, 'The horror! The horror!', has he reverted to his mother (or half-mother) tongue, English? or is Marlow translating from the French, for the benefit of his English listeners on the *Nellie*?

And is he likewise translating, 'Mistah Kurtz—he dead'?
Or is the manager's boy showing off his (pidgin) English?
There is some warrant for the 'silent translation' hypothesis.
When, for example, Marlow takes farewell of the doctor in
the sepulchral city who has examined his fitness to serve the
company, the old man concludes with some advice:

'Avoid irritation more than exposure to the sun. Adieu. How do
you English say, eh? Good-bye. Ah! Good-bye. Adieu. In the tropics
one must before everything keep calm.' . . . He lifted a warning
forefinger . . . 'Du calme, du calme. Adieu.' (p. 26)

What the reader infers from the slightly stilted phraseology,
and the switch to transparent, italicised, French, is that
Marlow has been translating throughout for the benefit of
his English listeners bobbing on the *Nellie* off Gravesend.

Du calme, du calme. Adieu is, to my ear, different not just
in sound but meaning from: 'I advise you to take it very
easy, old man. Good-bye. And *do* look after yourself.' The
difference, as best as I can pin it down, inheres in the rather
more authoritarian status and professional proprieties of
the Continental doctor, compared to his tweedier, man-to-
man affecting British colleague. So, too, there are significant
shades of difference between *l'horreur* (spoken by a Belgian
manager) and 'the horror' (spoken by an English manager). In
fact, it is not easy to imagine 'the horror, the horror' falling
easily off the English tongue without a melodramatic self-
consciousness.

Conrad sidesteps the problem by studiously avoiding
topographical names in his story. He raises his narrative
to a plane of abstraction where details of country, time, or
language are irrelevant. Even though, as Norman Sherry has
demonstrated,[3] the novelist's itinerary up the Congo can be
exactly traced, Conrad never offers a place name, a business
name, nor even—as far as I can determine—the name of the
'dark' Continent into whose heart Marlowe is penetrating (I
have encountered otherwise intelligent students who assume
the river in *Heart of Darkness* is the Amazon). Belgium and

Brussels are specifically *not* identified.

The wisdom of Conrad's 'no name' strategy is confirmed by the example of a lesser novelist. Edgar Wallace, 'the King of the Thrillers', visited the Congo in 1907 and was, like any true-born Englishman, sickened by Belgian atrocities. On his return to London, Wallace became a stalwart of the London branch of the Congo Reform Association. A fellow member suggested he might write a novel using his Congo experiences:

For the next three days he thought of nothing else. The Congo notes which he had made three years before were searched out and eagerly studied—the tribes, the customs . . . the fragments of Lomongo tongue . . . nothing remained but to clarify and elaborate his characters. The river need not be specifically the Congo, since his hero must be an Englishman and an empire-builder if possible into the bargain; no, an unspecified native territory in West Africa was best—impossible to identify on any map, yet containing all the romantic dangers of the Congo country.[4]

Wallace ran into exactly the same problem as Conrad: how could he get a quintessentially English (and morally decent) hero involved in a Belgian colonial location? Wallace solved the problem in his own way. He invented a Belgian Congo wisely administered by British colonists. The result was *Sanders of the River* (1910). As devised by Wallace, Mr Commissioner Sanders is a grey-haired, yellow-faced, wise old bird who has been 'called upon by the British government to keep a watchful eye upon some quarter of a million cannibal folk'—a task which he carries out with shrewd (and often draconian) efficiency. This is what Kurtz *would* have been, had the fellow been blessed with British nationality, pluck and upbringing. This is how African colonies *should* be run.

The Sanders stories all centre on stern and arbitrary acts of 'justice'—which the commissioner jovially administers with the assistance of his steamboat, his 'Houssa police', and, above all, his Maxim gun. The stories were immensely popular and *Sanders of the River* was filmed in 1935, with the American Marxist Paul Robeson as Bosambo and the future first president of Kenya, Jomo Kenyatta, as an uncredited extra—a most curious intertwining of colonial, political, literary, and film history.

With post-colonial enlightenment, *Heart of Darkness* is a more admired text than Wallace's Congolese thriller. The West has become rather shamefaced about Commissioner Sanders and his gunboat marauding up and down the river hanging ten a day.[5] Time, literary judgement and, one has to say, Western guilt have vindicated Conrad's narrative tactics—his bleaching his story into a stark black–white chromatography (European light, African darkness), fading out all identifiable topographic, national, and linguistic distinctions.

Nowadays, of course, we hear 'the horror, the horror' in our mind's ear with a sonorously American inflection: as uttered, that is, by Marlon Brando. Francis Ford Coppola's recycling of Conrad's story is historically appropriate, given the imperial status of America, and the diminished status of Britain and Belgium, in the late twentieth century. But arguably, by being too precise about time and place, the Coppola–Brando film falls into errors that Conrad's evasiveness artfully avoids. *Apocalypse Now* (1979) transposed *Heart of Darkness* to Indo-China during the Vietnam war. Captain Willard (played by Martin Sheen) is a Special Forces officer, sent to terminate 'with extreme prejudice' Colonel Kurtz (Brando)—another Special Forces officer who has gone 'rogue'. Kurtz is running a private guerilla war against the communists with a force of loyal *montagnards*.

Willard is assigned to go up-river into Cambodia, where deep in the jungle Kurtz has his headquarters. Coppola's narrative faithfully mirrors the familiar outline of *Heart of Darkness* and offers any number of direct echoes. The heads on stakes, the harlequin-Russian (played by a wholly spaced-out Dennis Hopper), the African princess all reappear. But, by being geographically and historically specific, the film gets itself into a fine mess, as described by Frances FitzGerald:

Of course, anyone who has spent any time in Vietnam would feel uneasy about Willard's journey from the start and become more uncomfortable as time goes by. Kurtz is said to have gone into Cambodia with a Montagnard army, yet there are no Montagnards in Cambodia for the simple reason that there are no mountains to speak of there. Willard's journey, we are told, begins in Nha Trang, and Kilgore's battalion surfs a beach that is surely in Central Vietnam. But you can't get to Cambodia from Central Vietnam by river because there are mountains in between (rivers don't flow uphill) . . . Because *Apocalypse Now* is fiction (and in no way naturalistic), Coppola has the perfect right to invent geography and depict imaginary tribesmen who, it appears, make ritual sacrifices before breakfast. However, the film loses interest as it strays from the realities of Vietnam—and the more it strays, the worse it gets as fiction.[6]

Famously, E. M. Forster declared that when we open the casket of Conrad's genius, we discover 'not a jewel but a vapour'. In *Heart of Darkness* vaporisation—wilful lack of specificity—would appear to have been the smart artistic option.

Tele-Murder

An amusing 1997 TV advertisement for British Telecom featured the bestselling novelist Jeffrey Archer. The great man was shown in his Thameside penthouse on the phone to his US agent, reading aloud his latest opus. The punchline showed the hardboiled, cigar-chomping Yank, having listened to the recitation of the whole novel, retorting, 'Sounds great, Jeffrey—but do you have anything with *dinosaurs* in it?' Fade out on baffled Archer physiognomy.

Although it did the author of *The Fourth Estate* no harm this was an advertisement not for fiction (whether Archer's or Michael Crichton's) but for the country's leading phone-service provider. One of the striking differences between the British and American booktrades is the relative status of advertising. Pick up the Sunday *New York Times* literary supplement and half its pages are occupied by screaming ads for the books of the week. The British *Sunday Times* supplement (like all the other nationals) is anaemic by contrast, with scarcely a paid-for advertisement to be seen.

One of the more quixotic attempts to pep up the sale of British fiction with the techniques of modern advertising, as pioneered by the Harmsworth 'yellow press', was Edgar Wallace's *The Four Just Men*. Wallace had made his name as a star reporter on the *Daily Mail* and resolved to apply the tricks he had learned in Fleet Street to the art of fiction. Mass production was the first challenge. Using a dictaphone and a platoon of secretaries—sustained by vast intakes of weak tea and nicotine—Wallace transformed himself into a 'human book factory'. When, in the 1920s, he hit his stride as a novelist there were jokes about the 'weekly Wallace', the 'daily Wallace' and (this being the period when London papers brought out several editions a day) the 'mid-day Wallace'.

The most interesting of Wallace's novels, from the marketing point of view, is his first: *The Four Just Men*. An archetypal 'thriller' (a genre Wallace made his own) it is written in pounding headline style, simulating the 'Blood-red placards, hoarse newsboys, overwhelming headlines, and column after column of leaded type' (p. 45)[1] of the newspaper world. 'His' paper, the *Daily Mail*, figures centrally in Wallace's plot as the 'Megaphone'.

Innovators traditionally have a hard time of it. Wallace ran into resistance in 1905 as he tried to sell his idea—a novel promoted by the 'stunts' that had proved so effective in Fleet Street. His brainwave was to combine the novel and the readers' competition. *The Four Just Men* is generically 'a locked-room mystery'—less a 'whodunnit?' than a 'How in God's name *did* they do it?'[2] A prize of £500 (Wallace initially wanted to make it £1,000) was to be split among any readers ingenious enough to guess how the four heroes killed their victim, Sir Philip Ramon, alone as he was in a heavily protected room, surrounded by bodyguards.

Failing to find a buyer for his project, Wallace enterprisingly set up his own company, the Tallis Press, in a one-room office. He went on to bombard the streets of the capital with placard, poster, and billboard advertising—all making play with his challenge to the reading public: how will the murder be done? He even tried to get the British cabinet minister Joseph Chamberlain to plug the book—as Gladstone had thirty years earlier for Mrs Humphry Ward's *Robert Elsmere*, and as Mrs Thatcher would one day do for her favourite novelist (despite his deficiency in the dinosaur department).

The story of *The Four Just Men* is, by the standards of detective fiction, brisk but banal. The quartet are indeterminately foreign vigilantes—*mousquetaires de nos jours*. Their self-imposed mission is to deliver 'justice', wherever the orthodox agencies prove to be inadequate. The just men are already

steeped in virtuous blood: among their victims they number
the East End clothier Bentvich, 'a sweater of a particularly
offensive type' (Jewish, of course), a corrupt judge in the
American West, and the Frenchman Herman le Blois, poet–
philosopher, guilty of 'corrupting the youth of the world with
his reasoning' (they are not bookish coves, these just men).

The Four Just Men pride themselves on their elegant
modus operandi. Their strikes are invariably prefaced by detailed warnings, public proclamations, and a hyper-ingenious
means of assassination in which they go out of their way to
make the law look asinine. They eschew bombs and other
techniques which imperil innocent bystanders. As the novel
opens, they have targeted the UK government. The English
are 'curious dull people', they condescendingly observe,
although not—like many of their Continental neighbours—
notably 'unjust'. None the less, the government of the day
proposes to bring in a measure which threatens the refugee
status of the venerable anarchist Manuel Garcia, a leader-
in-exile of the Spanish Carlist movement. For reasons which
are not gone into, the just men approve of Carlism.

Sir Philip Ramon, the British Foreign Secretary, is sent
a series of letters, advising him to withdraw the 'Aliens
Extradition (Political Offences) Bill'.[3] The threats are duly
given headline treatment by the *Megaphone*. The action
proper opens in Cadiz, where we are introduced to the
vigilante heroes. Despite their brand-name there are, we
discover, only three of them—'poor Clarice' having been
killed in the le Blois affair. They are: Gonsalez of the light-
blue eyes and restless hands; Poiccart—heavy, saturnine and
pathologically suspicious; and Manfred, with his grey-shot
beard and single eyeglass. All are masters of disguise. The
just men have recruited a low type of criminal, Thery, to
make up their number. He evidently has certain skills they
need. What skills? Somewhat later we learn that Thery's
specialism is 'stealing rubber'—which doesn't much help.

The main action occupies two weeks in August in London

in what we take to be 1905. The just men show they
mean business by disguising one of their number as an MP,
and smuggling into the Houses of Parliament 'an infernal
machine', capable of blowing up the whole establishment—
did they choose to use such a means to their end. Panic reigns:
'never since the days of the Fenian outrages had the mind of
the public been so filled with apprehension' (p. 20). Bombs are
not in prospect as the actual means of assassination. Neither
is gas, we discover ('this time', Gonsalez adds ominously). To
further their scheme the just men purchase a zinc-engraver's
business in Carnaby Street, with 'a stock of chemicals'. In the
workshop, Manfred shows his companions 'a box of polished
wood . . . and disclosed the contents'. But not, infuriatingly,
so that we the readers can see them. He adds, inscrutably,
'if Thery is the good workman he says he is, here is the bait
that shall lure Sir Philip Ramon to his death'.

A little later, Manfred rhapsodises on their dastardly
scheme, to Thery:

'You and I and Poiccart and Gonsalez will kill this unjust man in
a way that the world will never guess—such an execution as shall
appall mankind,—a swift death, a sure death, a death that will creep
through cracks, that will pass by the guards unnoticed . . . There
has never been such a thing done.' (p. 53)

Warming to the theme, Thery promises: 'let me find your
minister of state, give me a minute's speech with him, and
the next minute he dies' (p. 52). How?

The narrative climaxes on the evening that Sir Philip is to
introduce the second reading of the bill. Whitehall is black
with the helmets of policeman, brought in by van, train and
'every form of traction'. There has been nothing like it 'since
the atrocious East End murders' (of Jack the Ripper in 1887).
None the less, alone in his steel-shuttered, guarded, and
barricaded office in Downing Street, on the stroke of nine,
Sir Philip is found dead, as promised.

At the inquest Scotland Yard confesses itself totally baffled.
The only mark on Sir Philip's corpse is a small 'round black

stain' on his right palm. Meanwhile, Thery's body is also
found, dumped in the Romney Marshes, similarly unmarked
except that 'on his right palm [is] a stain similar to that found
on the hand of Sir Philip Ramon' (p. 98). It seems as if the
mysterious stains have been 'formed by an acid'—perhaps
'some subtle poison' is involved? How *was* the deed done?

Wallace's thriller, as first published in November 1905,
concluded with an enigmatic letter from the Four Just Men
delivered to the world through the *Megaphone*:

Sir Philip's death would appear to have been an accident. This much
we confess. Thery bungled—and paid the penalty. We depended too
much upon his technical knowledge. Perhaps by diligent search you
will solve the mystery of Sir Philip Ramon's death. (p. 102)

The narrative was thus left open-ended, as a challenge to the
ingenious reader. Had Wallace kept it so, he might have been
credited with the first *roman nouveau* in English.

Unluckily for the Tallis Press and its proprietor, within
three months so many readers came up with the solution to
the mystery of Sir Philip's death as to confront Wallace with
the prospect of bankruptcy and public charges of fraud. With
the help of Alfred Harmsworth and the *Mail* he finessed it,
and lived to write on—more prudently. On its part, *The Four
Just Men* went on to become a perennial bestseller, boosted
by film versions and (in the 1960s) a TV serial.

Wallace added an explanatory 'Conclusion' for the novel's
post-prize reprints. Inspector Falmouth goes to Sir Philip's
other London residence in Portland Place. There he discovers a 'table telephone' (at this date, a bell and speaker
instrument, not our more familiar cradled one-piece receiver
and mouthpiece) which has been burned and twisted. The
inspector calls an electrician who tells him that:

'Somebody has attached a wire carrying a high voltage—probably
an electric-lighting wire—to this telephone line; and if anybody
happened to be at [the other end]—'

He stopped suddenly, and his face went white.

'Good God!' he whispered, 'Sir Philip Ramon was electrocuted!' (p. 105)

There was, we apprehend, a direct land line between Sir Philip's London house in Portland Place and his office at 44 Downing Street. Such lines were, at this period, commonly single-wire affairs. Thery—whose expertise in 'rubber' made him an expert in insulation—connected the line to a live household socket, and rang Sir Philip (this was his deadly 'minute's speech with him'). By some unspecified clumsiness, Thery electrocuted himself—hence the black stain on his palm, a mark left by the scorched bakelite. At the other end, Sir Philip Ramon picked up the ringing phone. He received a similar (if less severe) electric shock and the corresponding stain in the palm of his right hand where he held the speaker part of his telephone. The jolt was sufficient to arrest his weak heart (something established earlier on by Wallace). It had been noticed that there were two dead sparrows on the window sill at Sir Philip's Downing Street office. It is now obvious to the inspector that these luckless birds must have perched on the 'live' telephone wire and copped it like the Home Secretary. Cunning.

There was no visible damage to the Downing Street phone, and in the excitement no one noticed it was dangling off the hook. Why, however, wasn't this instrument burned and twisted, like its counterpart at the other end of the line? The electrician explains (rather feebly): 'I have given up trying to account for the vagaries of electricity . . . besides, the current, the full force of the current, might have been diverted—a short circuit . . . ' (pp. 105–6).

As the records tell us, so many readers of *The Four Just Men* came forward with the right solution that Wallace faced the prospect of ruin. But, of course, the 'right' solution is hopelessly wrong. It is technological nonsense to rank with James Thurber's aunt who was convinced that dangerous quantities of electricity were leaking into her house from empty light sockets. Wallace's denouement depended on the total ignorance of the reading population about how phones work. Only tiny electrical charges are needed to carry sound from dispatching to receiving membrane. Even if hooked up, a domestic current of 220 volts would be wholly harmless by the time it reached 44 Downing Street, some three miles away. Birds perch with impunity on power lines. Nor could domestic current kill Thery, unless he was standing in a bucket of water and with the wires clamped between his teeth (and he is, after all, an 'expert' in insulation—which is why the just men brought him to England in the first place).

How did Wallace get away with it? Two reasons suggest themselves. This was the period of the infancy of the British telephone service. It was not until 1905 that the government fully nationalised the phone service into the Post Office, laying the ground for the necessary infrastructural investment. In 1905, there were only around 70,000 subscribers in England. The reading public had only a hazy idea of how Mr Bell's new-fangled invention worked—other than that electricity was involved. Nowadays, one suspects, many fewer readers would 'solve' Wallace's narrative conundrum for the paradoxical reason that they know more of the workings of telecommunications. Public ignorance is a valuable resource for the novelist; unfortunately, public education is always working against it.

There was some slight warrant for Wallace's gimmick in the observed fact that phones were dangerous things to be holding during thunderstorms. Robert Graves, for instance, recalls in *Goodbye to All That* that he was (in the 1920s) holding a telephone receiver when lightning struck. The charge grounded itself along the telephone cable, jumped the receiver's insulation, and gave him a shock which resulted in an anxiety condition lasting years. To avert this risk, the phone system eventually installed 'lightning arresters', designed to avoid such freak accidents. If, like Frankenstein, the just men could have arranged a convenient lightning bolt they might have achieved their end. Otherwise, the homicidal phone belongs with 'Beam me up, Scottie' and Luke Skywalker's light sword. Techno-fantasy.

It is not clear whether Edgar Wallace himself believed his techno-fantasy. Probably not. He had signally failed in his attempt to combine fiction and the Fleet Street stunt. But Wallace learned a valuable lesson with *The Four Just Men*— namely that no popular novelist ever went broke by over-estimating the gullibility of the reading public. At the end of his life, in 1932, Edgar Wallace was embarked in Hollywood on what was to be his most daring concept: the story of a gigantic gorilla, brought back from a South Seas island to New York, where it was to run amok and end up fighting the US Air Corps perched at the top of the Empire State Building. Unlikely, you may think? The public lapped it up, just as they did Michael Crichton's cloned dinosaurs, sixty years later.

===

What is the Professor's 'Stuff'?

===

If there is one essential critical text for the understanding of *The Secret Agent* it is Norman Sherry's *Conrad's Western World*.[1] By resourceful sleuthing Sherry—over twelve chapters—uncovers the 'originals' which inspired the novelist's 'Simple Tale'. In one small detail, however, Sherry's explications may mislead us. He assumes (as do most other commentators) that the 'stuff' (p. 71) which the Professor gives Verloc, wherewith to mount his explosive outrage on the first meridian, is dynamite.[2]

Dynamite is, paradoxically, a 'safe' explosive, and one whose useful applications (in mining, construction, and demolition) have far outweighed its criminal misuses. Developed and patented by Alfred Nobel (who magnanimously diverted a portion of his ensuing profits to his 'Prizes') dynamite represented a commercially viable way of stabilising the fearsomely volatile liquid TNT (tri-nitro-toluene), by mixing it with a suitably inert and solid base. Nobel's first successful compound used *Kieselguhr*—a clayey substance. The resulting 'stick', wrapped in waterproof cartridge paper, could be detonated only by a smaller, controlled explosion in the form of a percussion cap, an ignition fuse, or an electrical wire attached to a plunger. The beauty of dynamite was that it could be safely knocked, dropped, kicked or pounded without risk. You could fall over carrying a hundredweight of the explosive, and suffer nothing more than a sprained wrist. It was marketed as 'Nobel's safety powder'. TNT was something else. An unlucky sneeze might detonate it.

Nobel's (trademarked) name for his product was an inspiration. Of all the names for explosives (cordite, gelignite, semtex, C.4) it is the most resonantly poetic and memorable. In the early 1880s 'dynamite' was quickly adapted into common currency as shorthand for any bomb-maker's gear. Revolutionaries became *dynamitards*—even though cartoonists would forever show them throwing the traditional black metal ball with the short fizzing fuse sticking out at the top.

In *The Secret Agent*, the word dynamite is used loosely on three occasions. 'A dynamite outrage must be provoked' (p. 36), Mr Vladimir tells the appalled Verloc, as he outlines the new regime under which the secret agent is to operate. A little later, Comrade Ossipon is described as a 'moribund veteran of the dynamite wars' (p. 48). And as the Greenwich outrage reverberates through the corridors of power the 'great personage' (the Home Secretary, we apprehend) asks impatiently 'if this is the beginning of another dynamite campaign' (p. 136; he is thinking presumably of recent Fenian outrages).

In fact, it is clear that the Professor's 'stuff'—whatever it may be—is *not* dynamite (a commodity which it would have been much easier to acquire from a mining contractor, or a quarry stockroom, than a crazy anarchist chemist). As Conrad recalls in his 1920 'Author's Note', the central episode of *The Secret Agent* was based on 'the already old [in 1907] story of the attempt to blow up the Greenwich Observatory; a blood-stained inanity of so fatuous a kind that it was impossible to fathom its origin' (p. xxxiv).[3]

On 15 February 1894 Marcel Bourdin, a French anarchist, had prematurely detonated a bomb in Greenwich Park. Luckily he damaged only himself and some nearby trees. It was never established what his actual target was, nor how he intended to give himself time to escape (assuming that it was not a suicide mission). He survived the explosion—being able to whisper (in English, with a heavy French accent), 'Take me home.' But his hand was blown off, and he died thirty minutes later in hospital of horrific fragment wounds to his abdomen.

Bourdin's device was described in *The Times*, 16 February, as 'a bottle which had apparently contained an explosive mixture'. This explosive mixture—whose 'character' was initially mysterious to the authorities—was (accidentally) detonated. Fragments of glass were found in the vicinity, together with Bourdin's missing body parts. It was supposed Bourdin had stumbled—possibly on a tree stump—and the concussion prematurely detonated his bomb.

On 17 February, it was reported that there was new evidence as to the construction of the bomb in the shape of 'an all-important piece of iron, with five parallel grooves upon the inner side'. The metal fragment had been extracted from the wound in Bourdin's stomach. Its shape suggested 'the lip of a stone bottle' (or a metal container), about the 'size of a penny piece'. This piece of metal clearly worked against the 'glass bomb' hypothesis. And *The Times* was perplexed by the grooves in the iron fragment—'perfect circles' not 'spiral' in form. They could not be a screw top, and—plausibly—had something to do with the timing device. By 19 February, the paper's special correspondent felt on safer ground with the explosive, reporting confidently that 'the bomb was charged with picric acid . . . a remarkably powerful explosive'. The paper continued: 'any person with a small knowledge of chemistry can make an engine of destruction out of a sardine box or an old saucepan'—but, it warned, 'expert assistance' would be required for the detonator and timing mechanism.

Bourdin's bomb was clearly not dynamite based. Nor, powerful as picric acid is, was it anywhere near as powerful a charge as that which disintegrates Stevie who (having 'stumbled', as it is supposed, 'against the root of a tree') is 'blown to small bits: limbs, gravel, clothing, bones, splinters—all mixed up together'. As Inspector Heat recalls with gratuitous relish, 'they had to fetch a shovel to gather him up with' (p. 210). Most of Bourdin was intact.

Picric acid was an explosive favoured by the European military for artillery shells before the commercial availability of TNT. The disadvantage of picric acid and its derivatives was that they corroded metal containers (such as shell casings) and formed new, and unstable, chemical combinations. Hence the explosive needed to be kept in glass. If Bourdin's 'infernal machine' was picric-based, the combination of glass and metal fragments was logical. The circular grooves and the nature of the detonator remained mysterious.

It is clear from Conrad's narrative that, whatever explosive the professor has secreted on his body, it is not dynamite, and may well be picric acid. He keeps it, as he tells Ossipon, 'In a thick glass flask' (p. 65). When the time comes, it will be detonated with the same kind of pneumatic rubber ball used at the time in flash photography. There will be a twenty-second interval (the period marked in the studio by 'say cheese!'). Not one to hide his expertise in such matters (he was, after all, once a university lecturer) the professor gives his anarchist colleagues a detailed description of the other 'infernal machine' he manufactured for Verloc:

'As he wanted something that could be carried openly in the hand, I proposed to make use of an old one-gallon copal varnish can I happened to have by me. He was pleased at the idea. It gave me some trouble, because I had to cut out the bottom first and solder it on again afterwards. When prepared for use, the can enclosed a wide-mouthed, well-corked jar of thick glass packed around with some wet clay, and containing sixteen ounces of X2 green powder. The detonator was connected with the screw top of the can. It was ingenious—a combination of time and shock. I explained the system to him. It was a thin tube of tin, enclosing a—'. (pp. 75–6)

At this tantalising point, the Professor's exposition is interrupted, never to be resumed.

I do not know much about the home-manufacture of explosive devices, nor I think did Joseph Conrad. What he did was to throw together all the information he had gleaned from newspaper accounts of Bourdin's explosion. The 'sardine can' becomes a one-gallon varnish can. The glass casing required for the brilliantly yellow liquid picric acid is retained. But,

since the explosive is 'green powder' rather than yellow
liquid, glass would seem superfluous. Nobel's *Kieselguhr*
makes an entry as the wet clay packing—again superfluous;
it would make more sense to surround the bomb with cotton
wool or nails. The mysterious 'lip' extracted from Bourdin's
stomach resurfaces as the varnish-can's mouth. And what
was the detonator on Stevie's bomb? We shall never know.
But there may be a clue in the Professor's 'thin tube of tin'.
Conrad, I suspect, had come across the following description
of a time-delay detonator in the *Deutsches Offizierblatt*, 1906:

In France an entirely different solution of the difficulties connected
with the construction of long-range time fuses has been worked out.
The time composition, which is a mixture of pulvérin and gum lac, is
filled into a lead tube, which is then drawn out by passing through
a number of draw plates until its diameter is reduced to a few mil-
limetres. This tube, which burns very regularly, is wound in a spiral
inside the fuse. To set the fuse, this tube is stabbed at the appropriate
point, whereby the flame is caused to impinge on the priming at the
proper time. The tube can, of course, be made of any desired length.[4]

The professor's 'thin tube of tin' is a version of this French
tubular timer. What one supposes is that: (1) screwing down
the top of the can detonates a small cap which ignites
the combustible substance compressed in the tube; (2) the
contents of the tube are measured to burn for twenty minutes,
before reaching the 'X2 powder'. The device needs careful
handling since an unlucky jolt could forestall the whole
process. As the Professor surmises, Stevie either screwed
down the cap too early, or dropped the can.

It is clear that the Professor's device is based on Bourdin's
tin and glass 'machine', with some Conradian refinements
in the business of the detonator. It is clear, also, that the
Professor's 'stuff' is the product of 'home industry' not Mr
Nobel's Swedish factories. Is the Professor's 'stuff', then, 'stuff
and nonsense'? Not quite. But neither is it an explosive device
in the Freddy Forsyth class.[5]

'War? What War?'

In his 'Foreword' to *Women in Love*, D. H. Lawrence recalls the circumstances of the novel's composition:

The novel was written in its first form in the Tyrol, in 1913. It was altogether re-written and finished in Cornwall in 1917. So that it is a novel which took its final shape in the midst of the period of war, though it does not concern the war itself. I should wish the time to remain unfixed, so that the bitterness of the war may be taken for granted in the characters. (p. xli)[1]

Because of its 'obscenity' *Women in Love* could not find a publisher until 1920. Lawrence used the interval to redraft, polish, and emend his text. The novel's strata of composition thus straddle pre-war, mid-war, and post-war: without ever directly mentioning the war.

Lawrence's striking phrase 'I should wish the time to remain unfixed' recalls another great novel of war, Kurt Vonnegut's *Slaughterhouse Five*, and its opening line: 'Billy Pilgrim has come unstuck in time.'[2] But Vonnegut's 'unstuck' narrative is a device by which eventually to come closer to the reality of world war, epitomised in the dreadful Dresden raid of February 1945. Lawrence's 'unfixed' narrative seems instead to want to erase or repress the 'Great War' from public memory. To create a world in which its effects, but not the thing itself, are present.

Lawrence's foreword poses a challenge to the reader. Realistic fiction, if it is to be realistic, must carry in its fabric historical markers: the action will be precisely 'dated' by fashion (the Brangwen girls' 'grass-green' stockings); technological advances (the wedding at the beginning of *Women in Love* has horse-drawn carriages, Gerald Crich has a motor-car which he loans to Birkin); background detail (in the period 1914–18, every street in every town in England would have men in furlough khaki or invalid blue uniforms).

Film-makers have to be even more precise about such things than novelists. In his big-budget 1969 adaptation of Lawrence's novel Ken Russell opted decisively for a post-war setting. His screenplay featured war-memorial services (invented by Russell, not Lawrence), characters doing the wild knee-knocking mid-1920s 'Charleston' dance, flamboyantly jazz-age clothing, 1930s automobiles. Russell's justification for setting *Women in Love* so late was enlarged on by the actor Oliver Reed, who played Gerald Crich, in a TV chat show promoting the film. Reed argued, plausibly, that the industrial world in which Crich operates is clearly that of 1919–30, a period of rapid mechanical modernisation and industrial strife.[3]

What historical markers can we find in the text of Lawrence's *Women in Love*, and what do they tell us? A time-line can be deduced from Gerald Crich's own *curriculum vitae*. He is, Gudrun tells Loerke, 'thirty-one' years old (p. 423). Elsewhere we are informed that as a young man 'he refused to go to Oxford, choosing a German university. He had spent a certain time at Bonn, at Berlin, and at Frankfurt . . . Then he must try war. Then he must travel into the savage regions that had so attracted him' (pp. 218–19).

Gerald's twenties have been action-packed. After university, he has explored the Amazon and held the Queen's (and possibly the King's) commission. As he tells Gudrun: 'I resigned my commission . . . some years ago.' Birkin adds, 'He was in the last war.' For some time he has been a 'Napoleon of industry . . . ruling over coal-mines' (p. 60). The 'last war' is, manifestly, the Boer War, 1899–1902. Gerald must have been no younger than his early twenties to have served, and if he is—at the time of his death in the Tyrol—thirty-one, the date must be around 1910. Oliver Reed would seem to be out by ten momentous years.

There are a number of other chronological markers; passing references, for instance, to Futurism, Nijinsky, and Picasso. These would seem to suggest a date after the 1910 Post-Impressionist Exhibition and Stravinsky's *Rite of Spring*, but before 1914. The narrative breathes the cultural atmosphere of the Edwardian high-noon. We may fancifully picture the Brangwen sisters rubbing shoulders with the Schlegels of *Howards End*. Ursula's own *curriculum vitae* supports this dating: she was at college during the Boer War (as we recall from *The Rainbow*) and is now twenty-six. This gives a setting of *circa* 1905.

This pre-war setting is further confirmed by the fashionability of things German. Winifred, the eerily precocious Crich daughter, calls her pet rabbit 'Bismarck'. This would have been regarded as positively traitorous after 1914 (the period in which the royal house of England furtively changed its names from 'Saxe-Coburg-Gotha' to 'Windsor', and from 'Battenberg' to 'Mountbatten'). After the outbreak of hostilities the Crich rabbit, we may be sure, would have been patriotically renamed 'Kitchener'.

There are, none the less, historical markers which point, somewhat less decisively, to a mid-war setting. Gudrun and Ursula regard a robin 'on the top twig of a bush, singing shrilly'. Isn't he, Gudrun observes ironically, 'a little Lloyd George of the air' (p. 260)? This remark would have lacked full resonance before Lloyd George's becoming war-time Prime Minister in 1916. There are passing references to two hit songs of the War—'It's a Long Way to Tipperary' and 'My Little Grey Home in the West'. Loerke 'hates' the sculptor Mestrovic (1883–1956), a reference that would make little sense before 1916. The fact that he tells Gudrun this in the Tyrol, a theatre of war in 1916, is one of the novel's typical historical perplexities.

The most perplexing reference, however, is found in the last chapter, 'Exeunt', as Birkin contemplates Gerald's frozen corpse:

he went in again at evening, taking a look at Gerald between
the candles, because of his heart's hunger . . . with a strange
whimpering cry, the tears broke out . . . Ursula who had followed
him recoiled aghast from him . . . 'I didn't want it to be like this,
I didn't want it to be like this,' he cried to himself. Ursula could
not but think of the Kaiser's: 'Ich habe es nicht gewollt.' She looked
almost with horror on Birkin. (pp. 476–7)

Kaiser Wilhelm's protestation that 'he didn't will it' refers, of
course, to the Great War.

Thematically, the remark fits well: both the Kaiser and the
'Napoleonic–Nietzschean' Gerald have come to grief through
blind faith in the power of 'will'. But historically the remark is
baffling. It was made on 25 June 1915—and could easily have
been communicated to Lawrence by Frieda, who might have
picked it up from German relatives.[4] But the fact that Ursula
has this German thought in the German-speaking Alps
would suggest that, logically, it could only happen some years
later. Nor could *she*, Ursula, lacking a spouse with friends in
high German places, know the Kaiser's pronouncements until
well after the event.

Probably Lawrence's 'unfixed' (for which read 'all over the
place') is the best solution.

James Joyce · *Ulysses*

═══

Who Moved Molly's Piano?

═══

A mischievously speculative article by Hugh Kenner in 1972 pointed to a teasing puzzle in *Ulysses*.[1] It pertains to what is, for Leopold Bloom, an over-riding cause for anxiety on 16 June 1904: namely the affair between his wife Molly and the 'masher', Blazes Boylan. Their singing together, Bloom 'knows', is the pretext for his cuckolding. The scene in question occurs in the 'Ithaca' section—the pseudo-catechismic, question-and-answer description of Stephen and Leopold drinking tea, having returned late at night to the Bloom household. Stephen leaves and Leopold is suffused with sadness as he stands in the garden, having come outside to bid farewell to his young friend. He looks upwards at the stars:

Alone, what did Bloom feel?
    The cold of interstellar space, thousands of degrees below freezing point, or the absolute zero of Fahrenheit, Centigrade or Réaumur: the incipient intimations of proximate dawn. (p. 625)[2]

Having mournfully reviewed a roll call of dead friends, as dawn breaks, Bloom returns into the house. He picks up a candle, and goes into the front room. He could, of course, find his way blindfold; he has done it so many times. But this occasion is painfully different:

What suddenly arrested his ingress?
    The right temporal lobe of the hollow sphere of his cranium came into contact with a solid timber angle where, an infinitesimal but sensible fraction of a second later, a painful sensation was located in consequence of antecedent sensations transmitted and registered. (p. 626)

This is to say, he bumps his head on the walnut sideboard.
The front-room furniture has been moved during the day; the
main change in the layout of the room is the piano over which
Boylan and Molly hang during their musical rehearsals (in
fact, rehearsals for more intimate duets). This instrument
now occupies the position formerly occupied by the sideboard.
Bloom, his head throbbing, contemplates the object at length:

A vertical piano (Cadby) with exposed keyboard, its closed coffin
supporting a pair of long yellow ladies' gloves and an emerald
ashtray containing four consumed matches, a partly consumed
cigarette and two discoloured ends of cigarettes, its musicrest
supporting the music in the key of G natural for voice and piano
of *Love's Old Sweet Song* (words by G. Clifton Bingham, composed
by J. L. Molloy, sung by Madam Antoinette Sterling) open at the last
page with the final indications *ad libitum*, *forte*, pedal, *animato*,
sustained, pedal, *ritirando*, close. (p. 627)

We never know who moved the furniture, or why. The
episode is, of course, a traditional joke which goes as far
back as literature itself, about the philosopher, who while
regarding the stars, falls into a pit. Leopold Bloom plays,
momentarily, the absent-minded professor.

Who moved the piano? Bloom has been out of the house
some five hours. It is unlikely that the Blooms' home help,
the less than Amazonian Mrs Fleming, could have done it; at
least by herself. And although Molly could have moved the
chairs in the room, Kenner deduces that the piano and the
sideboard would have been too much for her. Boylan must
have done it. Kenner goes on to speculate why she would
have had her lover do it. Because, he goes on to speculate,
she wanted to avoid, postpone, or somehow sabotage the
imminent sexual encounter with Blazes. The aim is to:

drain him . . . with exercise. She will postpone, perhaps evade,
the physical moment; certainly reduce it. Across her mind, as they
stand in the front room, flits her husband's frequent proposal to
move that sofa to the ingleside. Masterstroke! She will wear Boylan
down moving furniture, heavy furniture. And so, it seems, we are

to imagine Blazes Boylan, redfaced, putting his shoulder to the sideboard, tugging at the piano, lifting and carrying the sofa and majolica-topped table, relocating the heavy chair, the light chair . . . (p. 26)

It's a nice scenario; and—if accepted—it subverts the erotic ruminations of Molly in 'Penelope'; we should see these not as factual, Kenner suggests, but as 'pornographic' fantasy. The reality of what went on between Mrs Bloom and her lover was very different.

Slight as the evidence is, Kenner's suggestion is material. It depends, pre-eminently, on one common-sense 'fact'—namely that moving pianos is no light task; not woman's work but man's labour. One thinks of that delicious Laurel and Hardy silent film in which the two clowns, with comically catastrophic results, attempt to move a piano up a flight of stairs.

Kenner's essay was amusingly controverted by a woman Joycean, Margaret Honton, in the *James Joyce Quarterly*, four years later. Citing quantities of chapter and verse (as Joyceans love to do in their internecine wars) Ms Honton's *coup de grâce* was her womanly familiarity (and, by implication, Kenner's male chauvinist ignorance) of the realities of 'housework':

I should like to persuade Mr Kenner and his readers of the likelihood of the women's [i.e. Molly and Mrs Fleming] moving the furniture by saying that I have moved an extremely heavy upright piano (Wegman) any number of times since I was twelve years old. A short distance, yes. Gradually, yes. And singly, yes. My experience with heavy Victorian furniture is that most of the pieces are on castors, and some have handles—a sideboard would be a likely candidate for this—to facilitate moving. As for the bookcase, many a woman has moved larger cases than that by herself. One can take out the books first and replace them after the move, or venture to move the bookcase entire which usually necessitates picking up a few books scattered during the move.[3]

Professors, it would seem, are not just absent-minded; they also don't help much about the house.

━━

Mr Ramsay's Three-Decker

━━

Virginia Woolf's *To the Lighthouse* has a dramatically effective structure, illustrative of the novelist's Proustian preoccupation with time. The first two-thirds of Woolf's narrative (the eighteen sections of 'The Window') describe a single day in the late-summer holiday in the Hebrides of the Ramsay family—the crusty philosopher, his admirable wife, their eight children, and various house-guests. Tomorrow if the weather holds—which it will probably not do—the Ramsays may make an expedition by boat to the offshore lighthouse. The historical setting of this first section is not clearly specified but is reliably assumed to be around 1908. This date is supported by a string of historical markers: for example, the picture of a refrigerator which young James is playing with, references to the recently formed Labour Party (an event which took place in 1905), to X-rays, and so on.

The narrative mode of 'The Window' is ruminative and delicate. The second section of *To the Lighthouse*, 'Time Passes', is in violent contrast. The narrative now fast-forwards over the catastrophic events of the years after the languorous September day chronicled earlier. The tone is disruptive and harsh. The saintly Mrs Ramsay dies—the event warrants only a hurried parenthesis; the prettiest of the Ramsay daughters, Prue, dies a year after marriage; the cleverest of the Ramsay boys, Andrew, is killed in the First World War. Woolf's novel ends with a third section, 'The Lighthouse', chronicling another expedition to the lighthouse, years later, by the querulous and dislikeable Mr Ramsay and his two youngest children, Cam and James. The children are now some ten years older—James, for example, who was six in the first section, is now sixteen. Logically the reader assumes that the first and third sections of *To the Lighthouse* bridge a period from 1908 to 1919.

Having said this one should note that Woolf herself wrote in her manuscript that 'there need be no specification of date'. In the author's mind the historical background, we assume, was shrouded in a prophylactic vagueness. There are good biographical reasons for the vagueness. Woolf wrote the book in the mid-1920s, with the present (and the awful intervention of the Great War) much on her mind. But she was recalling holidays which the Stephen family took in the early 1890s (when she was around James's age).

However relaxed our view about *To the Lighthouse*'s chronology, the reader needs to 'see' the characters and their background in the mind's eye, and to do so one has to put them in a more or less visualised historical setting. One can't, for example, imagine Lily Briscoe in a low-cut Regency dress, or Mrs Ramsay with a bustle, or Prue with a punk hairstyle and a safety pin through her nose. Vagueness has its chronological boundaries. How then do we interpret what seems to be a significant exchange (in 'The Window') between Mr Ramsay and his radiant young house-guest, Minta Doyle, over the majestic *boeuf en daube*, which Mrs Ramsay has prepared for the candle-lit supper which crowns the day's proceedings? Minta finds herself seated alongside Mr Ramsay at supper. The venerable patriarch chaffs her for having lost a brooch on the beach, earlier in the day (something which distressed the young lady considerably):

How could she be such a goose, he asked, as to scramble about the rocks in jewels?

She was by way of being terrified of him—he was so fearfully clever, and the first night when she had sat by him, and he talked about George Eliot, she had been really frightened, for she had left the third volume of *Middlemarch* in the train and she never knew what happened in the end; but afterwards she got on perfectly, and made herself out even more ignorant than she was, because he liked telling her she was a fool. (p. 113)[1]

It's a vivid little vignette. But the business about the 'third volume of *Middlemarch*' is perplexing. And, one may note, in the manuscript of *To the Lighthouse* Woolf first wrote not 'in the train' but 'in the tube' (tube being twentieth-century slang for the London Underground). It was, of course, the habit of the Victorians to produce and consume their fiction in the majestic three-decker format. The three-volume novel, with its elegant binding, large type, and lavish leading, was—like the battleship after which it was nicknamed—an emblem of the age's imperial grandeur. The three-decker also suited the leisurely way in which the Victorians liked to consume their novels—as purveyed by the great leviathan of Victorian circulating libraries, Mudie's of New Oxford Street (the three-decker suited Mr Mudie as well; it meant that he could keep three subscribers happy at the same time with the same novel).

But the three-volume novel collapsed in 1893, after a run of seventy years, when the principal lending libraries (notably Mudie's and W. H. Smith) collaborated to boycott it. The three-decker was a rare bird by 1894 and wholly extinct by 1895. The libraries de-stocked, and resupplied their shelves with the handy 6s one-volume novel (forerunner of our 'hardback')—known for a few years as the 'single-decker'.

There are two puzzles hovering around Minta's three-volume *Middlemarch*. The first is glaring anachronism. It would be very strange to have a three-volume novel on the tube in 1908. They were not easily come by, the individual volumes were large and awkward, and it would be much easier to have a handy Blackwood 'Cabinet' pocket-size, one-volume reprint.

The other more intractable problem is that, unlike other Victorian classics of fiction, *Middlemarch* did not come out in three volumes. Eliot's novel was first published in eight serial parts, between December 1871 and December 1872 and then—very unusually—as a *four*-volume edition to coincide with the last instalment. Another four-volume edition came out in March 1873, followed by a one-volume edition in May 1874 which was, thereafter, the ubiquitously standard form of the novel.

There could be a sly joke here. That is—Minta doesn't realize that the third volume of *Middlemarch* doesn't get you to the 'end'. But this seems too deep an explanation. One needs, I think, to turn to the novelist's biography for illumination. Mr Ramsay—the patriarchal sixty-year-old philosopher who is so disappointed with himself and so unable to communicate with his family—is known to be based on Virginia Woolf's own father, Leslie Stephen (1832–1904), the distinguished late-Victorian man of letters. Everything about Mr Ramsay is old and musty. He is the 'Eminent Victorian' *par excellence*.

Stephen was, of course, a notable critic of George Eliot, in her own day—that day being the 1870s. What seems to have happened here is a bubble of anachronism. Suddenly, by the strength of his patriarchal aura, Mr Ramsay has temporarily retrojected Woolf's narrative into the late-Victorian era (Stephen would, of course, have been four years dead by 1908; and fifteen years dead by the last section of the novel, in which Mr Ramsay makes his great voyage to the lighthouse). If Woolf were consistent about time schemes, Minta should, of course, be reading the exciting new work of young Mr H. G. Wells or young Mr E. M. Forster, not stale old *Middlemarch* in its stale old multi-volume format. And Mr Ramsay should be with the three-decker in his grave.

Woolf blurs the point about the 'four-volume' novel, I would guess, because she wanted to make a general point about the Victorian era—an era associated indelibly with Mudie and the three-decker. Why then did Woolf not make it one of Eliot's novels that *did* appear in three volumes (such as *Adam Bede*, 1859; or *The Mill on the Floss*, 1860)? Because she wanted to make an allusion to *Middlemarch* which her cultivated reader would have picked up. The end of Eliot's novel offers an encomium on woman's extinction of self:

> Her [Dorothea's] finely-touched spirit had still its fine issues, though they were not widely visible. Her full nature, like that river of which Cyrus broke the strength, spent itself in channels which had not great name on the earth. But the effect of her being on those around her was incalculably diffusive: for the growing good of the world is partly dependent on unhistoric acts; and that things are not so ill with you and me as they might have been, is half owing to the number who lived faithfully a hidden life, and rest in unvisited tombs.[2]

Mrs Ramsay is just such a one whose effect on those around her is incalculably diffusive and who lives faithfully a hidden life. Her days are spent in discreet match-making and preparing majestic suppers for the family. She is a good, unobtrusive woman. On her part, as a young woman of the period (that period being Edwardian, not Victorian), Minta is happily ignorant of the Eliotan ideal of self-sacrificial womanhood which Mr Ramsay enjoins and which Mrs Ramsay embodies. Lily Briscoe—the artist who finally emerges as the heroine of *To the Lighthouse*—repudiates the Eliotan *via negativa* (as did Virginia Woolf, and—more abrasively—Lytton Strachey in *Eminent Victorians*, 1918).

Inventing for the purpose of her own novel a three-volume *Middlemarch* was an artistic necessity, one may assume. And Woolf, quite reasonably, relied on the fact that the multi-volume novel was so far in the past in 1927 that no one (apart from the odd crosspatch bibliophile) would notice her little liberty with strict literary history.

===

The Case of the Missing (or Not) Foreskin

===

Dorothy L. Sayers began her sequence of Lord Peter Wimsey novels in 1923, with *Whose Body?* She was at the time a young writer (just thirty), feeling her way into crime fiction as a part-time author (she kept her daytime job as an advertising copywriter with S. H. Benson until 1931). Like many first novels, *Whose Body?* is marked by the newcomer's unfamiliarity with the conventions of the literary genre in which she is working. The writing is not yet automatic. Sayers makes gaffes of a kind that an old hand, like Dornford Yates or G. K. Chesterton, would never perpetrate.

The novel's opening words, 'Oh Damn', are themselves daring at a mealy-mouthed time for English literature. As daring, for example, as Michael Arlen's '"Hell!" said the Duchess' with which his 1924 bestseller, *The Green Hat* opens or—to skip six decades—as daring as the 'Fuck! Fuck! Fuck!' with which the film *Four Weddings and a Funeral* opened in 1992. As he is introduced Lord Peter ('bally silly ass') is strikingly different from his later cosy incarnations (particularly as played by Ian Carmichael, in the 1970s TV production). As Sayers describes him: 'His long, amiable face looked as if it had generated spontaneously from his top hat, as white maggots breed from gorgonzola.' The simile suggests that Sayers (a literate and in later life affectedly donnish woman) had taken on board the two great modernist works of the time: *Ulysses* (1922, with its 'snot-green sea') and *The Love Song of J. Alfred Prufrock* (1917, with its evening 'spread out against the sky like a patient etherised upon a table').

As we first encounter him, Wimsey is on his way to a book

sale. He has his eye on two plums: a Wynkyn de Worde and a
Caxton. *En route* he discovers ('Oh damn!') that he has forgotten his catalogue and is obliged to turn the taxi back to his Al-
bany flat. There he is told by his 'man' Bunter that his mother,
the Dowager Duchess, is on the telephone. It transpires that
one of her 'people'—a humble retainer called Thipps—has
found a naked body in the bath of his Battersea flat. The
police have been called in. But knowing her son's 'hobby'—
amateur sleuthing—she suggests he might take a look.

The game is afoot. Sending Bunter to the book auction
in his place, Wimsey takes a taxi to Battersea. He duly
casts a monocled eye over the body in the bath. Whose is
it? Thipps has no clue, nor does he know how the thing got
there. He himself has a watertight alibi. Inspector Sugg, of
Scotland Yard (clodhopping, like all his kind), has jumped to
a conclusion that the body is that of a 'Hebrew financier'—
Sir Reuben Levy, a gentleman who has been reported missing
and whose description the corpse fits, apparently exactly.

The more perceptive Wimsey expertly scrutinises the
naked cadaver:

The body which lay in the bath was that of a tall, stout man of about
fifty. The hair, which was thick and black and naturally curly, had
been cut and parted by a master hand, and exuded a faint violet
perfume, perfectly recognisable in the close air of the bathroom. The
features were thick, fleshy and strongly marked, with prominent
dark eyes, and a long nose curving down to a heavy chin. The clean-
shaven lips were full and sensual, and the dropped jaw showed teeth
stained with tobacco. On the dead face the handsome pair of gold
pince-nez mocked death with grotesque elegance; the fine gold chain
curved over the naked breast. The legs lay stiffly stretched out side
by side; the arms reposed close to the body; the fingers were flexed
naturally. Lord Peter lifted one arm, and looked at the hand with a
little frown. (pp. 17–18)[1]

The gold pince-nez, carefully dressed hair, and the perfume
suggest Levy—middle-aged, rich, and not quite English
(particularly the Parma violets). But Wimsey, with the aid
of his monocle (in fact a Sherlockian magnifying glass) and

his silver matchbox (which doubles as an electric torch), looks more closely at some red blotches on the body. He also peers inside the corpse's mouth. He makes interesting discoveries.

Later, in conversation with the congenial Scotland Yard man Parker, Wimsey delivers his conclusion that Sugg is on the quite the wrong track with the 'Semitic-looking stranger'. Wimsey has detected that the red blotches are in fact flea-bites—the 'body' was vermin-ridden. The teeth are decayed from neglect—poor oral hygiene. The gold pince-nez correct the long sight associated with advanced age; a vigorous middle-aged man would be unlikely to need them. The fingernails are manicured, but the toenails are filthy and black. Wimsey leads Parker to the conclusion that the body in the bath is that of a working-class gentile, murdered, and 'washed . . . and scented . . . and shaved in order to disguise him' (p. 37).

Wimsey's deductions set up the teasing mystery announced in the novel's title. There remain, however, some loose ends in the opening episode. It was Sayers's first intention to have Wimsey seize on what would immediately strike the eye of one man looking at the naked body of another— the penis. Wimsey instantly noted what the dim Sugg had missed; namely that the 'body' was not circumcised, and therefore, whosoever it was, could not be Jewish. The author was firmly instructed by her publishers to remove this disturbing detail—disturbing, that is, to the cosy decorums of the English detective novel in its golden age.[2] This kind of thing might be very well in *Ulysses* (banned, of course, in 1923) but not in the world of Styles or Father Brown. *Whose Body?* was Sayers's first novel; it did the rounds of unimpressed publishers ('Sayers? Who's she?'); she had great difficulty finding one who would take her on; she submitted; a successful career was launched on a compromise. The gorgonzola maggots and the foreskins disappear.

═══

Who Killed Owen Taylor?

═══

Even by the standards of twist-a-minute hard-boiled detective fiction Raymond Chandler's plots are difficult to follow. Typically, to use his kind of simile, they have more holes than a Swiss cheese. The impenetrability of the plot of Chandler's first published novel, *The Big Sleep* (1938), gave rise to a famous literary anecdote.

The novel was filmed in 1946, by director Howard Hawks. This was the movie which 'made' the acting team, Bogart and Bacall. The couple fell in love during the shooting on the Warner lot, and married soon after. With *Casablanca*, *The Big Sleep* has become a classic of *film noir*. The image of 'Bogie'—fedora-hatted, smoking, above all *tough*—is a genre icon. As Chandler himself noted, for the rest of his career, Bogart retained 'something of Marlowe. He never lost it.'

During the shooting of the movie the director and his screenwriters (William Faulkner and Leigh Brackett)[1] ran into an apparently insoluble turn of plot—who killed the Sternwoods' chauffeur, Owen Taylor? Hawks duly sent a telegram to Chandler, asking for guidance. Who was the guilty party? Back came the telegram, 'NO IDEA'. 'I never figured out what was going on,' Hawks later despairingly observed.[2] The 'No Idea' wire makes a good (and much repeated) story. But it is likely that Chandler was disinclined to help William Faulkner, of whom he may have been a little jealous. In fact the Owen Taylor subplot, although murky, suggests that the novelist had thought about it in some detail and worked out a range of possible developments.

When he arrives at the imposing Sternwood mansion, in the upper Hollywood hills, Owen Taylor is the first person

Philip Marlowe sees as he looks around the grounds:

There were french doors at the back of the hall, beyond them a wide sweep of emerald grass to a white garage, in front of which a slim dark young chauffeur in shiny black leggings was dusting a maroon Packard convertible. (p. 9)[3]

Both slim chauffeur and maroon Packard (Carmen Sternwood's vehicle, as we learn) will figure later.

The chauffeur (unnamed at this stage) reappears in the scene in which Geiger is taking his dirty pictures of a naked and drugged Carmen. Marlowe is keeping a gumshoe's watch on things from the dark street outside. After shots and a scream, Marlowe hears two cars speeding away. In the house he finds the naked Carmen and Geiger's corpse: a live nymphomaniac and a dead fag. Perfect. A studio camera has been set up. Clearly Geiger was planning to supplement his income as a high-class pornographer with some further lucrative blackmail of General Sternwood.

The photographic plate is missing from the camera. Who now has it? Marlowe tidies up as best he can (there is some collateral mystery about Geiger's corpse, which disappears and reappears), and deposits a blanketed and snoring Carmen back at the Sternwood residence.

The next morning, Marlowe is called by his pal in the District Attorney's department, Bernie Ohls. An automobile has been driven into the ocean at 'Lido Fish Pier' (San Pedro, apparently—the harbour thirty miles from downtown LA). There is a body. The dead man proves to be Owen Taylor, the Sternwoods' chauffeur. The automobile is the Buick sedan of the older Sternwood daughter, Vivian. The cause of Taylor's death is mysterious. He has a broken neck—which may or may not be a result of the impact of the car hitting the ocean. The detectives' trained eyes soon perceive, however, that he was 'sapped' with a blackjack at some point before his death.

Evidently the Buick crashed through the end-of-the-pier barrier at high speed—having been driven straight down the whole length of the structure. This, then, is no 'accident'.

The 'hand throttle' (i.e. hand-operated accelerator—a device found on pre-war limousines, equivalent to today's 'cruise control') had been set halfway down. Unlike the foot-operated accelerator, this could have been done by someone other than the driver, who might then have thrown the car in gear and set it off, effectively driving itself, if the man at the wheel were unconscious. Taylor may well have been bumped off.

There is still no sign of the blackmail photo of Carmen in the altogether. If the dead man ever had it, he has it no longer. There are obvious mysteries here. The film chose to cut them short by making the Taylor crash manifestly accidental and wholly enigmatic. The death off the end of a fishing pier left too many threads hanging for Howard Hawks to clear up in his scanty 118 minutes of screen time. Nor was Chandler inclined to be helpful. In the film, Taylor is now forgotten. The audience's attention is directed to other more profitable matters.

In the novel, with its more spacious dimensions, further teasing details about Taylor ooze out over the following chapters. Police investigation reveals that a year or two ago he was arrested on a 'Mann Act rap'—the federal 'white slavery' law which prohibits the transport of minors for sexual purposes across state lines. As Ohls explains:

'It seems Taylor run Sternwood's hotcha daughter, the young one [i.e. Carmen], off to Yuma. The sister [i.e. Vivian] ran after them and brought them back and had Owen heaved into the icebox. Then next day she comes down to the DA and gets him to beg the kid off with the US 'cutor. She says the kid meant to marry her sister . . . So we let the kid go and then darned if they don't have him come back to work. And a little later we get the routine report on his prints from Washington, and he's got a prior back in Indiana, attempted hold-up six years ago. He got off with a six months in the county jail, the very one Dillinger bust out of. We hand that to the Sternwoods and they keep him on just the same. What do you think of that?' (pp. 46–7)

'They seem to be a screwy family,' Marlowe laconically replies. It later emerges that Carmen carries in her handbag a cute little pearl-handled .22 revolver, engraved 'Carmen from Owen' (this is the gun with which she has killed Rusty Regan, and will try to kill Marlowe).

What went on at Geiger's Hollywood bungalow, on the night of his murder, gradually emerges. Carmen was somehow enticed to the house. She was drugged on the premises with a mixture of ether and opium—taken for 'kicks' apparently. There is no need to slip this young lady anything. Carmen had driven herself to Geiger's place in her maroon Packard convertible, still gleaming presumably from the chauffeur's loving chamois.

Taylor, the same evening, had taken Vivian's car without permission. What was he doing in it? 'Nobody knows,' Vivian tells Marlowe. But we can make an educated guess. Geiger, having taken his photographs, would have needed someone to take the incapable young woman home. He, as prospective blackmailer, could hardly drop her off himself. So he phoned the chauffeur. Alternatively, Taylor was there all the time, and he was the bait that got Carmen to the house in the first place. It was their 'love nest', and had been used for such assignations before. This might also explain how it was Carmen came to be undressed. Failing some such explanation it is hard to see what Carmen was doing in Geiger's seedy joint and why a good-time girl like her would want to spend an evening there.

There was, however, another player in this game that no one knew about. In addition to Marlowe, Geiger was being tailed by Joe Brody. Brody's aim was to move in on Geiger's pornographic lending-library racket. Confronted later by a gun-wielding Marlowe, Brody insists, 'I *didn't* bop Geiger' (p. 73). It was Taylor.

According to Brody, the chauffeur broke into Geiger's place 'to have words with him, because Owen Taylor was sweet on Carmen, and he didn't like the kind of games Geiger was playing with her' (p. 83). When he saw the precise nature of the 'games' he lost his head and shot Geiger three times in the belly. If he was so 'sweet on Carmen' it would seem logical at this point for lover-boy to have taken her home, called the police, or at least covered the naked young lady up. Instead of which Taylor grabbed the photographic plate leaving the nude Carmen for someone else to take care of. A strange kind of sweetheart, we may think.

Clutching the photographic plate Taylor shot off at speed in Vivian's car, hotly pursued by Brody (hence the two cars which Marlowe heard). In a sharp turn off Sunset Boulevard, Taylor (according to Brody) skidded off the road. Brody 'sapped' him with his blackjack while he was still dazed, and took the plateholder 'just out of curiosity'. Why he should engage in a high-speed chase, simply in order to crack Taylor on the skull, and take nothing except an undeveloped negative of whose nature he is unaware is another can of narrative worms.

The suggestion is that when he came round from being sapped, Taylor was so suffused with remorse that, having heaved his heavy sedan back on the road, he drove it thirty miles to the coast to drive it off the road again into the Pacific. He committed suicide by accelerating at top speed (using the 'hand accelerator') along the Lido Fish Pier. It might well be an unpleasant death (drowning in a slowly sinking car) and it is hard to imagine a young hardened criminal inflicting it on himself. Taylor still has a revolver with three bullets in it (he plugged Geiger with the other three). If, as seems wholly unlikely that he would, he had resolved to kill himself, why not just blow his head off? Most likely, of course, is that young Mr Taylor would take off down the Pacific Coast Highway for Mexico, sell the car for as many pesos as he could get, and keep his head down until it was safe to come back.

This is how the narrative leaves things. Slightly further along than Howard Hawks and William Faulkner do in the film, but still tantalisingly unexplained. The Los Angeles newspapers report Taylor's death as suicide, and Marlowe lets sleeping dogs lie—or this dog at least. According to the papers, 'Owen Taylor had been despondent and in poor health. His family lived in Dubuque, and his body would be shipped there. There would be no inquest.'

Who then killed Owen Taylor? Owen Taylor himself? The business about poor health and despondency is hogwash; chauffeurs can't afford such luxuries. How did the papers come by it? From someone in the Sternwood household, obviously. As chauffeur, Taylor would have had his own keys to the Buick, but it is hard to believe that he could have taken the pride of the Sternwood auto fleet without someone in the house knowing. Or without permission from the car's owner, Vivian (a ruthless woman). Who put the fix in at City Hall, and ensured there was no inquest? A Sternwood, obviously— the family has 'pull'.

Above all, why, after killing Geiger, did Taylor take the photographic plate? Not to protect Carmen, we deduce. It's easy to destroy undeveloped negatives—all you have to do is expose the sensitised surface to the light. Why, on his part, did Brody go to the trouble of chasing after Taylor, and— having caught him—take the plate 'just out of curiosity'? A curiosity which led to having the plate developed (privately, of course; you can't expect a main-street druggist to hand over pictures of a naked woman without some query).

One doesn't have to be Marlowe to work out a more likely scenario than suicide. Taylor, we may plausibly deduce, was blackmailing the Sternwoods. On that trip to Yuma, he got something on Carmen that made it impossible for the family to dismiss him (even though, as a convicted felon, he could not legally have a commercial driver's licence, let alone a permit for the gun he was carrying). He was a pain in the Sternwood neck, ripe for rubbing out. Vivian had a friend, Eddie Mars, who specialised in such favours.

Taylor was, meanwhile, in cahoots with Geiger—and quite possibly with Brody. He shot the fat pornographer, in order to get the negative, seeing the chance of a really big score from General Sternwood. Carmen was in no position to testify against him. He had too much on her. In all probability, Taylor was also hooked up with Brody. The two men arranged to double-cross Geiger. They met on Sunset Boulevard by arrangement (no skidding car). Brody then double-crossed Taylor, knocking him out (for the police to find and nail for the murder), making off with the negatives.

What neither Taylor nor Brody knew was that Vivian had put a contract out on the chauffeur, with her pal Eddie Mars (Geiger's landlord, surprisingly enough). After Taylor was sapped and Brody had left the scene, one of Mars's heavies (Canino?) took the still unconscious Taylor down to the coast in the Buick (followed by a henchman in a second car) and staged the 'suicide'. If anyone had been prepared to pay Marlowe $25 a day plus expenses, he would have uncovered it all. But Taylor didn't matter that much. He was expendable— a bit player, he's ultimately as forgettable as Howard Hawks makes him in the film.

The question of course is—did Chandler expect the canny reader to work this out for himself? Or did he leave it there, as a kind of reserve plot, to fall back on, should the denouement require it? Or is it there to generate an enveloping narrative fog—like the pea-soupers in the Sherlock Holmes films? One can't know. And if Chandler wouldn't confide in Hawks or Faulkner, we never shall know.

Daphne du Maurier · *Rebecca*

═══

Where Was Rebecca Shot?

═══

Daphne du Maurier's romance is replete with enigma and unanswered questions left hanging artfully over the plot and its cunning denouement. Four puzzles stand out: (1) What are the second Mrs de Winter's Christian and maiden names, and what is her background? (2) Whose is the body which, at Edgecoombe, Maxim de Winter identified, two months after her disappearance, as that of his wife? (knowing, all the while, that Rebecca's corpse is lying underwater in the cabin of *Je reviens*, a few hundred yards from the boat house); (3) Why, in his last encounter with Rebecca, did Maxim fortuitously have a loaded gun with him? (4) If Mrs Danvers set fire to Manderley, Maxim's great house, what happened to her after this act of criminal arson?

The awkward anonymity and 'out-of-nowhere' character of the heroine–narrator of the story is not a puzzle which one would want solved. Her complete absence of history, past life or identity, her affectless character, create a vacuum to be filled with the unexpurgated presence of the dead-but-not-dead ('I shall return') Rebecca. In life the nameless one is less alive than dead Rebecca. The gimmick was respected by Hitchcock in his 1940 film (Joan Fontaine is listed as 'the girl') and by Susan Hill, in her authorised sequel, *Mrs de Winter* (1993).

Effective and novel-seeming as it is, one would like to know who first used the device of the omnipresent but nameless heroine–narrator, if not du Maurier. It seems to derive in part from the author's reading of Kafka. As with 'Josef K' in *The Trial*, it creates a striking vacuousness at the heart of the novel. In *Rebecca*'s case the effect is heightened by the narrative's being otherwise excessively and lushly descriptive. Du Maurier's 'no-name' trick is, one concludes, worth all the contortions which the dialogue has to perform to avoid accidentally dropping the girl's first name. But the fact that the main character was unnamed made it difficult to promote the film and Joan Fontaine's starring role. That Fontaine played 'Rebecca' has become one of popular culture's ubiquitous vulgar errors.

Hitchcock also had some difficulty with the other lady in the water.[1] Two months after Rebecca's disappearance— presumably at sea—a body was washed up 'Near Edge-coombe, about forty miles up channel' (the Bristol Channel, in the West Country). It is assumed by the authorities that she ('Rebecca') must have been drowned, 'trying to swim to shore after the boat sank' (p. 137).[2] The body was then taken by the tides on its long voyage up the tidal channel while undergoing its sea change.

Even the narrator–heroine, who is no yachtswoman, thinks this course of events is odd: 'I thought drowned people were found after two days. I thought they would be washed up close to the shore when the tide came.' Maxim went to court to identify the corpse and confirmed it was that of his wife. He must, one presumes, have knowingly falsified his sworn testimony, although it is not entirely beyond conceiving that he might have deluded himself that Rebecca's body had somehow drifted out of the closed cabin in which he left it, before scuttling the three-ton *Je reviens*. But perjury is the more likely hypothesis. It must have been touch-and-go: in the 1930s a lady like Mrs de Winter would surely have a wedding ring which must (mysteriously to the coroner's office) not have been on the corpse's left hand. If the body were so decomposed that the flesh on the fingers had sloughed off, by what means *did* Maxim identify it?

Some twelve months after this false identification, Rebecca's true body is found in the cabin of her yacht by divers investigating the wreck of another vessel gone down

on the cove's treacherous rocks just a few hundred yards
from Manderley. There are, even at this early stage, some
mysteries which the Edgecoombe coroner seems flagrantly to
have neglected: why, for example, the substantial three-ton,
wooden boat sank like a stone after capsizing without any
wreckage being washed up on any shore. Did Maxim hint to
the coroner that Rebecca had gone, solo, on a long voyage out
to sea?

Another puzzle is why, when the real Rebecca's corpse
is discovered, no-one seems in the slightest curious as
to who the other 'pseudo-Rebecca' can have been. The
magistrate, Colonel Julyan, instigates the most vigorous
(and patently corrupt) investigations into the second, actual
Rebecca corpse—culminating in the astonishing interview
with Dr Baker, the cover-up as to the circumstances of her
death, and the discreet advice that the de Winters might find
it convenient to spend a decade or two in Switzerland. But
no one (least of all the Colonel) seems to think, even as a
hypothesis, that the other woman may have been on the boat
with Rebecca.

This hypothesis has a far-fetched plausibility. The first Mrs
de Winter's lesbian tastes are clearly established. 'Rebecca
was incapable of love, of tenderness, of decency,' Max bitterly
recalls, 'she was not even *normal*' (p. 284; my italics). Mrs
Danvers is blunter: 'She despised all men. She was above all
that' (p. 356).[3] The other woman's presence on the boat would
explain how it might be that, at the time of the supposed
capsize, Rebecca was below decks with the cabin door closed
on her.

There is a second inquest for Rebecca, a second formal
identification of the corpse by Maxim, and a second interment
in the vault at Manderley. But there is no second inquest for
the nameless pseudo-Rebecca. And where is her disinherited
corpse laid to rest? In Potter's Field, presumably. Or perhaps
it is tossed back into the waves whence it came.

A connected hypothesis invites passing examination. Did

Maxim come on Rebecca *in flagrante delicto* with a *woman* in the boat house, and kill them both, unable to restrain himself on witnessing, in its full 'unspeakability', the Sapphic depravity of his wife? Obviously he would not have been able to stow both corpses in the cabin and sustain the accidental capsize theory when the wreck was eventually discovered (as he must have known it would be). The other body may have been left on deck, or taken up the coast in his own yacht, and deposited miles away at sea.

This leads on to the third of the puzzles: why did Maxim take a gun with him when he went down to the boat house for his last interview with Rebecca? And what kind of 'gun' (shotgun, rifle, or handgun) was it? His repeated mention that the single fatal 'bullet' went right through Rebecca, without scraping or smashing any bone, suggests either a rifle or a large-calibre handgun.[4] Anatomically, the route which the fatal round must have taken is through the soft tissue of the belly or abdomen (more of which later). Although we have no firm information on the matter, Maxim presumably served in the Great War, and would be a trained shot; he would also know how best to kill your man. The heart, or head, would of course be the logical target; unless he had an ulterior motive in what marksmen call a 'gut-shot'. It's very nasty—more so since Maxim now 'knows' that his wife is carrying a baby. He is ending two lives. Hitchcock in his film blurred the whole thing by having Rebecca start back at the sight of Max's fury, fall over, bang her head, and die accidentally. No gut-shot, no blood.

Why was Maxim so enraged as to want to go rampaging down to the boat house, gun in hand? He has no reason to suppose that Rebecca has a lover with her, after her return from London. As he tells his second wife: 'I came back after dinner, about half past ten, and I saw her scarf and gloves lying on a chair in the hall. I wondered what the devil she had come back for' (p. 290). '*Her* scarf and gloves': no one else's. Maxim's explanation to his second wife for storming

down to the boat house, fully armed, rings very hollow. He
claims to have suspected that she had a (male) lover with
her, probably the obnoxious Jack Favell: 'The thing had got
to be settled, one way or the other. I thought I'd take a gun
and frighten the fellow, frighten them both' (p. 290). If he
just wants to 'frighten' them, why take a loaded weapon? He
would, of course, have to insert the shells before rushing down
to the boat house; countrymen and ex-officers like Maxim do
not leave loaded weapons round the house. It is part of the
licence under which they hold them that they do not.

Maxim, as he recalls, found Rebecca alone, although it later
emerges that she had left an urgent message at Jack Favell's
flat, on leaving London a few hours previous. The message
bears interestingly on Maxim's account (he does not know
of its existence when he makes his confession to his second
wife). 'I tried to ring you from the flat,' Rebecca writes to Jack:

but could get no answer. I'm going down to Manders right away. I
shall be at the cottage this evening, and if you get this in time will
you get the car and follow me. I'll spend the night at the cottage,
and leave the door open for you. I've got something to tell you and I
want to see you as soon as possible. Rebecca. (p. 340)

The 'something' she has to tell him, obviously, is that she
has only months to live. Why tell Jack before anyone else?
Because, as he apprehends ('This cancer business . . . does
anybody know if it's contagious?', p. 385), the disease is
venereal in origin. If she has it, so does he. Dr Baker of course
is tactful on this aspect of Rebecca's disorder. Surprised by
Maxim in the boat house, according to his version of events,
Rebecca taunted him with the 'news' that she is pregnant by
another man. She will pass the child off as heir to Manderley.
There are numerous hints in the narrative that theirs is a
'blank', unconsummated union ('Our marriage was a farce
from the very first . . . We never loved each other, never had
one moment of happiness together,' p. 284).

Rebecca knows that this malicious invention will madden
Maxim and (again according to his account) she turns the

screw ruthlessly on her husband:

'If I had a child, Max . . . neither you, nor anyone in the world, would ever prove that it was not yours. It would grow up here in Manderley, bearing your name. There would be nothing you could do. And when you died Manderley would be his. You could not prevent it. The property's entailed. You would like an heir, wouldn't you, for your beloved Manderley? . . . Well, you heard me say I was going to turn over a new leaf, didn't you? Now you know the reason . . . I'll be the perfect mother, Max, like I've been the perfect wife.' (p. 292)

It is all too much for the cuckolded Max:

'She turned round and faced me, smiling, one hand in her pocket, the other holding her cigarette. When I killed her she was smiling still. I fired at her heart. The bullet passed right through. She did not fall at once. She stood there, looking at me, that slow smile on her face, her eyes wide open . . . I'd forgotten,' said Maxim, and his voice was slow now, tired, without expression, 'that when you shot a person there was so much blood.' (p. 293)

One notes, as a point of passing interest, that Maxim has clearly shot people before. And one notes how carefully he chooses his words: 'I fired *at* her heart.' He missed, of course. It is inconceivable that even a small-calibre bullet (a .22 round, say) could miss hitting a bone in the rib-cage on entry or exit. And it would have to be a very powerful gun indeed for the bullet to pass through the whole width of the (presumably corseted) body, causing enough damage to vital organs to kill the victim with one wound. If the bullet had remained lodged in the body it would, of course, have been found by the post-mortem.

Maxim is a liar on oath: a proven perjuror. And there are aspects of this which ring false. He intends to straighten things out 'one way or another', but he takes a loaded gun only to 'frighten the fellow'. Or possibly to frighten Rebecca as well. Why Rebecca should want to taunt him into killing her, before having had her little talk with Jack, is mysterious. As Maxim reconstructs the scene, it was she who was to blame. She manipulated him into pulling the trigger of the gun which, quite fortuitously, he happened to have with him. It is, of course, the classic (and often successful) defence of the wife-killer: 'She taunted me with my manhood, your Honour; a red mist came over my eyes and I didn't know what I was doing.' Justifiable homicide; three years' probation.

Then there is the business of the single shot that killed Rebecca. If, as Maxim says, the bullet went through her body, killing her without touching a bone, we have to assume that he shot her in the belly, above the pelvis and below the ribs. He claims to have aimed at her false heart. But, since the heart is an organ encased by bone, he clearly either missed or is lying. What seems more plausible is that with her cigarette-holding hand Rebecca pointed to her stomach, the lodging place for the embryonic heir of Manderley, and that is where Maxim shot her.

If we look through Maxim's terse, self-serving description to what more probably happened, it throws an unromantic light on the master of Manderley. Should we believe, in the first place, that he went down to the boat house simply to put the frighteners on Rebecca and her lover? What seems plausible, given Max's explosive temper (of which we are given many examples), is that he apprehended, from the coat and scarf, that Rebecca was in the boat house by herself, and went down intending to kill her. She pleaded for her life, claiming (falsely) that she was pregnant. It is the kind of ruse that would come naturally to her. Implacable, Maxim shot her in the stomach. With a great deal of cunning, it is possible for narrative to handle such scenes and retain some degree of sympathy for the murderer. I have witnessed an audience cheer, for example, at that last scene in the film *Fatal Attraction* where the pregnant *femme fatale* (played by Glenn Close) is shot in the stomach. But it would be hard, if we had a more candid account than Maxim de Winter's own, to see what he did as anything other than cold-blooded, premeditated murder.

As to the fire at Manderley, both the Hitchcock film and the

1995 TV version made it a grand climax, a kind of lesbian suttee. Mrs Danvers is shown, inside the house, setting the fire (hard to do, one would have thought, with a household full of servants). Mrs Danvers then immolates herself in the flames, in the shrine of Rebecca's bedroom. The suggestion is that they were lovers (unappetising as 'Danny' is, physically). Susan Hill makes Mrs Danvers the arsonist, but has her survive to return and persecute the second Mrs de Winter, ten years later.

In the novel, the fire is more enigmatic. The de Winters arrive by car, at four o'clock in the morning. Maxim is apprehensive. He has been informed that Mrs Danvers had a trunk phone call, and has packed up and left. As they approach Manderley, the narrator–heroine sees, as she thinks, the dawn rising in the west. But it cannot be. Are they perhaps 'northern lights'? Not in summer:

He drove faster, much faster. We topped the hill before us and saw Lanyon lying in a hollow at our feet. There to the left of us was the silver streak of the river, widening to the estuary at Kerrith six miles away. The road to Manderley lay ahead. There was no moon. The sky above our heads was inky black. But the sky on the horizon was not dark at all. It was shot with crimson, like a splash of blood. And the ashes blew towards us with the salt wind from the sea. (p. 397)

And so the novel ends. The questions remain. Who has done this vengeful act, set fire to Manderley? Rebecca, of course. *Je reviens*.

≡

Godfathers

≡

Anthony Burgess took mischievous pleasure in an Italian translation of George Orwell's *Nineteen Eighty-Four* which changed the first line 'It was a bright cold day in April, and the clocks were striking *thirteen*' into striking *'uno'* on the grounds that sensible Italian clocks don't go up to thirteen. My own favourite cock-eyed translation is a *Livre de poche* paperback of Graham Greene's *Brighton Rock*, which I saw in the 1960s, translated as *Les rochers de Brighton* with a cover illustration of what looked like the north face of the Eiger. I suppose *Le nougat de Brighton* or *Le bonbon-particulier de Brighton* would have been thought too perplexing for the Gallic reader.

'Rock'—that tooth-wrecking sweetmeat with the writing which goes right through (like guilt)—is one of those specifically English comestibles. Like the 'banger' sausage and Albion's beloved whale-oil ice-cream, Brussels will doubtless adjudicate that it must be more accurately renamed, if it has not already done so.

There are a number of puzzles in *Brighton Rock* which might be profitably pursued. There are even a couple arising from the novel's vivid opening sentence: 'Hale knew, before he had been in Brighton three hours, that they meant to murder him' (p. 5).[1] We are never enlightened, as far as I can make out, on two salient issues arising from this *mise en scène*. First, what is Pinkie's precise motive for killing this apparently inoffensive newspaper stunt man ('Kolley Kibber'), harmlessly distributing his cards around the crowds in Whitsun-holiday Brighton? Even in Brighton's criminal underworld—where cutthroat razors come to hand as readily as ice-cream cones—murder is a serious act, to be carried out only *in extremis*. Some treachery to do with the murder on St Pancras Station of Pinkie's patron, the gang-leader Kite, seems to be involved. But we are never clear how, why or to whom Hale–Kibber 'grassed', or what his double-cross was, if that is what it was. Why not go for whoever it was who actually murdered Kite, or ordered his murder?

Secondly, how was the deed—Hale's murder—actually done? We know precisely when it was done: between half-past one and two o'clock. Establishing an alibi for this half-hour involves Pinkie in his having to marry Rose (despite his loathing of sex) so that she cannot testify against him. After leaving Hale's body, Pinkie is evidently convinced that he *has* murdered Hale. But how? Surprisingly, after he is 'cut up' (post-mortemed) for the inquest, it emerges that Hale died of a heart attack. Was he smothered? Did he collapse on being threatened by Pinkie's razor or vial of acid? Was he poisoned? The inquest determines that he died of natural causes; and the body is promptly cremated. Why then is Pinkie so anxious that—against every fibre in his misogynistic body—he should marry Rose, to forestall her 'informing' on him. He's in the clear. There is no reason to have anything to do with the wretched 'poloney'.

These are dark spots, artfully introduced, one suspects, into the fabric of Greene's 'entertainment'. Something classily 'literary', that is, to distinguish *Brighton Rock* from the tell-all banalities of the Edgar Wallace school of thriller writing (Wallace's *The Ringer* seems to have been one of the inspirations for Greene's 'entertainment').

Beguiling as these enigmas are, I want to investigate a coincidence connected with names in *Brighton Rock*. The up-and-coming gang leader in the sea-side town, the new *capo di tutti capi* who embodies 'organised' crime, is called Mr Colleoni. Was he the inspiration, in name at least, for Mario Puzo's 'Godfather', Don Corleone, almost forty years later?

On a superficial level, the echo is strikingly suggestive.

Both arch-criminals are, apparently, of Italian origin. Both head 'syndicates', or business-style mobs. Both have an eerily calm statesmanlike manner in their thuggery. Corleone's most famous maxim is that the man with the briefcase can out-steal the guy with the gun, every time. He is moving high crime into white-collar 'respectability'. He is a business man ('this is not personal, but business' is one of Corleone's favourite apologies for any egregious piece of thuggery). So too with Greene's godfather. 'You are wasting your time, my child,' Colleoni tells Pinkie:

'You can't do me any harm.' He laughed gently. 'If you want a job though, come to me. I like push. I dare say I could find room for you. The World needs young people with energy.' The hand with the cigar moved expansively, mapping out the World as Mr Colleoni visualized it: lots of little electric clocks controlled by Greenwich, buttons on a desk, a good suite on the first floor, accounts audited, reports from agents, silver, cutlery, glass . . . the weekend at the Cosmopolitan, the portable dictaphone beside the desk, had not the smallest connection with Kite slashed quickly with razors on a railway platform . . . 'I'm just a business man,' Mr Colleoni softly explained. (p. 64)

So are they both business men. It would be easy to assume that Puzo somewhere picked up or half remembered this detail in Greene's gangster story. Mobsters are the same the world over. Etymologically, however, Colleoni and Corleone are coming from quite different places. Corleone is—manifestly—a variant of 'Coeur de Lion', Richard the Lionheart. The name connects with that ubiquitous high-school text in the American 1930s and 1940s (and Elizabeth Taylor-starring film of the early 1950s), Scott's *Ivanhoe*. The 'Don' is literally noble. A king, almost. In Scott's narrative, Richard (the black knight) is a benignly cunning manipulator of England's unruly barons—the *capi* or 'muscle' who run the country in his name. But Richard embodies, above all, 'heart'—bravery, honour, and fidelity to country; qualities similarly incarnate in 'Don' Corleone.

Greene's 'Colleoni' has a more vexed and ignoble deriva-
tion. In the first, 1938 version of *Brighton Rock* he was
conceived as 'a small Jew with a round belly'—a rootless
cosmopolitan in the aptly named Cosmopolitan Hotel—
surrounded by 'little Jewish bitches'. Greene tactfully altered
this after World War II by taking out the Semitic identification. 'Little Jewish bitches' became 'little bitches'; Colleoni is
described merely as 'small with a neat round belly'.[2]

With the removal of any taint of racial slander from
the characterisation of Colleoni there was also lost the
religious opposition between the small Jew's corrupt, bitch-
sniffing sensuality and Pinkie's austere, monastic, body-
hating Catholicism. More so since, by itself, the Italianate
name half suggests that Colleoni may be another lapsed
Catholic. When he revised his text for the 1970 Bodley Head
'Collected Edition' of his works, Greene (currently resident
in Antibes) inserted into the foreword to *Brighton Rock* what
looks like a deliberately misleading nod in this direction:

Colleoni, the gang leader, has his real prototype who had retired
by 1938 and lived a gracious Catholic life in one of the Brighton
crescents . . . I am sometimes reminded of him when I watch the
handsome white-haired American gangster, one of Lucky Luciano's
men, spending the quiet evening of his days between the Piazza of
Capri and the smart *piscine* of the Casino del Mar restaurant at
Piccola Marina.[3]

It is not easy to see how Colleoni, as originally conceived
in 1938, could have retired to a 'gracious Catholic life in
one of the Brighton crescents'. One assumes that Greene is
deliberately throwing up a smokescreen over the issue of
ethnicity.

Both the Italian and the Hebraic elements in 'Colleoni' are
less weighty, however, than another etymological element.
One of the refrains ringing through *Brighton Rock*'s narrative
is the broken-down lawyer Prewitt's despairing tag from
Marlowe's *Doctor Faustus*: 'Why, this is Hell, nor am I
out of it.' Brighton, we deduce, is Hell. Prewitt rolls off

a number of other Marlovian and Shakespearian lines, all cosmically pessimistic. Taken with Kolley Kibber (i.e. the playwright Colley Cibber, 1671–1751) and Kite (the name of a prominent character in Farquhar's *The Recruiting Officer*, 1706), we can reasonably point to a strand of allusion to 'old drama' in *Brighton Rock*. In Elizabethan, Jacobean, and Restoration theatre one frequently encounters the word 'cullion'—a derivative of *coglione*, or 'testicle'.

The *OED* gives two meanings (both archaic) for 'cullion': (1) a testicle, (2) a despicable fellow, a rascal. Greene, we assume, has darkened his design in *Brighton Rock* with colours taken from the Jacobean palette. Following this line, Colleoni ('despicable fellow') suggests something quite opposite to Corleone ('the lionhearted').

The etymology of Colleoni–cullion leads on to the decoding of another curious name in the novel—that of 'Pinkie' Brown, the seventeen-year-old villain–hero. 'Pinkie' is an odd first (or 'Christian') name. The word 'Pinkie' is normally only commonly used in twentieth-century speech for the 'little finger'. There is an obsolete verb, 'to pink' (again found in Elizabethan drama), which means to prick, or stab. This might seem appropriate for a razor-boy; but I am unconvinced this was anywhere in Greene's mind when he devised the name.

Pinkie is, clearly, a nickname, not a baptismal or given name (it would be interesting to know under what name he marries Rose in the Registry Office scene; we are not told). It seems as a child, Pinkie was found a street-waif coughing on the Palace Pier, 'in the bitter cold, listening to the violin wailing behind the glass' (p. 218). He was befriended by Kite, half gangster (a version of the recruiting sergeant), half carrion-hunting bird of prey. Kite, for obscure reasons, adopted him, and brought him to Billy's, and—presumably— gave him the name 'Pinkie Brown'. Why did a middle-aged Brighton mobster recruit a child into his gang? Why did not the local police or social services take an interest? Kite's

motives for being philanthropic are vaguely guessed at by
Pinkie: 'God knows why . . . perhaps because a man like Kite
needed a little sentiment like a tart who keeps a Pekinese'
(p. 218).

Homosexual motives are hinted at by that comparison with
the whore's lap-dog. It would explain, among other things,
Pinkie's subsequent loathing of everything sexual; it would
also explain his fanatic loyalty to Kite's memory, and his
self-destructive need to avenge him, by killing Hale. Did Kite
abuse, molest, or even caress Pinkie in a way that has scarred
him for life? A hinted answer may be found in the puzzling
name. By the conventional 'I-mutation' process, by which 'u',
over historical time, becomes 'i', we can read 'Pinkie' as a
version of 'Punk[ie]'. 'Punk' is a a familiar term in Jacobean
drama denoting (1) a prostitute, (2) the passive and typically
younger partner in a sexual relationship. The term survives,
oddly, in this second sense in American prison argot. To
become a con's 'punk' is to become his sexual slave. It is a
role traditionally reserved for boys, and 'sissies'.

As regards Corleone and Colleoni, any resemblance is—
for once, and genuinely—'entirely coincidental'. The homony-
mous godfathers are as different, we may conclude, as a lion's
heart and a vulture's testicles.

Lucky Jim's Happier Ending

It was David Lodge who identified the 'turning point' in *Lucky Jim*.[1] For most of the narrative the hero, Jim Dixon, compensates for the drabness of being a fourth-rate history lecturer (probationary) at a third-rate 'redbrick' by means of a richly compensatory inner life. He cultivates a mental world inhabited by a menagerie of his particular enemies—notably Professor Welch and his family—on whom he visits imaginary indignities. Jim *thinks* his satire, in the spirit of *esprit de l'escalier*. It can be deliciously funny, but it is essentially Pooterish—revenge in the head. Jim—an archetypal angry young man—expresses his anger in fantasies about stuffing his professor down a lavatory ('pulling the plug once, twice, and again, stuffing the mouth with toilet-paper', p. 10),[2] by making aggressive 'faces' (his gorilla face is a speciality), solitary boozing, and equally solitary 'long jabbering belches'.

The point at which Jim turns is in the climactic encounter with Bertrand Welch, his rival for the rich and pretty Christine Callaghan. Bertrand, who has come to Jim's rooms to warn him off, is bested in some farcical fisticuffs. In his moment of triumph, Jim puts his glasses on again, 'feeling good':

Bertrand caught his eye with a look of embarrassed recognition. The bloody old towser-faced boot-faced totem-pole on a crap reservation, Dixon thought. 'You bloody old towser-faced boot-faced totem-pole on a crap reservation,' he said. (p. 209)

As Lodge points out, it is a significant moment. Private aggression has become public self-assertion. Jim, at last, is an angry young *man*. In light of this the ending of the novel may strike the reader as unsatisfactory. Following his hilariously drunken lecture on 'Merrie England' and the even more hilarious bus ride to the railway station, Jim gets the pretty girl, the plum job with the industrialist Julius Gore-Urquhart, and is set to be happy ever after. Lucky Jim indeed.

Lucky Jim was a first novel, and Amis was evidently some time in finding a publisher for it. It came out in 1954 but, as keen-eyed readers will note, is clearly set in the 1949–50 period.[3] Amis (a young lecturer at the time) was in the habit of reading out his work in progress to friends in various provincial universities—friends alert to the novel's many in-jokes about provincial universities (Jim's college is, clearly, Leicester, where the novel's dedicatee, Philip Larkin, was currently an assistant librarian). I have been told by one of those privileged auditors (at Reading, where Amis's friend John Wain was an assistant lecturer) that the embryonic novel had a different, and less formulaic, conclusion. Jim was dismissed (as he is in the published work) by Welch. But his final act was to call his professor up on the phone, and fart explosively into the receiver.

It would be in character. The emancipated Jim is a violent man. He revenges himself on his fellow lodger, Johns, by furtively scooping up a handful of insurance policies from the college administrator's desk and burning them in the building's furnace. It will, in probability, mean dismissal for Johns and—if found out—might well land Jim Dixon in the dock and not inconceivably in clink. For such a reprobate, breaking wind into a phone is no big thing (although one would not like to be the next person to use the instrument).

In 1954, a novelist might get away with a 'long jabbering belch', but the other was out of the question. Irvine Welsh was still forty years in the future. It is standard practice in Hollywood to try out alternative endings for movies on representative audiences before putting a film out on general release. *Lucky Jim* is, forty-five years after its first publication, still in print and selling healthily. Which ending would the public of 1998 prefer?

William Golding · *Lord of the Flies*

<hr>

Piggy's Burning(?) Glasses

<hr>

If there is one most notorious error of fact in the twentieth-century novel, it is William Golding's cock-eyed optics and pyrotechnics in *Lord of the Flies*. Fires and firemaking figure centrally in Golding's plot. The signal bonfire (which is allowed to go out at the very moment a plane flies over head) marks the critical breakdown of the boys' co-operative civilisation on the island. The forest fire, which Jack sets to smoke out Ralph at the climax of the narrative, marks the culminating triumph of savagery.

The instrument by which Golding's children master fire is Piggy's 'specs'. The discovery scene is one of the novel's memorable moments. The boys realise they have no matches. Some of them vaguely remember (from *Coral Island*, doubtless) a trick with two sticks, but no one quite knows how it is to be done. Enter from the forest Piggy, the tubby Prometheus, 'the evening sunlight gleaming from his glasses':

Jack pointed suddenly.

'His specs—use them as burning glasses!' . . . There was pushing and pulling and officious cries. Ralph moved the lenses back and forth, this way and that, till a glossy white image of the declining sun lay on a piece of rotten wood. Almost at once a thin trickle of smoke rose up and made him cough. Jack knelt too and blew gently, so that the smoke drifted away, thickening, and a tiny flame appeared. The flame, nearly invisible at first in that bright sunlight, enveloped a small twig, grew, was enriched with colour, and reached up to a branch which exploded with a sharp crack. The flame leaped higher and boys broke into a cheer.

'My specs!' howled Piggy. 'Give me my specs!' (pp. 39–40)[1]

One is led to deduce that Piggy is short-sighted and, without his glasses, he is virtually blind. All he can see is 'blurs, that's all. Hardly see my hand—' (p. 40).

The 'discovery of fire' scene exactly parallels its counterpart in Golding's source text, *Coral Island*. It is sunset. Ralph, Jack and Peterkin are preparing themselves for their first night on the coral island:

> But it now occurred to us, for the first time, that we had no means of making a fire.
>
> 'Now, there's a fix! What shall we do?' said Peterkin, while we both turned our eyes to Jack, to whom we always looked in our difficulties. Jack seemed not a little perplexed.
>
> 'There are flints enough, no doubt, on the beach,' said he, 'but they are of no use at all without a steel. However, we must try.' So saying, he went to the beach, and soon returned with two flints.[2]

They are, indeed, of no use. Not even when struck against a piece of hoop-iron or the back of the axe can a useful spark be produced. Suddenly, Peterkin has an inspiration: '"Oh I have it!" he cried, starting up; "the spy glass—the big glass at the end is a burning glass!" "You forget we have no sun," said I' (p. 30). Jack finally hits on the solution: a bowstring with which to revolve a stick of wood so fast and hard that by friction against another piece of wood it will eventually ignite tinder.

Peterkin would seem to be more observant than William Golding; he knows that it is the magnifying lens, at the far end of the telescope, which will work, not the minifying (if that's the right word) lens at the eye-end of the instrument. It is also clear that Golding must have had this passage in mind when he devised the parallel scene in *Lord of the Flies*. He echoes, verbatim, the 'burning glass!' exclamation. And the reader is informed, on four occasions, that (as on Coral Island) it is dusk and that the sun is 'slanting', that it is 'almost horizontal', and that 'the shadows are thickening fast'. It is almost as if Golding is stacking the cards against the plausibility of the scene with Piggy's specs as burning glass by recalling Peterkin's failure.

The crucial optical flaw in William Golding's account of Piggy's Promethean specs was explained in an article by T. Hampton, in *Notes and Queries* (July 1965). The fire-raising scene was 'impossible', Mr Hampton pointed out, because 'The lenses used to correct myopia are diverging lenses and so will not bring the rays of the sun to a focus. Had Piggy been long-sighted then he would have been wearing converging lenses, which will focus light to a point.'

It is, perhaps, a feeble defence to note that Golding does not specifically indicate in his text what Piggy's sight problem is. But the circumstantial evidence (his not being able to see his hand in front of his face, for example, without his glasses) confirms Hampton's myopia surmise. One might also mount a forlorn defence, as I have suggested, by pointing to the way in which Golding, apparently knowingly, weakens the scene by stressing the setting sun. Quite likely William Golding, like most of us, was ignorant of the differences between diverging and converging lenses. But he would know that you need strong sunlight for the focussed beam to ignite wood.

In his essay, 'Literature and the Matter of Fact', Christopher Ricks argues that we should take the anomaly seriously: 'Piggy's shortsightedness, and the glasses which counter it, are central to the architectonics of the book.' Ricks thinks the error represents a salutary cutting down to size of William Golding: 'I continue to think *Lord of the Flies* an extraordinary achievement,' Ricks concedes, 'especially for a first novel; but there was already present, if the early readers had eyes to see and were not myopic, the hubris and the overbearing which damaged his later novels.'[3] If Golding comes a cropper, so much the better.

Piggy's specs crop up again in Julian Barnes's *Flaubert's Parrot* (1984). The novel's hero, Geoffrey Braithwaite, has heard an earlier version of 'Literature and the Matter of Fact', given as a lecture 'some years ago' at the Cheltenham Literary Festival (from later exchanges, it is clear that there was such a lecture, and Barnes heard it):

It was given by a professor from Cambridge, Christopher Ricks, and
it was a very shiny performance . . . Its theme was Mistakes in Literature and Whether They Matter . . . Two examples particularly
struck me. The first was a remarkable discovery about *Lord of the
Flies*. In the famous scene where Piggy's spectacles are used for the
rediscovery of fire, William Golding got his optics wrong. Completely
back to front, in fact.[4]

It's definitely an error, Braithwaite–Barnes concedes, but
'does it matter?' Not much:

With Piggy's glasses I should think that (a) very few people apart
from oculists, opticians and bespectacled professors of English would
notice; and (b) when they do notice, they merely detonate the error—
like blowing up a small bomb with a controlled explosion . . .
Mistakes like William Golding's are 'external mistakes'—disparities
between what the book claims to be the case and what we know the
reality to be; often they merely indicate a lack of specific technical
knowledge on the writer's part. The sin is pardonable. (pp. 77–8)

The shiny professor thinks it's cardinal; the irate novelist
thinks it's pardonable.

One could sidestep the issue by pointing out that much
licence is extended to boys' books. In R. M. Ballantyne's *Coral
Island*, for example, there is one of the most famous sole-
cisms in Victorian fiction—the 'Coconut Lemonade' blunder
(Ballantyne assumed, never having been to the tropics, that
coconuts grew on palms unhusked, as one finds them in English grocers' shops; as absurd a conception as Walt Disney's
bread-and-butterflies).[5] No one holds it against *Coral Island*,
any more than the boys' ludicrously improbable victory over
the shark. Such liberties are allowed in adventure stories
for boys. The technique by which Jack lights the fire, with a
bowstring and two pieces of wood, verges on the fantastic. It is
unlikely that an English schoolboy, attempting the operation
for the first time, could pull it off. A bushman might after
many years' practice. But, as I say, one does not press boys'
books too hard on such things.

On the other hand, Ricks surely has a strong point.

Although the error was first pointed out in the little-read columns of *Notes and Queries* (a journal normally restricted to university libraries), it has seeped out into general consciousness. It is not just oculists who nowadays perceive the blunder. Even A-level candidates blithely trot it out and feel they have done something significant by doing so. Once pointed out, it does material damage. The 'controlled explosion' needed to demolish the error in the reader's mind is reaching car-bomb dimensions. On the other hand, so central is the contested possession of the fire-making specs to the plot, it is hard to see how it could be easily mended, even if some meddler (now that Golding has gone) were impertinent enough to attempt such a thing. And, at the end of the day, *Lord of the Flies* is not—like its Victorian source—a boys' book with such books' generous licence; it is a book for adults about boys.

There are, if one looks carefully at it, a number of other improbabilities which we have to swallow in *Lord of the Flies*. How did all those children survive (none seems to be injured) after their passenger plane was shot down, and not a single adult? There is some perfunctory reference to a 'passenger tube', which we are to suppose was parachuted down, like the nose-cone of a space rocket. It is probably as well the novel did not dwell on this machinery.

Although Ballantyne's optics are firmer than Golding's (in that the Victorian novelist knows one lens from another) the modern novelist's geography is much more plausible, as are the flora and fauna he describes. *Coral Island* is set in a vaguely described 'Pacific Ocean' of the romantic imagination. Ballantyne's description of how his boys get there is skimpy. Ralph Rover, brought up on the west coast of England, is of an incurably roving disposition. He embarks, as a fifteen-year-old seaman, on the *Arrow*, bound for 'the islands of the Pacific Ocean'. Two other cabin boys become his inseparable friends, Jack and Peterkin. The *Arrow* rounds 'terrible' Cape Horn safely, but is wrecked by a storm among the coral islands of the Pacific. Whereabouts in that vastest of oceans, we never know. At the end of the novel, the nearest port of call is, apparently, Tahiti. What line of trade the ship is in is not made clear. It could be slaving, or 'blackbirding'.

Prior events are described even more briefly in *Lord of the Flies*, but more accurately if we trouble to reconstruct them. The jet plane, full of juvenile evacuees, is evidently directed towards the relative safety of Australasia. Europe is, by the time the children land on the island, a theatre of nuclear war and they have got out just in time. Piggy has overheard 'grown-ups' say an atom bomb has hit England (it would be nice to think it is that bomb which Orwell describes in *Nineteen Eighty-Four* hitting Colchester, in 1951). But how have they landed on this tropical island, with its coral reef? Whereabouts on the globe is it? *Coral Island*'s Pacific Ocean? That would be the automatic assumption, and it is often made. In a random sweep through my college library, for example, I have come up with three 'authorities' who assert, confidently, that Golding's island, like Ballantyne's, is in the Pacific or 'South Seas'. The Macmillan 'Casebook' chapter on *Lord of the Flies* opens:

William Golding's *Lord of the Flies* is a retelling in realistic terms of R. M. Ballantyne's *The Coral Island*. A group of boys, shot down during some kind of atomic war, are marooned on an island in the Pacific.[6]

The island is *not* in the Pacific, although Golding mirrors many of Ballantyne's descriptions of its lagoon, its reef and the adventures involved in exploring its interior. Mark Kinkead-Weekes and Ian Gregor, in their *William Golding: A Study* (London, 1967) are nearer the mark in their observation that 'the aircraft has been attacked, probably over the Sunda Sea, and has released its detachable passenger tube to crash-land in the jungle of a convenient island.'[7] The Sunda Sea is just south of Borneo. Kinkead-Weekes and Gregor (who were in consultation with Golding while writing their monograph) seem to be drawing on knowledge of the early manuscript version of *Lord of the Flies* (then known as 'Strangers from Within'), in which the location was precisely given as near New Guinea and Borneo.

None the less, as finally rewritten for publication, we should assume that the island is neither in the Pacific Ocean nor the Sunda Sea. The main clue is fragmentary but conclusive. Jack Merridew, when Simon has an epileptic fit, dismisses it with a heartless: 'He's always throwing a faint . . . He did it in Gib, and Addis' (p. 20). One assumes from this that the haven to which the children are being evacuated is Western Australia.

The itinerary suggested by Jack's remark is logical, in the era before long-haul jets (*Lord of the Flies* is evidently set in 1951–2, shortly after the USSR developed an arsenal of atomic weaponry, in the late 1940s). The first leg of the plane's trip is to Gibraltar. There, they refuel. The second leg is to Addis Ababa in Ethiopia. There follows a third and last leg across the Indian Ocean, to Western Australia. At some point on this last stage of the flight, the plane has been intercepted by Soviet, or Chinese, long-range fighters.

The boys' 'escape tube' has come down in the Maldives, or the Seychelles, on one of the numerous coral islands in the Indian Ocean. This it is which explains how it is they are picked up by a British cruiser, steaming out of an East of Suez base—probably in Ceylon. It also explains why there is so much air traffic over their 'desert' island. This part of the globe, being a main theatre of conflict, is nowhere near as out-of-the-way as a Pacific coral island would be. And the Sunda Sea would be an impossibly long leg for an aircraft flying from Addis Ababa in the early 1950s—although at some point in his planning for the novel that may be where the boys were intended to come down. William Golding may not, as Christopher Ricks maintains, have been much of an oculist. But he had served in the Royal Navy during the war and had sailed the seven seas.[8] Myopic he may have been on the eye-chart, but he knew his maritime charts.

═══

Old Men Forget

═══

Ernest Hemingway's long-short story, *The Old Man and the Sea*, published to critical acclaim in 1952, laid the way for the award of the author's Nobel Prize two years later. It is a story of ordeal and epic endurance, written in sparse, semi-allegorical style. The old man of the title is a Cuban fisherman. The date is some point in the 1940s—pre-Castro. The old man is of that generation which still sees the United States (following the 1897 war with Spain) as liberators, not Yanqui oppressors. The oppressor in this story is not America, but life—the human condition. The narrative opens with a precise description of how long the old man, Santiago, has held out against adversity:

He was an old man who fished alone in a skiff in the Gulf Stream and he had gone eighty-four days now without taking a fish. In the first forty days a boy had been with him. But after forty days without a fish the boy's parents had told him that the old man was now definitely and finally *salao*, which is the worst form of unlucky, and the boy had gone at their orders in another boat which caught three good fish the first week.(p. 9)[1]

Fish means the big fish, marlin.

The old man is utterly alone in the world. He has outlived his family. On shore the boy, who has been forbidden to sail with him, still visits and brings him food. The two of them discuss another marathon—one which is almost as long as that of the old man's eighty-four days without a fish. It is, we assume, summer 1941. Joe DiMaggio, the New York Yankees baseball player, is embarked on one of his great seasons. 'I would like to take the great DiMaggio fishing,' the old man says. 'They say his father was a fisherman' (indeed, he was).[2]

The Joe DiMaggio reference points us towards what was evidently a tricky problem for Hemingway in writing *The Old Man and the Sea*. Joe DiMaggio's great years were 1939 to 1947. But the Cuban population would only have heard of him, one assumes, during the amazing 'run' of summer 1941, in which he hit safely in fifty-six consecutive games, from 15 May through 16 July. War was declared in November 1941. DiMaggio volunteered in February 1943, and was in the services until 1945. He was voted a 'most valuable' player in 1947 and was still playing heroically (against his doctor's orders) in 1949. In this 'comeback' season he became a national hero again when he helped bring the Yankees to victory over the Red Sox, in early summer. A number of references to the 'bone spur' which was crippling DiMaggio in 1949 and to the Red Sox suggest that Hemingway may have this very recent date in mind. But that raises the problem of what has happened to the Second World War. They surely heard of it in Havana? And surely it must have impacted on the then not-so-old man's life? The setting feels more pre-war than postwar.

Whatever the year, the old man goes out, once more, alone to do battle with *la mar* (what Cubans call the sea 'when they love her'). Drifting in the Gulf Stream, he hooks the biggest marlin of his life, two feet longer than his skiff:

The old man had seen many great fish. He had seen many that weighed more than a thousand pounds and he had caught two of that size in his life, but never alone. Now alone, and out of sight of land, he was fast to the biggest fish he had ever seen and bigger than he had ever heard of. (p. 63)

The ensuing struggle with the fish lasts a Biblical three days. It pits the old man against the marlin, against scavenging sharks, and against *la mar*. In the largest sense, it is a struggle against life itself. He fortifies himself with two thoughts. One is of the American baseball player: 'I must have confidence and I must be worthy of the great DiMaggio who does all things perfectly, even with the pain of the bone

spur in his heel' (p. 68).[3] The other thought is of an athletic
feat of his own:

As the sun set he remembered, to give himself more confidence, the
time in the tavern at Casablanca when he had played the hand game
with the great negro from Cienfuegos who was the strongest man on
the docks. They had gone one day and one night with their elbows
on a chalk line on the table and their forearms straight up and their
hands gripped tight. Each one was trying to force the other's hand
down onto the table. There was much betting and people went in
and out of the room under the kerosene lights and he had looked at
the arm and hand of the negro and at the negro's face. They changed
the referees every four hours after the first eight so that the referees
could sleep. Blood came out from under the fingernails of both his
and the negro's hands and they looked each other in the eye and
at their hands and forearms and the bettors went in and out of the
room and sat on high chairs against the wall and watched. The walls
were painted bright blue and were of wood and the lamps threw their
shadows against them. The negro's shadow was huge and it moved
on the wall as the breeze moved the lamps.
     The odds would change back and forth all night and they fed the
negro rum and lighted cigarettes for him. Then the negro, after the
rum, would try for a tremendous effort and once he had the old man,
who was not an old man then but was Santiago *El Campeón*, nearly
three inches off balance. But the old man raised his hand up to dead
even again. He was sure then that he had the negro, who was a fine
man and a great athlete, beaten. And at daylight when the bettors
were asking that it be called a draw and the referee was shaking his
head, he had unleashed his effort and forced the hand of the negro
down and down until it rested on the wood. The match had started
on a Sunday morning and ended on a Monday morning. Many of
the bettors had asked for a draw because they had to go to work on
the docks loading sacks of sugar or at the Havana Coal Company.
Otherwise everyone would have wanted it to go to a finish. But he
had finished it anyway and before anyone had to go to work. (pp.
68–70)

     The 'hand game' (otherwise called 'arm-wrestling' or 'In-
dian wrestling') is not (yet) an Olympic sport, and average
readers—although they will know the rudimentary rules—

will not know how contests work at the highest level. Some clarity on the issue can be had from an abysmally inferior Sylvester Stallone film *Over the Top* (1987). Based on what is, apparently, a Las Vegas 'world championship arm-wrestling championship', it features the muscled one as a Rocky-like no-hoper who none the less comes from nowhere to win (what next? the *Time Out* reviewer sardonically asked, 'caber tossing?'). If one credits the film, which is, one assumes, founded on actual contests at Las Vegas, the bouts tend to be short and explosive. The violent bursts of muscular effort required cannot be sustained more than thirty seconds or so.

One can wonder at the young Santiago's formidable biceps, and his amazing stamina. But perhaps even more at his iron bladder. I have never been to a bar in Casablanca (this, incidentally, is Casablanca in Havana, not Rick's joint, in North Africa). But one thing I know about bars everywhere is that a lot of drinking goes on in them—and a lot of necessary unloading of that drink. We are to assume here that for a period of twenty-four hours neither contestant relieves himself. Cigarettes are lighted for them, and rum fed into the Negro's mouth. Referees change every four hours. But no break for the rest room. One of the folk-tales about the 'best orator of his generation', Enoch Powell, was that he always made his speeches with a full bladder, thinking it added that extra (rather panicky) note of urgency to his oratory. But, thank God, his speeches did not go on for twenty-four hours.

The contestants in the Casablanca bar could, of course, wet themselves, un-*macho* as it might seem in such a setting. Sanitation would not be an over-riding consideration in a Havana water-front dive. But—as any man knows— it is difficult to keep other parts of the body clenched while relaxing the urethral muscles. Nor is it easy to focus your mind on something else while relieving yourself. And urination, biologically, is a sign of fear or defeat. Either party opening his bladder would be vulnerable, at that critical moment, to a sudden push by his opponent, catching the hot ammoniac whiff in his nostrils and instinctively sensing weakness.

It is not that Hemingway—a man's novelist if there ever was one—is shy about mentioning bodily functions. He blithely informs us that, when he has to, the old man urinates over the side of his boat during the epic fight with the fish. But he could not do so, of course, at moments when strenuous muscular effort or concentration were required.

Do we credit the old man's recollection of his *mano-a-mano* battle with the Negro, or is it a kind of 'fisherman's tale'; 'heroic exaggeration', as it is called in epic poetry? Or is his memory playing him false? Old men forget. There are other hints that the old man's recollection may not be entirely reliable. Talking to the boy, like the old sailors to the young Raleigh in the Millais picture, he claims when himself a ship's boy in Africa to have seen 'lions on the beach in the evening'. This recollection is picked up in his dreams, the night before he sets out on his voyage:

He no longer dreamed of storms, nor of women, nor of great occurrences, nor of great fish, nor fights, nor contests of strength, nor of his wife. He only dreamed of places now and of the lions on the beach. They played like young cats in the dusk and he loved them as he loved the boy. He never dreamed about the boy. (p. 25)

I disbelieve in these lions gambolling on the beach, visible to any passing Cuban fisherman. And I am sceptical about that day-long arm-wrestling contest. In the old man's mind, dream, fable, and personal deed have apparently merged. At least, with the skeleton to prove it, the big fish is real.

═══

Humbert's First Crime

═══

Lolita ('The Confessions of a White Widowed Male') is written in the form of a prison journal: part admission, part self-exculpation, part plea-bargain with the reader. Humbert is, we apprehend, facing a charge of murder: not child abuse (if it were the 1990s, rather than the early 1950s, the paedophilia might well attract a heavier penalty than the entirely justified homicide of Clare Quilty). In so far as Humbert has a credible line of defence, it seems to be one of *crime passionnel*: he did what he did for love. Love, that is, of a twelve-year-old girl. A secondary, and riskier, line of defence is that she made him do it (Your Honour).

If one follows the large contours of Humbert's criminal career it seems to run thus: he comes to the New World of America to take possession of an inheritance from his *oncle d'Amérique*. He has been fixated on 'nymphets' (girls on the brink of puberty), ever since his traumatic coitus interruptus on the beach with Annabel. But prudently he has held his inclinations in check. Now a *rentier* and dilettante man of letters, Humbert lodges with a widow, Charlotte Haze, in the nowhere town of Ramsdale. Infatuated with her pubescent daughter, Lolita, he marries the widow—although he secretly despises her and her crass American ways. He plans, ineffectively, to murder her. What then is not clear. Whether, that is, he intends to have his way with Lolita, or merely enjoy a Platonic 'possession', limited to close contemplation, some voyeurism and furtively intimate caressing—all this side of the law (at least, as it was applied in the lax early 1950s). Humbert's hand is forced when, rushing out into the night after reading his private journal (Humbert is a great one for writing things down), Charlotte is run over.

The widowed Humbert picks up the orphaned Lolita from the summer camp ('Camp Q') where she has been boarded. On their first night at the Enchanted Hunters Hotel, where they are obliged to share a room, Humbert discovers that Lolita is not, as he fondly thought, an American maiden. She has been, he discovers, 'debauched' at the camp, by the proprietor's oafish thirteen-year-old son, Charlie Holmes. Humbert's indignation at the non-existence of the innocence he was planning to violate is comic:

Suffice it to say not a trace of modesty did I perceive in this beautiful hardly formed young girl whom modern co-education, juvenile mores, the campfire racket and so forth had utterly and hopelessly depraved. (p. 133)[1]

Other sordid details emerge, notably Charlie's habit of frugally recycling 'a fascinating collection of contraceptives which he used to fish out of a . . . nearby lake . . . called Lake Climax' (p. 137; an interesting detail, since it indicates that Lolita is post-puberty; what prophylactics does Humbert use?).

It is clear, from Humbert's account, that Lolita is taking charge. She seduces him, on the morning after they have arrived at the hotel. He is insistent on the point:

Frigid gentlewomen of the jury! I had thought that months, perhaps years, would elapse before I dared to reveal myself to Dolores Haze; but by 6 she was wide awake, and by 6.15 we were technically lovers. I am going to tell you something very strange: it was she who seduced me. (p. 132)

There ensues the Beardsley episode, in which Humbert (masquerading to the local town as a solicitous single parent) methodically prostitutes Lolita, giving her pocket-money in return for increasingly degrading sexual services. She betrays him with the even more predatory Quilty, and the scene is set for the climactic murder for which Humbert will pay the price (it being the late 1940s, the 'chair' awaits).

It is not easy to defend Humbert—even with his command of literary circumlocution his acts are vile. Nor has the book benefited from the growing distaste (moral panic, some would say) for paedophilia ('pederosis', in Humbert's terminology) in the last forty years. Nowadays Humbert would be much more likely to get a 'true' life sentence (i.e. thirty years or more) for what he did in Beardsley (systematic and repeated sexual exploitation of his under-age step-daughter) than for what he did at Quilty's mansion on the Grimm Road. With a sympathetic jury, and an ostensibly clean criminal record, Humbert might even 'walk' for ridding the world of Clare Quilty. A lawyer in 1998 would advise him thus: 'Say *nothing*, absolutely *nothing* about your relations with your step-daughter: let me inform the court that this degenerate abducted Lolita, used her sexually, gave her to his friends to use, and forced her to act in degrading pornographic movies. You found out what happened, and shot him. We'll win.' The less 'White Widowed Male' confession, the better for Humbert. Had he survived, the wise course would have been to tear up his manuscript and flush it down the cell toilet.

But confess Humbert does (before dying, untried, of a heart attack). The one thing in his favour is that, in the final analysis, it was she (Lolita) who began it all in the Enchanted Hunters Hotel. She was more 'debauched' than he was. When it comes to murdering Charlotte, for instance, Humbert finds that his nerve fails him. It might also have failed him when it came to seducing Lolita—had the little wanton not taken the initiative. He may *au fond* be a fantasist and nothing more. This ties in with Humbert's larger, quasi-theological belief, that 'nymphets' are succubi, demons sent to torment middle-aged males. They *know* full well what they are doing.

With this in mind, I want to look at the first of Humbert's molestations of Lolita, if that is what it is. It is not easy to disentangle from the obliquities of Humbertian prose. It takes place in Chapter 13 (significant number). It is a Sunday morning in June. 'Lo' sits alongside 'Hum' (soon to be her 'dad') on the pretext of reading his magazine. He is in his pyjamas and robe, she in her Church frock. She takes the magazine, and throws her legs across his lap. He is in 'a state of excitement bordering on insanity; but I also had the cunning of the insane'. He manages to 'attune' his 'masked lust' to her 'guileless limbs'.

Talking fast, he increases the 'magic friction'. Her legs 'twitch' as they lie across 'my live lap'. She is eating an apple (significant detail) and as she throws the core in the fender 'her young weight, her shameless innocent shanks and round bottom, shifted in my tense, tortured, surreptitiously laboring lap'. He imagines himself 'a radiant and robust Turk, deliberately, in the full consciousness of his freedom, postponing . . . the moment of actually enjoying the youngest and frailest of his slaves'. As he comes to climax, she shows him a bruise on her 'lovely nymphet thigh', which 'my huge hairy hand massaged and slowly enveloped—and because of her very perfunctory underthings, there seemed to be nothing to prevent my muscular thumb from reaching the hot hollow of her groin'. She twists away, 'while I crushed out against her left buttock the last throb of the longest ecstasy man or monster had ever known' (pp. 59–60). He wipes his brow (and, we apprehend, other parts of his anatomy) with a handkerchief of multicoloured silk, and goes upstairs to take his bath.

The technical term for this, I believe, is 'frottage', from the French *frotter*, 'to rub'. Humbert has brought himself to climax. But is it indecent assault, or decently discreet masturbation? Is this crime, or merely 'thought-crime'—sex in the head? It depends on what Lolita perceives, and to what degree she was conscious, complicit or even provocative. We never know. This episode—which is, in its way, grossly sexual—is none the less wholly inscrutable. Certainly, once confessed, it would go into the charge sheet as Humbert's first crime. Whether it belongs there, or in the innocent (because verbal) fantasies of his journal is another question.

===

When Is Gilbert Pinfold's Ordeal?

===

Evelyn Waugh subtitled *The Ordeal of Gilbert Pinfold* a 'Conversation Piece'. A truer title might be what the author playfully (with an allusion to one of his less favourite novelists) called his first chapter: 'Portrait of the Artist in Middle-Age'. Written between February and October 1956 and published in 1957, the novel—in its opening sections— offers, in the person of the blimpish novelist Gilbert Pinfold, a mirror image of Evelyn Waugh 'At the beginning of this fifty-first year of his life' (p. 10). Warts predominate:

His strongest tastes were negative. He abhorred plastics, Picasso, sunbathing, and jazz—everything in fact that had happened in his own lifetime. The tiny kindling of charity which came to him through his religion sufficed only to temper his disgust and change it to boredom. There was a phrase in the thirties: 'It is later than you think', which was designed to cause uneasiness. It was never later than Mr Pinfold thought. At intervals during the day and night he would look at his watch and learn always with disappointment how little of his life was past, how much there was still ahead of him. He wished no one ill, but he looked at the world *sub specie aeternitatis* and he found it flat as a map; except when, rather often, personal annoyance intruded. Then he would come tumbling from his exalted point of observation. Shocked by a bad bottle of wine, an impertinent stranger, or a fault in syntax, his mind like a cinema camera trucked furiously forward to confront the offending object close-up with glaring lens; with the eyes of a drill sergeant inspecting an awkward squad, bulging with wrath that was half-facetious, and with half-simulated incredulity; like a drill sergeant he was absurd to many but to some rather formidable. (pp. 14– 15)[1]

The narrative opens with two apparently neutral events
which will reverberate through the body of the novel. Mr
Pinfold, as a British novelist of note, is interviewed for
the radio by the BBC. Men from Portland Place, with all
their electronic apparatus, invade his squirearchical isolation
in 'Lychpole, a secluded village some hundred miles from
London'. Here it is that Pinfold lives with his wife (who runs
their farm) and their numerous children.

The Pinfolds are meanwhile in regular social contact with
a neighbour, Reginald Graves-Upton, 'a gentle, bee-keeping
old bachelor', who believes in a device called 'The Box' which
exercises 'diagnostic and therapeutic powers. Some part of a
sick man or animal—a hair, a drop of blood preferably—was
brought to The Box, whose guardian would then "tune in"
to the "life waves" of the patient, discern the origins of the
malady and prescribe treatment' (p. 12). Mr and Mrs Pinfold
(devout Catholics) regard the Box and its keeper with good-
natured scepticism.

The 'ordeal' in Pinfold's life is precipitated by his inju-
dicious habit of supplementing prescribed medicine with
a private supply of powerful sleeping potions. Assaulted
by a cocktail of barbiturates the hero's health deteriorates
alarmingly. His face turns purple, movement becomes clumsy
and painful. He determines to go on a cruise to the tropics to
recover himself—ocean voyages have always been propitious
for his writing and he will take his half-completed work
in progress with him. His wife—who is preoccupied with
some fields they have recently recovered from a troublesome
tenant—does not accompany him.

On his sea journey, Mr Pinfold continues recklessly to dope
himself. He begins to hear voices which he assumes come
through the air ducts of the vessel (the ominously named
Caliban). The voices take on an increasingly threatening
tone and Mr Pinfold's behaviour becomes increasingly odd.
He is soon in the throes of full-blown paranoiac delusion—a
condition which Waugh describes with amused objectivity.

The BBC and the Box figure centrally in his delusions. Finally, after a hailstorm of bizarre radiograms home, he is rescued by his wife, the cause of his breakdown is diagnosed, he cuts back on his medication and recovers his senses.

The Ordeal of Gilbert Pinfold records an actual breakdown which Waugh suffered, as the biographies tell us, between January and March 1954. The episode was triggered by an overdose of bromide and was irrationally associated in Waugh's temporarily deranged mind with a couple of interviews which he did for BBC radio with (as he thought) aggressive and impertinent questioners. In correlating Pinfold's and Waugh's experiences (as all biographers have) one discovers an odd anomaly. It can be outlined through what looks like a series of time-line contradictions in the chronology of *The Ordeal of Gilbert Pinfold*.

The visit of the obnoxious BBC men is given a precise date. It follows 'soon after' Mrs Pinfold recovers her farmland, 'at Michaelmas 1949' (p. 18). That is, late summer (September 29 is the Michaelmas 'quarter day'). It is in the winter of that year that Pinfold's health collapses and just after Christmas, 1950, that the shattered novelist embarks on his ill-fated health cruise on the SS *Caliban*.

Soon after this point, however, very strange things happen with the time setting—stranger than can be accounted for by the hero's raging mental problems. At the captain's table, the second night out, a deranged Mr Pinfold regales the bemused company with personal anecdotes about politicians of the day:

At one time or another he had met most of the Government Front Bench. Some were members of Bellamy's whom he knew well. Oblivious of his audience he began to speak of them with familiarity, as he would have done among his friends. (p. 44)

This is very odd. Mr Pinfold, we are earlier told, cleaves to an 'idiosyncratic toryism'. (Bellamy's seems to be a clear pseudonym for Waugh's own club, White's.) The Government over 1949–50 was, however, Labour. (This was the period, apparently, when Waugh liked to read the *New Statesman*, because he found the rage its Socialist twaddle provoked in him perversely pleasurable.) It is difficult to imagine a middle-aged backwoodsman like Pinfold being friendly with the likes of Cripps, Bevan, or Bessie Braddock, or their sharing a club in St James's. On his part, Waugh *was* very friendly—from his early manhood—with a number of front-benchers in the Churchill (1951–5) and Eden (1955–7) administrations.

The anachronisms continue. They are not so obtrusive as to impede the reader, but they are troublesome if we keep an eye out for them. In one of the more elaborate of Pinfold's delusions, for example, he fantasises an 'international incident' between Spain and England, as the *Caliban* steams past Gibraltar. The theme is taken up by his voices, now apparently emanating from a couple of crusty generals:

'It's nothing short of a blockade. If I were in command I'd call their bluff, go full steam ahead and tell them to shoot and be damned.'

'That would be an act of war, of course.'

'Serve 'em right. We haven't sunk so low that we can't lick the Spaniards, I hope.'

'It's all this UNO.'

'And the Americans.'

'Anyway, this is one thing that can't be blamed on Russia.'

'It means the end of NATO.'

'Good riddance'. (pp. 87–8)

The North Atlantic Treaty Organisation was set up in April 1949. At this point (if it means 'the end of NATO') it has evidently been in existence for some time. A little later the voices refer to some 'missing diplomats' (friends of Pinfold's) who have decamped to Moscow. This seems a clear reference to the Burgess and Maclean scandal of May 1951.

Finally one's suspicion that the narrative has slipped forward half a decade are confirmed in a late hallucination, as Gilbert resolves to leave the ship at Port Said. The voices are furious:

'You can't go, Gilbert. They won't let you off the ship. The doctor has you under observation. He'll keep you in a home because you're mad, Gilbert . . . You haven't the money. You can't hire a car . . . Your passport expired last week . . . They won't take traveller's cheques in Egypt . . . ' 'He's got dollars the beast.' 'Well, that's criminal. He ought to have declared them. They'll get him for that.' 'They won't let you through the military zone, Gilbert' (this was in 1954). 'The army will turn you back. Egyptian terrorists are bombing private cars on the canal road.' (p. 138)

If 'this was in 1954' how does the reader account for the fact that a short three months ago, in Lychpole, it was 1949?

One can speculate. Initially, it would seem, Waugh retrodated his ('Pinfold's') 'ordeal', so as to put it decently in the past; something from which he was long recovered. But as he got into the story, with its irresistible charge of personal recollection, he slipped into 'real time'. Without noticing, the date slipped forward five years. What began as a conversation piece, became—*malgré lui*—a confession. Was Waugh aware of the slippage? Did he leave it in, as a clue to the reader to 'read through' the fiction to the fact lying beneath? *The Ordeal of Gilbert Pinfold* is, as Martin Stannard points out, 'an ingenious and deceptive autobiographical document'[2] and such a trick would not be out of character.

═══

The Fourth Clockwork Orange

═══

The personal circumstances and vexed post-publication career of Anthony Burgess's *A Clockwork Orange* are well known. The novel was written under death sentence, on receiving a (happily false) diagnosis of brain tumour in January 1960. Thinking he had a bare twelve months to live Burgess, in a do-or-die spurt of creativity, turned out five novels to provide for his future widow. This 'pseudo terminal' year's work amounted to 'very nearly E. M. Forster's whole long life's output', Burgess complacently noted, on being reprieved.[1]

The central episode in *A Clockwork Orange*, the droog-gang's rape of the writer F. Alexander's wife, was based on an episode in Burgess's own past. He describes it tersely in his autobiography. It was 1944 and his wife Lynne had been working late at the Ministry of War Transport:

Leaving the office at midnight she had been set upon by four men who, though in civilian dress, were evidently GI deserters. Their accents were southern. The attack was not sexual but in the service of robbery. The four snatched her handbag and one of them tried to pull off her tight gold wedding ring. He was prepared to break or even cut the finger. Lynne screamed to no response of help. Her screams were stilled by blows. She remembered being kicked before losing consciousness. She was pregnant and she aborted.[2]

Lynne Burgess suffered long-term trauma and died in 1968 of chronic alcoholism. Although he was overseas at the time, serving with the army in Gibraltar, her husband was racked with guilt and remained so all his life.

According to Burgess, 'a novel is primarily an entertainment that should primarily entertain its author'.[3] In *A*

Clockwork Orange, on the brink as he thought of death, he chose to 'entertain' himself by probing his feelings of guilt and his inexpungible fascination with the assault on his wife (against whom he had the co-alcoholic's sporadic but homicidal feelings of aggression). In the novel the novel-writing victim, 'F. Alexander' (sometimes called 'F. Alex') is concatenated by name with his victimiser, 'young Alex', the novel's hero. The points being made by this playful confusion are: (1) that sin is a stage which must be passed through on the way to virtue; (2) that free will is the means by which the passage is achieved.[4]

The striking feature of *A Clockwork Orange* for its first readers was its being delivered by young Alex ('Your Humble Narrator') in an invented teenager's argot; part *Finnegans Wake*; part London, Moscow and New York street-talk; part Romany dialect. Imposing as it did the strain of learning a new language *A Clockwork Orange* was badly received on its first publication in the UK. With some exaggeration, Burgess claimed that no British critic liked it. But *A Clockwork Orange* went down extremely well with the huge campus readership in America. Perversely, the American publisher, Norton, insisted on dropping the last chapter. As Burgess impotently protested, the cut distorted the narrative's vindication of free will.

Astutely, the American film-maker Stanley Kubrick bought rights on the novel (which Burgess had earlier parted with for a 'few hundred dollars'). Kubrick went on to direct a sensationally successful movie, released in 1970, starring Malcolm McDowell (it was a further vexation for the novelist that some American critics assumed that he—Anthony Burgess—was an 'invention' of Kubrick's). The film-maker transposed Burgess's 'young thug of the future'[5] from the Teddy Boys of the 1950s, who had inspired Burgess, to the Woodstock-generation anarchists of the late 1960s. By 1970, as Burgess ruefully noted, the 'future' foreseen by him in 1960 had already passed into remote history.

Burgess, with grudging praise for its cinematic stylishness, called Kubrick's adaptation 'Clockwork Marmalade'.[6] As part of his screen treatment, Kubrick picked up on the Alex–Alexander concatenation, renaming his hero 'Alex Burgess' (this detail was slyly inserted into the margins of the film, in glimpsed newspaper headlines). Burgess relished the joke, but objected to the way in which the film made his novel into a 'pornograph'—especially in the balletic, 'Singin' in the Rain' rape scene. Kubrick's celebration of 'chic' violence stripped the narrative of its religio-moralistic conclusion (as an American, Kubrick claimed never to have read the novel's 'missing' last chapter).

After its release in Britain the film of *A Clockwork Orange* was held to be responsible for a spate of copy-cat crimes. A familiar kind of moral panic was triggered, with the tabloid press in the lead. In disgust Kubrick pulled the film from British (but not American) distribution. To this day, the film remains an 'underground classic' in the UK. Riding its notoriety, the book was reissued and became a cult classic in Britain—ten years after sinking without trace. But, to Burgess's rage, it was reissued, *à la mode américaine*, less the all-important last chapter.

There are, then, three *Clockwork Oranges*—Burgess's original 1962 novel, the truncated American and 'book-of-the-film' text, and Kubrick's 'marmalade' version. And, if we want to be curious on the subject, there is a fourth *Clockwork Orange*. When Alex, Dim, Pete and Georgie invade 'Home' (as F. Alex's home is logically but unimaginatively called) they find the author at work on a book called *A Clockwork Orange*, of which he has written only a small part.

What is this book? Between trashing the Alexander home and gang-raping Mrs Alexander, Alex contemptuously reads out a portion of the work in progress, for the delectation of his fellow droogs:

I looked at its top sheet, and there was the name—A CLOCKWORK ORANGE—and I said: 'That's a fair gloopy title. Who ever heard of

a clockwork orange?'[7] Then I read a malenky bit out loud in a sort
of very high type preaching goloss: '—The attempt to impose upon
man, a creature of growth and capable of sweetness, to ooze juicily
at the last round the bearded lips of God, to attempt to impose, I say,
laws and conditions appropriate to a mechanical creation, against
this I raise my sword-pen—' (p. 21)[8]

On his return to Home, 'cured' by the 'Ludovico technique',
Alex discovers that F. Alexander has now finished and
published *A Clockwork Orange*. He idly picks up the book
and leafs through it:

I could not viddy what the book was about. It seemed written in a
very bezoomny like style, full of Ah and Oh and that cal, but what
seemed to come out of it was that all lewdies nowadays were being
turned into machines and that they were really—you and me and
him and kiss-my-sharries—more like a natural growth like a fruit.
F. Alexander seemed to think that we all like grow on what he called
the world-tree in the world-orchard that like Bog or God planted,
and we were there because Bog or God had need of us to quench his
thirsty love, or some such cal. I didn't like the shoom of this at all.
(p. 124)

As best we can make out, F. Alexander's *A Clockwork
Orange* is not a novel but a tract on Burgessian themes. And,
from the fragments Alex gives us it's pretty awful stuff—
bezoomny cal ('mad shit'). What point is Burgess making? A
typically self-wounding one, I think. It was one of his famous
practical jokes in the early 1960s to adopt a pseudonym
(Joseph Kell) and review his own fiction savagely. When he
wrote *A Clockwork Orange* Burgess was forty-three years
old. Alex is fifteen. He builds into his novel the obvious
criticism: what does a middle-aged windbag with a bee in
his bonnet about free will have to say to, or what can he
know about, a juvenile delinquent? What is the 'message' of *A
Clockwork Orange* ('all lewdies nowadays were being turned
into machines') other than sub-Catholic platitudinising? You
don't have to say it: Anthony Burgess (through his *alter egos*,
Alex and Alexander) has taken the words out of your mouth
and set them in the novel.

═══

James Ballard's Auto-Erotics

═══

Crash had a bumpy ride to the British screen in 1997—having to fight its way through innumerable bans. But one aspect of the process was smooth. David Cronenberg reported that James Ballard 'loved' the movie. And, the director went on to claim, the story transplanted perfectly from early 1970s outer London (where Ballard's *Crash* is set) to mid-1990s Toronto (where Cronenberg's *Crash* was shot).

None the less, as with poetry, much gets lost in the translation. Elizabeth Taylor, for instance. Cronenberg was admirably courageous about Ballard's 'obscenity' (even if he, or James Spader, balked at the final male-on-male buggery). But, however tall he stood against moralistic licensing authorities, Cronenberg (as it seemed) bottled out ignominiously at the prospect of showbiz lawyers. Although she's never mentioned in the film, *Crash*-the-novel revolves obsessively around an Elizabeth Taylor fetish. Robert Vaughan, the mad doctor, designs the last act of his life as a *Liebestod* pile-up on London Airport's perimeter, in which he will achieve an orgasmic death-fuck with the fragrant star of *National Velvet*. The essence of Ballard's plot is contained in the novel's opening paragraph:

Vaughan died yesterday in his last car-crash. During our friendship he had rehearsed his death in many crashes, but this was his only true accident. Driven on a collision course towards the limousine of the film actress, his car jumped the rails of London Airport flyover and plunged through the roof of a bus filled with airline passengers. The crushed bodies of package tourists, like a haemorrhage of the sun, still lay across the vinyl seats when I pushed my way through the police engineers an hour later. Holding the arm of her chauffeur, the film actress Elizabeth Taylor with whom Vaughan had dreamed

of dying for so many months, stood alone under the revolving
ambulance lights. As I knelt over Vaughan's body she placed a gloved
hand to her throat.[1]

Crash is not a novel which hides behind the 'any resemblance . . . coincidental' shield. James Ballard wilfully
removes that defence by calling his hero–narrator James Ballard. This, we apprehend, *is* Liz Taylor, not some namesake.
Vaughan has stalked and furtively photographed her for
months. As it happens, Taylor frequently worked in England
in the 1960s and early 1970s, a period when her relationship
with Richard Burton was at its most fraught.

It is amazing that James Ballard's original publishers,
Jonathan Cape, let him get away with the Taylor business.
Only at one point in the novel is there any evidence of publisher's nervousness. It comes when Vaughan is fantasising
about the death-love-crash with Seagrave, the stunt driver
who shares his Taylor fetish:

Seagrave smiled through the smoke. He ignored his wife, who was
trying to calm him, and stared with level eyes at Vaughan. 'I know
who I'd start with . . . '
  'Maybe.' [said Vaughan]
  '. . . I can see those big tits cut up on the dash.' Vaughan turned
away abruptly, almost as if he were afraid of Seagrave stealing a
march on him. (p. 81)

The ellipses were, I would guess, imposed by the publisher.
Whose 'big tits' these are is made clear later in the narrative
when Seagrave indeed steals a march on Vaughan by wiping
himself out in a kamikaze crash, dressed in full Elizabeth
Taylor drag.

Fantasies about death trysts with Elizabeth Taylor are
unthinkable for an above-ground film-maker. Cronenberg
does his best by substituting a parallel erotic riff between
Seagrave and Vaughan about Jayne Mansfield's 'big tits
cut up on the dash'. You can't libel the dead, so there's no
legal risk. But Mansfield was hugely lacking in class; tacky,
in a word. The climactic collision in the film is altered so

that Ballard's wife, Catherine, is Vaughan's target. It gets
Cronenberg out of his libel fix, but it remains a weak section
of the screenplay. There is no mention of Taylor in the movie.
This is a fetish film that dare not name its central fetish.

There is another aspect of the Taylor business which
crucially distinguishes book from film. Date-markers identify
Ballard's narrative as set in 1973, exactly when it was
published. In 1972, Taylor hit 40. If not quite an old
banger at the period of Vaughan's love-death-crash, she was
getting close. But Ballard, on all the evidence, likes ageing
glamour. And from his writing for *Drive* magazine in the
early 1970s, his preference as a motorist is for 'veteran'
automobiles—because of the naked 'danger' they embody.
They are death traps and don't hide the fact. There have
been three revolutions in British motoring since 1973, none of
them to Ballard's taste. One is the shrinking of the car which
came in with post-'oil-shock', fuel-efficient designs. Another is
the concerted campaign for safety, pioneered by Ralph Nader.
The third is the completion of the British motorway network.

Ballard is addicted to big, old, gas-guzzling, unsafe at
any speed, cars and distrusts motorways as much as he
distrusts safe sex. The cars which feature in *Crash*-the-
novel are ostentatiously dangerous. They would be illegal
on today's roads. Ballard's cars have protruding door handles
which castrate their victims; chromium quarter-light latches
that scoop out eyeballs; non-collapsible steering columns
that impale luckless drivers; bonnet mascots that eviscerate
occupants shot like bullets through non-shatterproof wind-
screens. There are seat belts in *Crash*—but wearing them
is anything but mandatory. The only occasion on which one
is used in the narrative is for some in-car bondage with the
S&M-loving Renata.

This leads on to the main gap between novel and film. Look
again at the first paragraph. If you visualize the approach of
today's driver into Heathrow, the collision which Vaughan
plans is physically impossible. The M4 divides traffic with a

crash barrier so solid that you would need a Chieftain tank
to mount a head-on collision.

Vaughan, however, is not driving the M4 but the old
Western Avenue—the route which led to 'London Airport'
before it was Heathrow International. The Western Avenue
now merges seamlessly into the M40 at Chiswick. But, as it
is pictured in the novel, this road swings right by the mouth
of the airport. Along its six-lane length it is bordered by seedy
all-night cafés, cheap hotels, and prostitutes' pitches—all of
which have been swept away by the sanitising motorway.

Crash commemorates the precise historical moment in
the early 1970s when the new motorway system obliterated
England's old arterial roads—more particularly the climactic
moment when the M4 finally connected with Heathrow's
runways. Ballard was profoundly uneasy about these new
motorways, and the soulless, disinfected corridors they
created. In an essay of 1971, he called them 'the twentieth-
century's equivalent of the Pyramids, but do we want to
be remembered in the same way as the slave-armies who
constructed what, after all, were monuments to the dead?'

I wish *Crash* the film well (although, at the time of writing,
it still hasn't got a general release and will never, I suspect,
get a video certificate). And I'm glad Ballard likes it (more, I
suspect, than he liked Spielberg's *Empire of the Sun*). But
it would be a pity if Cronenberg's blood, glitz and sperm
spectacle does not obscure the *nostalgie de la boue* of Ballard's
original vision: its addiction to fading film stars, veteran
motor-cars, and Britain's single-carriageway roads, with all
their dirt and danger.

===

Poirot's Double-Death

===

The long birth of Agatha Christie's last Poirot novel, the detective's 'curtain call', is well known. In the early days of the war, Christie—like many other brave Londoners—refused to leave the capital, while at the same time fully realising that she might die in the Blitz. It was a point of honour. In those uneasy months it must have seemed if not the end of the world, the end of old England. The England, that is, of Styles, and of the country-house ethos celebrated in the genteel crime fiction of which, by 1939, Agatha Christie was the acknowledged 'Queen'.

Christie wrote her message-in-a-bottle for posterity in the form of a valedictory Poirot and Miss Marple novel. Having written them, the manuscripts were placed in a suitably bomb-proof safe, 'in anticipation of my being killed in the raids, which seemed to be in the highest degree likely as I was working in London', as she serenely put it.[1] Hitler would have no easy victory over her.

The Poirot novel was *Curtain*, the detective's 'last case', as the subtitle puts it. It is necessarily his last, since—invalid throughout—he dies in the last chapter. Happily, Christie's apprehensions proved unfounded. London discovered it could 'take it'; the tide turned and the allies won the war against Fascism. Miss Marple and Poirot were permitted to live on and make the world safe for England's decent middle classes.

Christie in the last, richly productive phase of her writing life turned out a string of a dozen or so Hercule Poirot mysteries between 1945 and 1975. None of the faithful (and growing) band of readers who snapped them up as soon as they were published knew, of course, that the Belgian detective was 'dead'—his remains lying peacefully interred in the bomb-proof safe.

The effect now as we look back on the corpus of post-war Poirot novels is similar to that in Quentin Tarantino's film *Pulp Fiction* (1996) in which Vince (the John Travolta character), having been killed by Butch (the Bruce Willis character), is brought back in the framing coffee-shop scene. He has his long metaphysical discussion with Jules (the Samuel L. Jackson character) on the meaning of life while, all along, we 'know' he is already dead. It adds a strange *sub specie aeternitatis* edging to the scene.

In the mid-1970s, Dame Agatha Christie, now in her eighties and ennobled for her services to literature, decided that it was *really* time to draw the curtain, to carry out Poirot's thirty-five-year belated obsequies. In 1975, *Curtain* was taken out, dusted off, and published. It is pleasant to record that it became the third-bestselling novel of the year in America and a huge bestseller world-wide.[2] Christie had never been more popular—nor had Poirot, his image boosted by a number of big-budget films, in which he was played (over-played, one might complain) by such actors as Peter Ustinov and Albert Finney. Christie was signing off at the top of the tree.

But what, exactly, was implied by 'dusting off'? So as not to make nonsense of those 'posthumous' Poirot narratives *Curtain* had to have all obtrusive chronological reference filleted out. Christie is usually engagingly factual about time and place dimensions in her novels. Take, for instance, the opening sentences of the 1935 Poirot novel, *The ABC Murders* (Arthur Hastings, as usual, narrates):

It was in the June of 1935 that I came home from my ranch in South America for a stay of about six months. It had been a difficult time for us out there. Like everyone else, we had suffered from world depression. I had various affairs to see to in England that I felt could only be successful if a personal touch was introduced. My wife remained to manage the ranch.

> I need hardly say that one of my first actions on reaching England was to look up my old friend, Hercule Poirot.
>
> I found him installed in one of the newest type of service flats in London. I accused him (and he admitted the fact) of having chosen this particular building on account of its strictly geometrical appearance and proportions.[3]

This introduction fixes the setting three ways: with a precise date (synchronised with first publication), by reference to the post-1929 world slump, and by allusion to the new apartment blocks springing up in London.

All the evidence of the narrative suggests that, after exhumation, the manuscript of *Curtain* was rigorously purged of any such dating reference. For its readers in 1975, it was (by default) as much a novel of 1975 as *The ABC Murders* was a novel of 1935 for *its* first readers. But there were problems; Poirot's age is one. Even at the beginning of the 1935 narrative he is getting on in years (not to say ancient) and, to the astonishment of Hastings, reduced to dyeing his hair. Well retired he takes on the occasional case only to keep his 'grey cells' active. No dye needed in that department.

We were introduced to the dapper little detective as a Belgian war refugee at the Essex country house, Styles Court, in 1916. He was already retired from the *Sûreté* and—as his 'biographer' estimates—must have been born 'between 1849 and 1854'.[4] One can, with a little strain, picture him as a dashing eighty-something in 1935. The 120-year-old (as he must be) in 1975 requires a truly heroic suspension of disbelief.

If we read *Curtain* with this question in mind: what sense of period, or *mise en scène*, do we get? In fact, we get very little sense of period at all: *Curtain* is to vintage Christie what distilled water is to Beaujolais; it lacks all historical salt or savour. Someone—the author, her amanuensis, or editors at Collins—erased 'time' from the narrative. It creates a remarkable effect—a kind of historic weightlessness.

Despite the keen eyes and sharp scissors of the erasers,

a few dated details slip through. The action is (appropriately for a valedictory performance) set in the country house where we first met Poirot. A minor character—musing on the most recent murder—is made to remark how closely it recalls the Styles affair 'of twenty years ago and over' (p. 158).[5] That affair, as we very precisely know (from references to World War One), took place in 1916. The afterthought 'and over' could hardly mean fifty years.

Other markers, what few there are, suggest something a little bit later than the 1930s. There is a war-time 'billeted' feel about Styles. The general absence of service-aged characters conduces to this feel, as does the austere 'guest house' catering, the general run-down feel of the place: 'the drive was badly kept and much overgrown with weeds growing up over the gravel; [the house] badly needed a coat of paint' (p. 9).

About Arthur Hastings's children we are told that: 'one boy was in the Navy, the other married and running the ranch in the Argentine. My daughter Grace was married to a soldier and was at present in India' (p. 8). This manifestly predates August 1947 and Indian Independence (as do other references in the text to serving Indian civil servants). Arthur Hastings still has his ranch in Argentina—unlikely if he had been in the country during the socialist-revolutionary Perón regime.

Hastings married in 1923, and his daughter Judith—who figures centrally in the narrative and is, for a while, a suspect—is just twenty-one and has recently been awarded her BSc. If it were now 1975, Hastings and his wife would have had to have procreated her in their mid-fifties. At one point, Hastings becomes alarmed that Poirot might be short of money, and asks, 'I say, Poirot, you're not—er—hard up, are you? I know the war hit investments very badly' (p. 16)—which suggests a period in the 1950s, at the latest.

But which war is Hastings thinking of? Elsewhere, Poirot

refers in passing to 'your Mr Asquith in the last war' (p. 72). By 'last' he means, of course, the 1914–18 conflict (Herbert Asquith was Liberal Prime Minister, 1908–16). World War Two must either currently be going on, or not yet have broken out. There is no reference to Winston Churchill in the text.

There are some cosmetic touches clearly designed to sketch in a post-World War Two setting—a passing reference, for example, to the 'rows of council houses' (p. 9) which nowadays disfigure the village of Styles St Mary. But the general ethos of Styles—its valets, night-nurses, dinner gongs, and daring silk 'negligées'—all point backwards. Appropriately so.

Poirot, we should accept, died at some point in the 1939–45 War, among another generation of refugees, in his old stamping ground. All those postwar cases in which he rails against 1950s Teddy Boys, 1960s strikes, and the changing times are so many fictions, nothing more. He could not have been there. Like John Brown, he's mouldering in his grave.

===

The Hitchcock Hallmark

===

Alfred Hitchcock, famously, organised his cine-narratives around what he called a 'MacGuffin'—a dominant gimmick, or 'hook'. In *Psycho*, for example, the MacGuffin is that Norman Bates's mother did it—but Norman Bates's mother is Norman Bates. Hitchcock's movies can be seen, in their totality, as an assemblage of tricks, gags, quirks, mannerisms, and hallmark gimmicks of the MacGuffin kind. For this reason, he lends himself both to homage (reverent imitation—everywhere found in French New Wave film) and parody (irreverent imitation) such as Mel Brooks's *High Anxiety* (1977).

One of the more eccentric Hitchcockian hallmarks, his thumbprint in the butter, so to call it, is the intrusion into his films of his own rotund little self as a 'cameo', or background 'extra'. Knowing that somewhere, in some corner of the story, we will see the director *in propria persona* keeps the audiences on their toes. It also reminds them of who the 'director' is and his god-like powers (this is *my* story—*I* can break its rules whenever I choose). In his long-running TV series, 'Alfred Hitchcock Presents', it was his practice to *compère* the gothic-horrific narrative with clownish 'intros'. His cockney-sparrow persona had outgrown its status as a mere 'extra'. It was now the lead.

In the films the Hitchcockian intervention is sometimes Prufrockian; he is seen, that is, swelling a prologue or as part of the walk-on décor. In *Blackmail*, he is glimpsed reading a newspaper on the subway; in *The Shadow of a Doubt*, he is playing bridge on the train; in *Strangers on a Train*, he is seen alighting with a double-bass. In *Psycho*, he walks by wearing an absurd Texan hat. In *The Birds*, in an early scene in the pet shop, he is briefly glimpsed walking outside with two tiny dogs. Elsewhere he can be seen as a pedestrian or as a passenger on the trains that feature in many of his movies. In *Rebecca* (as I recall), he makes a fleeting appearance waiting impatiently outside a telephone kiosk. Sometimes the intrusion is self-mocking as, for instance, his reproduced appearance(s) in the 'before and after' newspaper advertisement for the weight-loss treatment, 'Reduco', in *Lifeboat*. Sometimes the intrusion is hyper-ingenious. *Rope*, for instance, is a claustrophobic drama which takes place, effectively, in a single room with half-a-dozen characters. There are no crowds, no outside shots. Alfred Hitchcock's round figure appears, if we are alert enough to see it, as a neon shop-front design, glimpsed through the apartment window (another theory has it that he 'doubled' for one of the more portly characters in a rear-shot).

Novelists are, on the whole, wary about confusing fiction with their real-world selves—perpetrating those intrusions of self which Henry James called 'suicidal'. The tricksy campus novel is an exception to the Jamesian rule. Campus novelists love to probe and transgress the blurry boundaries of fictional representation.

A version of the Hitchcock gimmick is slyly inserted into Malcolm Bradbury's *The History Man*, one of the most distinguished products of English campus fiction. The novel is well known beyond the limited circuit of academic readers who traditionally relish the genre's in-jokes. *The History Man* triggered a mania among the viewing public when televised in 1982, starring a wonderfully slimy Anthony Sher as Howard Kirk ('the thinking man's J.R.', as Sher–Kirk was labelled, with reference to another TV mania of the time, the soap opera *Dallas*).

Bradbury's career has been unusually diverse. A distinguished literary critic (largely responsible for the development of American literary studies in the UK) he had a concurrent interest in sociology. Born in 1932, Bradbury had also written three well-received novels by 1975—all widely spaced in time. *Eating People Is Wrong* came out in 1959 (it is set in a provincial university, recognisably Leicester, where Bradbury was an undergraduate); *Stepping Westward* came out in 1965 (it is set on an American campus, reflecting a year's study at Indiana University); and *The History Man* (1975). This last is set at 'Watermouth', a 'new', post-Robbins campus, reminiscent of the University of East Anglia, where Bradbury had held the chair in American Studies since 1970, and where—with the novelist Angus Wilson—he founded an advanced course in creative writing in 1969. From their MA classes a corps of younger novelists emerged over the years, bearing the Bradbury–Wilson stamp: writers such as Ian McEwan, Rose Tremain, and Kazuo Ishiguro.

Bradbury's reading of British postwar cultural history has been enunciated *ex cathedra* and is centrally embodied in his fiction. He believes that 'liberalism', of which the most distinguished practitioners are E. M. Forster in Britain and Lionel Trilling in America, was destroyed by a new barbarism (cannibalism, as Bradbury pictured it) in the 1950s and 1960s. After 1956, the year of Suez and Hungary, eating people was no longer wrong. Bradbury's bleak vision of Britain's Brave New World was a premonition of the selfish hedonism of the 'swinging' 1960s and—further along—the Thatcherism 'enterprise culture' (whose effect on universities Bradbury satirises in *Cuts*, 1987).

The defeat of humane, Forsterian liberalism is the pathos at the heart of Bradbury's comedy. In terms of intellectual disciplines, he associates the new barbarism with the social sciences and their 'relativist' moral values. *The History Man*'s hero is a child of the times, the sociopathic sociologist, Howard Kirk. Kirk incarnates the new shiny barbarism and its triumph over the liberal values represented—feebly—by Watermouth's 'civilised' English department. In the course of the narrative Kirk persecutes, and finally has expelled,

Carmody—a Blimpish English 'major' (Watermouth has adopted American ways) who stands in his path. Dressed, with absurd anachronism (it is the 1970s) in a blazer and scarf, with short-back-and-sides haircut, and a touchingly out-of-date belief in 'fair play', Carmody offers a trenchant critique of Kirk's methods: 'getting all the radical students to your parties, and feeling them up, and getting them involved in causes and demos, and then giving them good grades. But the ones who won't play your game, the ones like me, you give them bad grades' (p. 139).[1] True enough, but Carmody is spitting into the wind of history.

Carmody, by clandestine photography, gets irrefutable evidence of Kirk's 'feeling up' his female students, and secures the backing of his English tutor, Miss Callendar, in his search for 'fairness'. Kirk promptly seduces the not unattractive Callendar. Now his sexual slave, she subsequently does his bidding. Goodbye fairness, goodbye Carmody.

Miss Callendar has a friendly colleague (and, we deduce, admirer) in the department, who makes a late brief intrusion into the narrative. It occurs at a high-point in the action when Kirk—in some urgency—calls on Miss Callendar (still something of a stranger to him) in her departmental home ground. He raps on her door:

There is no response, so he knocks and waits again. The door of a room adjoining opens a little; a dark, tousled-haired head, with a sad visage, peers through, looks at Howard for a little, and then retreats. The face has a vague familiarity; Howard recalls that this depressed-looking figure is a lecturer in the English department, a man who, ten years earlier, had produced two tolerably well-known and acceptably reviewed novels, filled, as novels then were, with moral scruple and concern. Since then there has been silence, as if, under the pressure of contemporary change, there was no more moral scruple and concern, no new substance to be spun. The man alone persists; he passes nervously through the campus, he teaches, sadly, he avoids strangers. (pp. 204–5)

This unnamed lugubrious novelist made an appearance (or an almost-appearance) at an earlier party of Howard's. The girl he came with says, *en passant*: 'He's a novelist . . . he's gone home to write notes on it all' (p. 87).

There has been a huge amount of speculation about who Howard Kirk really *is*. The commonly received view is that Kirk *is* the sociologist and broadcaster Laurie Taylor; something that has provoked wryly comic essays on the subject by both Bradbury and Taylor himself.[2] No one, as far as I know, has commented on this irruption of a self-portrait into the text. The *curriculum vitae* and the sad, hush-puppy physiognomy, the tousled-hair, are, of course, unmistakably those of the man himself, Malcolm Bradbury (I claim my five pounds).

It is an extraordinarily self-deprecating vignette—both in its lineaments and in the impotence of the 'novelist' to intervene. Even Forster, while he might not aspire to betray his country, felt he could help his 'friends'. This novelist (although, like Carmody, he has his 'notes') is powerless to intervene. He can only watch, in a condition of impotent comic gloom. What good will a novel do? What good is a novelist? You can't fight 'History'.

There has always been an interesting interplay between the fictions of David Lodge and of Malcolm Bradbury. *The British Museum Is Falling Down* (Lodge's satire on London University in the 1950s) has a wry dedication to Bradbury, but for whom, he implies, he would not have tried a comic novel. Both Malcolm Bradbury and David Lodge have been drawn, as a spin-off from their campus-novel fame, into the world of TV drama: they have emerged from the ivory tower into the 'industry'. The television adaptation of *The History Man* was hugely successful in 1982. Bradbury went on to win show-business awards (and huge viewing figures) for his adaptation of Tom Sharpe's black Cambridge comedy, *Porterhouse Blue*. David Lodge, *inter alia*, has among his credits another hugely successful dramatisation of Dickens's *Martin Chuzzlewit* in 1994.

In *Therapy* (1995)—a 'TV-world' novel written the year

after *Chuzzlewit*, Lodge introduces his own, very Lodgeian version of the Hitchcock hallmark. It is even more discreet than Bradbury's intrusion of Bradbury into *The History Man*. An important, but easily missed, clue is given in the *pro forma* 'no resemblance' declaration in the novel's prelims:

The locations of events in this novel are the usual mixture of the real and the imaginary, but the characters and their actions are entirely fictitious, with the possible exception of the writer–presenter of a television documentary briefly mentioned in Part Four.[3]

Few readers bother with the mechanical apparatus of their novel, but if we start digging in Part Four what do we find? The narrative of *Therapy* takes the form of a jaundiced journal by a successful TV sit-com writer, Laurence 'Tubby' Passmore, who has a bad case of mid-life crisis and a 'trick knee'. Neither physiotherapy nor psychotherapy provide effective relief. The leading Catholic novelist of his generation, Lodge makes it clear that only spiritual remedies will cure Tubby.

Part Four, the last section of *Therapy*, takes the characteristic Lodgeian form of an anti-climax, or artful petering out. Passmore finds himself in the Pyrenees: 'cruising up and down the roads of northern Spain'. He has embarked on a quixotic search for an old girlfriend, Maureen Harrington. He treated her shabbily when they were youthful lovers. Now he craves 'absolution'. Tubby and Maureen finally get together and jointly make a pilgrimage to Santiago. A miraculous cure for the trick knee is in prospect—as well as other divine interventions.

'At Cebrero,' Tubby records, 'we ran into a British television unit making a documentary about the pilgrimage.' Things have gone badly for them so far. But the discovery of two English-speaking pilgrims is, for the programme-makers, a heaven-sent opportunity—their own little miracle:

'Stop!' cried the director. 'Don't say any more. I want to film this. Go and get David, Linda,' he added to a freckled, sandy-haired young woman clutching a clipboard. David, it appeared, was the writer–presenter of the programme, but he couldn't be found. 'He's probably sulking because he had to actually *walk* a bit this morning,' muttered the director, who was also confusingly called David. 'I'll have to do the interview myself.' (p 304)

The grumpy writer–presenter 'David' never makes his entry, nor is referred to again. But it is not hard to work out what his second name is.

If David Lodge's Hitchcockism is self-effacing to the point of invisibility, Martin Amis's is in-your-face flamboyant. In *Money* (1984), the autobiographical narrator, enigmatically called 'John Self' (he has a friend called 'Martina Twain'), is a porn-and-pulp merchant, with one foot in London and the other in New York. In a London pub, the Blind Pig, Self has an odd encounter:

I was just sitting there, not stirring, not even breathing, like the pub's pet reptile, when who should sit down opposite me but that guy Martin Amis, the writer. He had a glass of wine, and a cigarette— also a book, a paperback. It looked quite serious. So did he in a way. Small, compact, wears his rug fairly long . . . (p. 87)[4]

Self decides to make conversation: 'Sold a million yet?' (No); 'Your dad, he's a writer too, isn't he?' (Yes). One thing leads to another, and Self gets stroppy: 'I didn't much like his superior tone, come to think of it, or his tan, or his book. Or the way he stares at me in the street' (p. 88). They part, without actually coming to blows, but awkwardly.

Again, the self-portraiture of the artist is extravagantly self-deprecating. In Amis's case it has an added fascination in light of its eerily accurate prophecy of what was to come. Notably the 'Money' furore about the £450,000 advance in 1994 for *The Information* (1994), with all the attendant accusations about 'selling out'.

I would guess that Martin Amis was less influenced by his slightly older campus novel *confrères* than by the much older American novelist Kurt Vonnegut, specifically a little joke in *Slaughterhouse Five* (1969). The moment in question occurs as Billy Pilgrim, captured in the Ardennes, is being taken as a prisoner of war to Dresden ('the safest air-raid shelter in Germany', as he is assured). The novel climaxes on the horrific fire-bombing of 13 February 1945. But that is in the future (or possibly the past—Vonnegut's narrative is 'unstuck in time'):

The Americans arrived in Dresden at five in the afternoon. The boxcar doors were opened, and the doorways framed the loveliest city that most of the Americans had ever seen. The skyline was intricate and voluptuous and enchanted and absurd. It looked like a Sunday school picture of Heaven to Billy Pilgrim.

    Somebody behind him in the boxcar said, 'Oz.' That was I. That was me. The only other city I'd ever seen was Indianapolis, Indiana. (p. 148)[5]

This is the second entry that Kurt Vonnegut Jr makes into the novel. Earlier, in the camp latrine, he is overheard complaining that he has just 'excreted everything but his brains' (p. 125). On both occasions it tears a tiny slit in the fictional fabric.

One can come up with strategic reasons for these novelists' use of this device. As with Hitchcock it is a wilful demonstration of narrative power. It is also a playful testing of the elasticity of 'fictionality'—at what point does it snap? These *in propria persona* interruptions are, we may say, tiny explorations of the blur which separates fictional microcosm and factual macrocosm. With Vonnegut, the effect is rather like that of the Renaissance artist modestly but insistently inserting himself among the crowd of spectators watching a crucifixion. Amis's use of the device is more extravagant— more confidently Hitchcockian. Bradbury and Lodge are very British, very discreet. Most interesting is, where did the device come from? Who was the first to attempt this trick? I would like to think it was Hitchcock, and that it made a trans-genic jump from film to novel.

===

Echoes of the Six-O'Clock News

===

Despite novelists' pretensions to be visionaries, Cassandras and prophets, fiction (even science fiction) has a poor record as regards accurate prediction. Nor is it much better as a truth-teller. Who, for instance, wanting to know the truth about Bill Clinton, would go to *Primary Colors* rather than Matt Drudge, cyber-muckraker *extraordinaire*?

Occasionally, however, one finds eerily prophetic moments in the most unlikely novels and a quality of truth-telling entirely overlooked by the newspapers. In *Naked Lunch*, for instance—a novel written in the 1950s and published in the UK in the early 1960s—William Burroughs (as his biographer Ted Morgan records), predicted:

the coming of a viral venereal disease that originates in Africa, as AIDS is believed to have done. It starts in Addis Ababa and spreads from New Orleans to Capetown. The disease shows a predilection for blacks, but whites are not immune. There is no treatment. 'Males who resign themselves up for passive intercourse to infected partners . . . may also nourish a little stranger.' This may have seemed fantastic when it was published in 1959, but in 1988 [when Morgan is writing] it's just an echo of the six o'clock news.[1]

If crazy Bill Burroughs *did* foresee the 'gay plague' in the early 1950s he was thirty years ahead of medical science. The Disease Control Centre at Atlanta did not identify AIDS until 1984. Its African origins were only established (hypothetically) later in the decade.

Frederick Forsyth's bestselling thriller, *The Odessa File*, was published in 1972. It is dedicated to 'all Press reporters'—a corps to which Forsyth himself belonged until the runaway success, a few months earlier, of *The Day of the Jackal*. This second novel is a story of the Nazi SS 'underground railway', 'Odessa', and its highly successful attempts, after World War Two, to smuggle out its members to safety.

Forsyth's novel is set in 1963–4. A 'good German', Peter Miller (an oddly English name, one might think), goes deep undercover to penetrate Odessa and contrives to bring it down, with some timely assistance from the Israeli secret service, Mossad. *The Odessa File* did well for its author. It was one of the three bestselling novels he wrote in less than three years (the third was *The Dogs of War*, 1974), establishing him as the premier thriller writer of his generation.

The Odessa File was promptly filmed (1974), efficiently but not quite as successfully as *Jackal*, with Jon Voight playing the dogged Miller. On the whole, this second novel—like many second novels—has not lasted as well as its predecessor. Two aspects of *The Odessa File* have, however, lasted. Indeed they have suddenly in the late 1990s become burningly topical: namely, the 'Hitler's Willing Executioners' thesis, and the 'Swiss Gold' discoveries.

An 'author's note' prefacing *The Odessa File* thanks informants who cannot be named—for prudent reasons, presumably. This is a routine gambit in thriller writing, and often means nothing. In Forsyth's case, however, it may well be trustworthy. At the very least, Forsyth's novel is historically contentious. Time and again he insists that guilt for the Holocaust should be directed not at the German population, but specifically and solely at the SS. Himmler's black-uniformed thugs were 'the army within an army, a state within a state': a cruel army and a corrupt state. Forsyth's novel roundly asserts that 'of the crimes against humanity committed on the German side between 1933 and 1945 probably ninety-five per cent can accurately be laid at the door of the SS' (p. 320).[2]

This apologia, supported by the novel's 'good German' hero, Peter Miller, is an extreme version of the proposition attacked in Daniel Goldhagen's bestselling (and highly controversial)

1996 study of German guilt, *Hitler's Willing Executioners*.
Goldhagen asserts, vehemently, that 'eliminationist anti-
Semitism' was rampantly universal in Germany, from 1933
to 1945. It was the state, not Himmler's 'state within the
state', which did the crime and should be held accountable
by history. Goldhagen would reverse Forsyth's ratio: 95 per
cent of Nazi crimes against Europe's Jews can be laid at the
door of the German population. The SS was simply their tool.

This is a currently topical element in *The Odessa File*, but
hardly prophetic. Another element does, I think, uncannily
anticipate something that was, supposedly, 'discovered' in the
same year as Goldhagen's book was whipping up international controversy in 1997. In his 'Foreword' to the novel,
Forsyth refers to the 'vast sums of SS gold [which] were
smuggled out and deposited in numbered bank accounts' (p.
281). Later in the text, he expands on how the vast sums
were accumulated:

Out of [the] luggage of six million people, thousands of millions
of dollars worth of booty was extracted, for the European Jews
of the time habitually travelled with their wealth upon them,
particularly those from Poland and the eastern lands. From the
camps entire trainloads of gold trinkets, diamonds, sapphires,
rubies, silver ingots, *louis d'ors*, gold dollars, and bank-notes of every
kind and description were shipped back to the SS headquarters
inside Germany. Throughout its history the SS made a profit on its
operations. A part of this profit in the form of gold bars stamped with
the eagle of the Reich and the twin-lightning symbol of the SS was
deposited towards the end of the war in the banks of Switzerland,
Liechtenstein, Tangier and Beirut to form the fortune on which
the Odessa was later based. Much of this gold still lies beneath
the streets of Zürich, guarded by the complacent and self-righteous
bankers of that city. (p. 320)

A little later, the narrative refers to the 'gold teeth fillings,
which were yanked out of the corpses with pliers and later
melted down to be deposited as gold bars in Zürich' (p. 321).
Still later (p. 390) the novel alleges that the 'Zürich deposits'
constituted the huge reserves of capital used to finance the

'staggering Economic Miracle of the fifties and sixties'. The *Wirtschaftswunder* was just another war crime.

At the time the novel came out, 1973, all this was generally seen as so much thriller fantasy. There was, in the 1970s, a vogue for 'the nightmare that would not die' novels—gothic-paranoid romances about the survival of Bormann, Mengele or even Hitler. These monsters had lived on, and were at this moment, with their SS minions, plotting a Fourth Reich. If any thoughtful readers took note of what Forsyth was alleging about Swiss banks, it was written off as fantasy of the 'Boys from Brazil' kind. Or irresponsible slander.

Forsyth's 'fiction' about Swiss–Nazi gold received stunning confirmation in 1996. Documents (picked out of the garbage by a sharp-eyed janitor, who was subsequently persecuted for being 'unpatriotic') revealed that Swiss banks had, indeed, colluded with the Nazis to squirrel away huge quantities of looted, mainly Jewish, gold. Assailed by massive newspaper publicity in the United States, the complacent and self-righteous bankers of Switzerland came clean. They held, and had continued to hold after the war, assets plundered from the Nazis' Jewish victims. Nor had they made it easy for survivors or their relatives to reclaim their property (as a 1997 book by Tom Bower on the subject confirmed). That property included, it emerged, gold yanked from camp-inmates' jaws and melted into ingots, stamped—as Forsyth described—with the tell-tale insignia.

After pressure by the World Jewish Congress in May 1996 a committee of experts was appointed to look into the matter in the US. In October of that year, Gizella Weisshaus, a Holocaust survivor, filed a $20-billion class-action suit in Brooklyn federal court against two Swiss banks. The suit charged the banks with holding and hiding large amounts of gold, and other assets, deposited before and during World War Two by Jews who hoped to safeguard their property from Nazi confiscation.

In December 1996 the Swiss Parliament approved a

law to set up an international Committee of Experts to oversee an exhaustive investigation of all Swiss dealings with Nazi Germany. Vigorous damage-limitation exercises were undertaken by Switzerland's beleaguered (and no longer complacent) bankers: contrite full-page advertisements were taken out in the *New York Times*; fast-track reparation schemes were set up, ambassadors were briefed to appear on American television offering an *amende honorable*.

For the casual reader of the British and American press, it would seem that this story had broken just now in 1997 (probably, one might think, as a consequence of relaxations of secrecy brought about by the end of the Cold War). In fact, it had been scooped all those years before by Frederick Forsyth, working from information supplied by his unnamed informants. Readers of the *Odessa File* already *knew* all these awful things about the Swiss banks—although, of course, they could not trust their knowledge since it had come from that most tainted of sources: a novel.

It all recalls a wry comment by William Burroughs, in London in 1967. As his biographer, Ted Morgan, recalls, the Beat novelist:

occasionally went to Sonia Orwell's, where he once ran into Stephen Spender . . . looking very hangdog because it had recently come out that the C.I.A. was backing his magazine, *Encounter*. Burroughs said he had 'known it for years but everyone said he was paranoid.' (p. 450)

But, as they say, being paranoid doesn't necessarily mean you're wrong. Just that you're crazy.

===

The Curious Career of Rambo's Knife

===

In 1972, David Morrell—a college English teacher turned popular novelist—published *First Blood*. Morrell had an unusual pedigree for a writer of male-action fiction. He holds a PhD in American Literature and from 1970 to 1986 was employed as a teacher in the English Department at the University of Iowa. Dr Morrell good-naturedly accepts the title given him by one facetious reviewer: 'the mild-mannered professor with the bloody-minded visions'. With Morrell's academic credentials in mind one can detect suggestive connections between Rambo and Thoreau (notably the latter's 'life in the woods') and even with Rimbaud, the poet who returned to Africa's heart of darkness and was never heard of again. Doubtless at this moment a PhD is being written about David Morrell PhD.

First Blood is a crisp thriller with a contemporary (for 1972) social twist—namely the problem of what to do with the returned soldiery who had, for the first time in US history, come home from abroad in defeat. Nixon's 'Peace with Honor' was, as everyone realized, a 'tricky Dicky' slogan coined to mask the fact that the Americans had committed that most heinous of American crimes: they had lost. There could be no ticker-tape, no parades, no home-coming parties, no 'respect'.

First Blood opens with the cameo of a drifter—a 'Vietnam vet', as we learn—who has drifted into Madison, a small town in Kentucky: 'His name was Rambo, and he was just some nothing kid for all anybody knew' (p. 11).[1] He has long, unshorn hair and a beard. He is, throughout the narrative, 'a kid'—in his early twenties, as we apprehend, and physically slight. Rambo is 'moved on', as so much human trash, by the sheriff, Wilfred Teasle. Teasle is himself a Korean war veteran, decorated for gallantry at the Choisin Reservoir battle in December 1950. He has a Distinguished Service Cross, proudly displayed in his office. He, of course, got his main-street parade in Madison and the gratitude of the American people for having saved the free world from the Commies.

The nothing kid resolves not to be moved on: 'In fifteen goddamn towns this has happened to me. This is the last. I won't be fucking shoved any more' (p. 22). One thing leads to another: imprisonment, jail break, a cop gets his throat cut with the open razor meant for the kid's beard. Rambo it emerges, is an ex-POW, and was tortured by the North Vietnamese. He does not like jails. It further emerges that he is a graduate from the élite Special Forces, Green Beret training school, where he was a prize student of the top instructor, Colonel Trautman. 'Kid' though he may be, Rambo has a Medal of Honor awarded for gallantry in Vietnam—it is a higher order of decoration than Teasle's DSC.

A deadly duel in the Kentucky hills develops between Teasle and Rambo. It is also a contest between generations, and between an American soldier of the old school and an American guerilla—a fighter who has picked up some useful dirty tricks from his Vietcong opponent.

There is much blood but no super-heroics in Morrell's novel. Rambo sneakily kills a number of deputies, state police and National Guard soldiers. Finally run to ground, Rambo returns to the town with a supply of dynamite, stolen from a mine, and blows Madison to bits. There is a final *de rigueur* shootout between Colonel Trautman and Chief Teasle versus the 'kid'. Trautman delivers the *coup de grâce*, blowing Rambo's head off with a shotgun. Minutes later, Teasle dies of a heart-attack. His last thoughts are 'of the kid'; he is 'flooded with love for him' (p. 256). Opponents, they have achieved *in articulo mortis* that most desired of male conditions, they have 'buddy bonded'.

First Blood was well received and was hailed as timely (for 1972) by reviewers. Like all Morrell's fiction, the novel was efficiently written, with a good command of pace and suspense. Film rights were acquired, although no film appeared until 1982. When it finally made the screen it had been remodelled as a showcase for its star Sylvester Stallone. The Italian Stallion played Rambo less as a kid than a pumped-up super-hero, an American Gladiator.

Stallone (who co-wrote the screenplay) retained the main lines of Morrell's story, but made crucial narrative changes. Although massively more physical, Stallone's Rambo is significantly less lethal. His killings are all 'collateral', as when he (ludicrously) brings down a police helicopter by throwing a rock at it. Under his carapace of muscle the film's Rambo is a gentle giant. In the final shootout—in which he favours an M-60 heavy machine gun rather than dynamite—Stallone's Rambo contrives to destroy the town without incurring any visible civilian casualties.

In the film 'John' Rambo (as he is renamed) survives. Teasle is ambiguously seen being carried out on a stretcher. He may not make it. The screen version climaxes on a final confessional scene between Trautman and Rambo: 'In Nam,' the lachrymose vet complains, 'I commanded a five-million dollar [helicopter] gunship. Now I can't get a job parking cars.' Trautman does not kill his protégé, but wraps a paternal arm about him and takes him out to safety and—as we assume— a healing course of psychotherapy in some Vets' Hospital. The insurance companies will pick up the tab for rebuilding Madison.

By 1983 the shame of failure in Vietnam had been, if not expunged (only Desert Storm would do that), diminished to the level that it could be lived with. This, however, created a number of chronological anomalies, glossed over in the three Rambo movies. The first in the sequence is clearly set in 1972–3. Young Vietnam vets weren't drifting into small American towns in 1982. They were middle-aged bums on skid-row. But if *First Blood* the film is set in 1973, it makes nonsense of its successors. In *Rambo: First Blood Part II* (1985), John Rambo—after a short spell in prison (he does not look a day older)—is sent to rescue MIA (Missing In Action) American soldiers who have been held ten years or more in Vietnamese prison camps. It must be the early 1980s. And in *Rambo III* (1988), the hero—still not looking a day older—is doing battle with the Russians in Afghanistan. It must be the late 1980s. And, if we date his age from the first in the series, John Rambo must be getting on for fifty: he should have hung up his sweat band, knife and kevlar jock-strap long ago. But, of course, he is not in his fifties. Hollywood's *elixir vitae* has kept him forever young.

That there were two film sequels was due to the producers' (Andrew Vajna and Mario Kassar) sagacity in not following their source text by killing Stallone–Rambo, and to the extraordinary popularity of the film, and Stallone's performance in it. Like Rocky, Rambo struck a sympathetic patriotic chord. Stallone's hero was 'all-American'. President Reagan saw *Rambo II* in his private White House cinema, and emerged with the memorable wisecrack: 'Now I know what to do about Gaddafi.' Overseas 'Rambo' was adopted as journalistic shorthand for 'Ugly American' machismo. The Libyan president's views are not recorded.

The Rambo image took root in different ways in different cultures. In America, one scene in particular sowed a seed. Stallone introduced into his narrative an episode in which Rambo is shown taking a needle and thread out of the handle of a massive knife which he always carries with him. He uses it to sew up a gaping wound in his arm (there is, incidentally, no such knife in the novel). This scene, and other uses of the knife in the film, identify it as a 'survivalist' tool. Rambo does not use it to kill, but to live. He kills many with the bow and arrow, his favoured weapon in *Rambo II*, but they are all Vietnamese, Russian or Chinese.

'Survivalism' is a peculiarly American outgrowth of the

Cold War—based as it is on the belief that after a nuclear holocaust America would need to rediscover pioneer skills and tools. Survivalism, as an ideology, is still nurtured by a loose constellation of 'far right' extremist groupings: the libertarians, the militias, the Identity Christians, the White Aryans, and the neo-Nazis. Go into any of the Survivalist bookstores to be found all over America and, looming over the manuals on how to make bombs from fertiliser, avoid paying your income tax or make a silencer for your Uzi, you will often see a picture poster of bare-chested, sweat-banded Rambo and his mighty knife. As remodelled by Stallone, Morrell's hero has become the patron saint of the survivalist nuts. And the Rambo knife is its prime cult object.

Morrell, opportunistically, latched on to the films' success. He produced to order 'novelisations' of both the *Rambo II* and *Rambo III* screenplays (1985, 1988). So inferior are they to *First Blood* that one would like to think them ghost-written. Both, however, have revealing 'Author's Notes'. After a declaratory 'In my novel *First Blood*, Rambo died. In the films, he lives,' and thanks to all concerned (including Stallone), Morrell gets on to the important business of the knife. In the foreword to *Rambo II*, he asserts that 'The weapons used in this book (and used in the film) exist. They are functional. More, they are works of art'. The Rambo 'work of art,' Morrell notes,

was created by Jimmy Lile, 'the Arkansas Knifesmith,' Route 1, Russellville, Arkansas 72801. Mr Lile also made the now famous knife that was used in the movie *First Blood*. The present knife is somewhat different, though equally dramatic. As with the *First Blood* knife, one hundred marked and serial-numbered *Rambo* copies have been sold to collectors. An unnumbered slightly different version of both knives is available to the public. A six-inch *Rambo* throwing knife is also available.[2]

In *Rambo III*, another knifesmith has won the franchise. As Morrell notes, 'The knife used in *Rambo III* was created by Gil Hibben, P.O. Box 24213, Louisville, Kentucky 40224. Three hundred and fifty marked and serial numbered copies have been sold to collectors. An unnumbered slightly different version is also available.'[3]

The books were bestsellers, the films broke box-office records, and the three Rambo knives sold like hot cakes. Rambo was good for everyone. Morrell, Stallone and the knifesmiths of America all enjoyed a bonanza.

In Europe it was somewhat different. The hero's knife—for Morrell 'a work of art', and for American survivalists a tool no more sinister than a Phillips screwdriver—was seen in Britain as an instrument of murder, *tout court*. 'Rambo knives'—so called—were the target of parliamentary legislation and police crackdown. Every so often, the British public gets into a furious tizzy about some criminal weapon: in the 1860s, it was the 'garotte' (or strangling cord, as used by London muggers); in the 1930s, it was the open razor (as wielded by the razor gangs of Brighton and Glasgow); in the 1950s it was the 'cosh' (as wielded by teen age 'cosh-boys'); in the 1960s, it was the 'flick knife'; in the 1980s and 1990s, it was the turn of the 'Rambo knife' to drive the British law-abiding public and their Fleet Street tribunes into paroxysms of fear. So fierce was the campaign against the cult of the Rambo knife (particularly after the shocking murder of school-teacher Philip Lawrence) that even carpet-layers were advised not to carry their innocent Stanley knives to work with them, for fear of arrest and prosecution.

Even more horribly, in Hungerford in England in 1987, a misfit called Michael Ryan went on a murderous rampage. Known to local townspeople as 'Rambo', Ryan played the part out only too faithfully. On the afternoon of 19 August he accoutred himself in homage to his screen idol, took his legally owned AK-47 and shot up his town, as Rambo had been shown shooting up Madison in the 1984 film. With the difference, of course, that Ryan was going for people not buildings. Sixteen innocent citizens were slaughtered before Ryan shot himself dead.

'Spree shootings', of the kind that were common in America, had never hitherto taken place in England. Until 1987, it was fondly thought they never would. Rambo Ryan's rampage led to a ban on automatic weapons. And the equally shocking shooting spree by Thomas Hamilton in Dunblane in 1996 inspired that most draconian of British laws on firearms, the 1997 act abolishing handguns altogether in England. In March 1998, you could go to prison for ten years for owning a .22 pistol that would scarcely damage a cream puff. And there was talk of banning airguns. What next? Water pistols?

It was oddly paradoxical. In America the Rambo films had been very good for knifesmiths. They were also good for gunsmiths (the bulk of American sheath-knives are sold through gunshops). The National Rifle Association (the American gun-owners' lobby) loved Rambo. The survivalists canonised him. He helped put thousands, if not hundreds of thousands, cf lethal weapons into legal circulation. In Britain, by contrast, Rambo played his part in the total disarmament of the populace.

Were They There?

A critic, with more patience than most, has calculated that *Gravity's Rainbow* has over 400 characters—which must be something of a record. Thomas Pynchon's story line is as complex as the dramatis personae is numerous. It is London, 1944. The capital is under attack from V-2 rockets. Early versions of IRBMs (Intermediate Range Ballistic Missiles), V-2s (*Vergeltungswaffe II*—'Revenge Weapon 2'), punctured the atmosphere so fast—five times the speed of sound—that there was neither aural nor radar warning. The impotent British authorities informed a sceptical London population that the V-2 explosions were caused by faulty domestic gas supplies. Londoners responded with wry jokes about 'flying gas mains'.

Gravity Rainbow's hero, so to call him, is Lieutenant Tyrone Slothrop. An American serviceman, attached to the mysterious unit ACHTUNG, Slothrop was subjected, years ago, to Pavlovian conditioning by Dr Laszlo Jamf. As a mysterious consequence of this process, V-2 strikes are precisely forecast by his sexual encounters—or more specifically his erections—in London. His erections are many and random. Where his penis rises, the rockets fall. High command knows about Slothrop's precognitive abilities and Slothrop is used by PISCES, another special forces unit, as a kind of early-warning system.

Pynchon's novel spirals off in innumerable directions—principally in a chase for the *Schwarzgerät*, a quasi-mystical bionic directional device, built into the most advanced generation of rockets. Thematically, everything in *Gravity's Rainbow* is tied together by the author's 'paranoid' logic—an explanatory scheme by which chaos makes sense, if only one can uncover the conspiracy (the 'They') that controls it.

Gravity's Rainbow is a novel of bizarre, but never (to the paranoid mind) random, connections. Typical of the novel's general procedure is a late section of the novel entitled 'Shit 'N' Shinola'. It relates to a subplot which finds the drug dealer Säure using Slothrop (in his secondary character as 'Rocketman') to carry merchandise across recently liberated Europe. The episode ponders the insult—still current in US Army slang—that someone guilty of some particularly egregious ignorance doesn't know 'shit from Shinola': Shinola being American patented brown shoe-polish. To the careless eye it looks like the other. The idiom parallels the British Army equivalent, 'he doesn't know his arse from his elbow'.

Säure, believes, along with the non-commissioned masses of the US Army, that shit 'n' Shinola are as different as chalk and cheese. Never the twain shall meet. But, as the narrative demonstrates, they sometimes do:

Well there's one place where Shit 'n' Shinola do come together, and that's in the men's toilet at the Roseland Ballroom . . . Shit, now, is the color white folks are afraid of. Shit is the presence of death, not some abstract-arty character with a scythe but the stiff and rotting corpse itself inside the whiteman's warm and private own *asshole*, which is getting pretty intimate. That's what that white toilet's for. You see many brown toilets? Nope, toilet's the color of gravestones, classical columns of mausoleums, that white porcelain's the very emblem of Odorless and Official Death. Shinola shoeshine polish happens to be the color of Shit. Shoeshine boy Malcolm's in the toilet slappin' on the Shinola, working off whiteman's penance on his sin of being born the color of Shit 'n' Shinola. It is nice to think that one Saturday night, one floor-shaking Lindyhopping Roseland night, Malcolm looked up from some Harvard kid's shoes and caught the eye of Jack Kennedy (the Ambassador's son) then a senior. Nice to think that young Jack may have had one of them Immortal Lightbulbs then go on overhead—did Red suspend his ragpopping just the shadow of a beat, just enough gap in the moiré there to let white Jack see through, not through to but through *through* the shine on his classmate Tyrone Slothrop's shoes? Were those three ever lined up that way—sitting, squatting, passing through? Eventually Jack and Malcolm both got murdered. Slothrop's fate is not so clear. It may be that They have something different in mind for Slothrop. (p. 688)[1]

We can decipher this digression with the aid of *The Autobiography of Malcolm X* (1965), specifically Chapter 3, 'Homeboy'. In 1940, Malcolm Little (as he then was) had moved to Boston. Through his friend, Shorty, 'Red' (as Malcolm was nicknamed, for his copper hair) got a job in the men's room ('the shitter') in the Roseland State Ballroom.[2] There he contrived to earn up to twelve dollars a day (a large sum for a Negro at that date) cleaning white kids' shoes. No Negroes were allowed into the dance-hall itself, except on special nights, when the ballroom was made available for their 'lindy hopping'. Shoeshine 'boys' like Red and Shorty made their main money selling rubbers, dope, setting up 'black chicks' for 'whiteman'. Malcolm worked at Roseland till Pearl Harbor, at which point he moved to Harlem, which was to be his base for the rest of his life and where, as Malcolm X, he was to die.

It may be that J. F. Kennedy, a senior at Harvard and recently returned from London (where his father had been Ambassador to the Court of St James's), did, like the Harvard kids Malcolm refers to, go to Roseland. And if he went there, did he sit on the elevated, throne-like chair, and have his shoes cleaned in the men's room? History does not know and is silent; paranoia says yes. The coincidence is too powerful for it *not* to have happened.

Malcolm and Jack's destiny intertwined again, twenty years later. On 22 November 1963, the President was assassinated: momentously, Malcolm X declared it was a case of 'the chickens coming home to roost'—a remark that provoked fury among the white American population and censure from blacks. As Malcolm's autobiography records, he even received death threats from his own sect, the

Black Muslims—threats sanctioned by its leader, Elijah Muhammad. Malcolm was eventually assassinated a couple of years later, on 21 February 1965. Another chicken had come home to roost. What 'They' have in mind for Slothrop is not revealed. But it is noteworthy that both Slothrop and Kennedy were 'rocketmen'. It was the President who had his finger on the button during the 1962 Cuban missile crisis.

There are pretty convergences here which tickled the novelist's fancy. The paths of these two leaders—Democratic, lily-white President and Black Supremacist—as different as shit and Shinola one would think, crossed; not once but twice—in the Roseland ballroom, and by death from the assassin's bullet (in neither case, incidentally, were the 'behind the scenes' men who had masterminded the killings satisfactorily identified; more grist to the paranoid mill).

The 'Shit 'n' Shinola' episode partners an earlier episode at Potsdam in July 1945, when the victorious allies met to slice up postwar Europe. Slothrop, alias Rocketman, is discovered carrying a bag of hash for Säure. Reporters, politicians and showbiz personalities are all over the place, as are the great men of history: Churchill, Truman (Roosevelt has just died) and Stalin. Slothrop finds himself in the garden outside the imperial hunting lodge at Babelsberg, where the conference is being held. A balcony is over his head; a picture of that balcony can be seen in the photograph of Chairman Stalin shaking hands with President Truman, at 3:04 p.m., 18 July, in Charles Mee's authoritative account, *Meeting at Potsdam* (New York, 1975). It is teeming with rain in the novel, as it was at Potsdam. As Lord Cadogan, a member of the British entourage, recorded on the 17th, 'it got hotter and more oppressive [in the] afternoon, till a thunderstorm burst at about five . . . there was a most frightful squall'. Standing in this downpour, Slothrop wishes, forlornly, he had a pipe to smoke some of Säure's weed.

Above Slothrop, at eye level, is a terrace and espaliered peach trees in milky blossom. As he crouches, hefting the bag, French windows

open and someone steps out on this terrace for some air. Slothrop
freezes thinking *invisible, invisible* . . . Footsteps approach, and
over the railing leans—well, this may sound odd, but it's [*] Mickey
Rooney. Slothrop recognizes him on sight, Judge Hardy's freckled
madcap son, three-dimensional, flesh, in a tux and am-I-losing-
my-mind face. Mickey Rooney stares at Rocketman holding a bag
of hashish, a wet apparition in helmet and cape. Nose level with
Mickey Rooney's shiny black shoes, Slothrop looks up into the lit
room behind—sees somebody looks a bit like Churchill, lotta dames
in evening gowns cut so low that even from this angle you can see
more tits than they got at Minsky's . . . and maybe, he even gets
a glimpse of that President Truman. He *knows* he is seeing Mickey
Rooney, though Mickey Rooney, wherever he may go, will repress
the fact that he ever saw Slothrop. It is an extraordinary moment.
(p. 382)

They part wordlessly, 'Mickey Rooney with his elbows on that
railing, still watching'. The star makes no other appearance
in the novel.

Had the narrative been cut off where I have put the
asterisk, no one in a million years would have guessed,
I think, who the celebrity was who was about to appear.
Slothrop *knows* he saw the diminutive star of the Andy Hardy
movies. Do we? There is a certain plausibility to Rooney's
walk-on appearance. As one commentator put it, 'Absolutely
everyone' was at Potsdam; 'it was the last great beano of the
war'.[3]

Whether or not he was with 'everyone' at Potsdam, Rooney
was certainly in occupied Germany at the time. The *New York
Times*, in June 1945, has reports of his giving performances
for American and Soviet officers. High blood pressure had
kept him out of the services in the early years of the War,
but in 1944 he took a second physical, and passed. The
star did his basic training in Fort Riley, Kansas, and was
assigned to the so-called 'Jeep Theatre'. As Rooney puts it in
his autobiography, 'I travelled 115,000 miles, entertaining in
the European Theater of Operations. I saw little danger and
a lot of mud.'[4]

He did win a Bronze Star—for what he does not tell us. More to the point, Rooney—not by nature a secretive man (he is amusingly indiscreet about his regiment of glorious wives)—is suspiciously taciturn about what he actually *did* in Germany in 1945: 'This is not the place', he mysteriously says, 'for a discussion of the Army. I did better than some, worse than some, and when the time comes we'll get to it.'[5] The time never comes. What *was* he doing over there in Germany? Did he sign an official secrets document? Is this what is muzzling the normally garrulous fellow?

It's no use asking Thomas Pynchon (although I have sent him a letter on the subject). A world-class recluse, Pynchon does not answer letters (although I'm told he's listed in the New York telephone directory). I wrote to Mr Rooney asking if he were, by chance, at Potsdam in those epoch-making days in July 1945. I received from him a photograph inscribed, 'To John, from Mickey, with best wishes'. What does it mean?

═══

What Sea?

═══

Iris Murdoch's *The Sea, The Sea* was a worthy winner of
the Booker Prize for 1978. A luxuriantly descriptive work,
Murdoch's novel is narrated in the form of a private journal
kept by Charles Arrowby, a spiritually desiccated 60-year-
old man of the theatre. He has retired to a coastal house
at 'Shruff's End', to 'find himself' and write a minimalist
cook-book ('the four-minute cook book'—Charles likes things
neat and tidy). The image which recurs to Arrowby is that
of Prospero, having sorted everything out on his island,
retreating to a hermit's cave to put his life in final order.

Life, however, pursues Charles to his retreat. He experiences visions of sea serpents, a traumatic *rencontre* with his
first love, much violence, and visits to his eyrie by almost
every character whose past has crossed with his during his
worldly career. The novel ends with an enigmatic spiritual
rebirth, or reincarnation, and Charles's return to the world.

The novel, like the title, is dominated by the sea. The direct
allusion is to 'Thalassa, Thalassa'—the shout that echoed
through the forlorn Greek army (as narrated in Xenophon's
Anabasis), when they finally came in sight of the Black
Sea. Murdoch's narrative is dominated by beautiful and
wonderfully various seascapes. But what sea?

Charles is informative, in the most pedantic way, about
every detail of his life. We know, for example, much more
than we want to know about his maternal grandparents.
But, in a novel dominated by seascape, his oceanography
is abysmal or knowingly deceitful. We do not know where his
coastal refuge actually *is*—its geographical (or even its broad
regional) location.

The opening paragraph of *The Sea, The Sea* informs us 'we are in the north' (p. 1).[1] But, from the loose context, this could mean no more than that Britain is in the northern hemisphere. It is by no means clear, on a cursory reading, what sea is it that is so often and so vividly described by Charles: the North Sea, the Channel, the Irish Sea, the Atlantic. One can turn up some more solid evidence in the physical features of the shore alongside Shruff's End. The British Isles offer many different kinds of coast: from the sandy beaches of the North-East, the muddy estuaries of East Anglia, the harder and more eroded sea-board of the West, reaching into the stormy Hebrides. Charles makes very clear that *his* coast is not just rocky, it is extraordinarily so. Charles goes into geological fine detail:

This rocky coast attracts, thank God, no trippers with their 'kiddies'. There is not a vestige of beastly sand anywhere. I have heard it called an ugly coast. Long may it be deemed so. The rocks, which stretch away in both directions, are not in fact picturesque. They are sandy yellow in colour, covered with crystalline flecks, and are folded into large ungainly incoherent heaps . . . There are also flowers which contrive somehow to root themselves in crannies: pink thrift and mauve mallow, a sort of white spreading sea campion, a blue-green plant with cabbage-like leaves, and a tiny saxifrage thing . . . a feature of the coastline in that here and there the water has worn the rock into holes . . . At one point, near to my house, the sea has actually composed an arched bridge of rock under which it roars into a deep open steep-sided enclosure beyond. (p. 5)

There are some other internal clues, which we can knit together. Late in the novel, Charles makes a motor trip to London. It is accomplished in few enough hours that, after an early start, he still has time to do things in the capital in the afternoon. A motorway is mentioned (the date is, one assumes, early 1970s, although one cannot be sure). One deduces a trip of 200 miles or under.

Another, firmer clue may be deduced from what seems to be a description of an evening seascape, early in the narrative.

The sun is described sinking in the West—or at least so one would assume from the luminescence on the horizon:

It is evening. Thick lumpy slate-blue clouds, their bulges lit up to a lighter blue, move slowly across a sky of muddy and yet brilliant gold, a sort of dulled gilt effect. At the horizon there is a light, glittering, slightly jagged silver line, like modern jewellery. Beneath it the sea is a live choppy lyrical goldeny-brown, jumping with white flecks. (p. 26)

Were it the east coast, that last line of light would be over land, not sea.

The locals who drink in the nearby pub, the Raven, do not speak with any identifiable accent. But, interestingly, cider ('too sweet and rather strong', p. 452) seems to be the drink most prominently on offer at another pub, the Black Lion. From the rockiness, the distance from London, the West Country tipple (but no 'Mummersetshire' accents), and the fall of the sun, one would assume that Charles has taken his retirement in the West Country. But not the deepest West Country. Somewhere in easily reached Dorset, perhaps.

Against this, there is that pesky 'northern' reference; and a profusion of references to plants, rock formations, and such things as seals (associated with the North-East) which complicate easy location. Peter Conradi, Murdoch's biographer, has been resourceful enough to question a geographer colleague on the subject. The evidence of the rocks, the flora and fauna suggests, Conradi reports, locations in the north, south, and east of England.

It's perplexing but oddly satisfying aesthetically. One assumes that Murdoch is not picturing any particular 'sea', but—as the title insists—*the* sea. The element, that is, not an identifiable oceanic region. When those soldiers of Xenophon's saw the ocean—it was not a shout of 'the Black Sea, the Black Sea' that rippled down their ranks. It was the mysterious, life-giving mass of water from which all life emerged and with which, after a long march through desert waste-lands, they had been reunited.

═══

Who Invented Cyberspace?

═══

There is innocent pleasure in looking back, from the standpoint of the past's future, at the forecasts of the 'futurologists', so revered in the 1960s and 1970s. The most intellectually respectable was Herman Kahn (immortalized as Dr Strangelove). The most commercially successful practitioner of the new clairvoyant science was Alvin Toffler with *Future Shock*. A 'runaway bestseller' of 1970, Toffler's portentous gaze into the future was taken very seriously by politicians and pundits. It was, C. P. Snow opined, a 'remarkable' work: 'No one ought to have the nerve to pontificate on our present worries without reading it' (I like 'ought').

Toffler made a heap of money from *Future Shock*, and good luck to him. But his predictions about the world of 2000 and after are so off-base that, frankly, Mystic Meg has him beat every time. With hindsight and a hollow laugh, we can see Toffler as one in a long series of Utopian optimists—and, above all, a booster for American consumerism.

Gazing into his crystal ball, Toffler foresaw large portions of the world's population at the turn of the century (i.e. now) living on the ocean floor, or on pontoon cities, grazing contentedly on the harvests of 'aquaculture' (fishburgers?). Global climate would, he prophesied, be micro-controlled. One would be able turn sunshine on and off, like a set of patio lights.

Riffling through one's yellowed 1970 paperback, it is what Toffler did *not* foresee that strikes one most forcefully. To wit: global warming, depletion of the ozone layer, AIDS, downsizing, women's liberation. Most strikingly, in his 600 pages, Toffler makes no more than a dozen passing references to the computer. When he does parenthetically turn his attention to it, Toffler sees the computer as (1) nothing more than a superior calculating machine or abacus; (2) a kind of futuristic butler-cum-secretary; something, that is, to help the busy *man* with *his* busy schedule. Take, for instance, the following hilarious prediction:

A case in point is the so-called OLIVER [On-line Interactive Vicarious Expediter and Responder] that some computer experts are striving to develop to help us deal with decision overload. In its simplest form, OLIVER would merely be a personal computer programmed to provide the individual with information and to make minor decisions for him. At this level, it could store information about his friends' preferences for Manhattans or martinis, data about traffic routes, the weather, stock prices, etc. The device could be set to remind him of his wife's birthday—or to order flowers automatically. It could renew his magazine subscriptions, pay the rent on time, order razor blades and the like.[1]

Razor blades? What they? His *wife's birthday*? *Flowers*!

The Internet and the World Wide Web are, as we come into the third millennium, the focus of our 'future shock' forecasts. Doubtless they will be as myopic as those of Alvin Toffler thirty years ago. None the less, all experts seem to agree, 'cyberspace' is the new frontier. As regards the question in the title of this chapter, the prefix 'cyber' (as in 'cybernetics' and 'cyborg') is attributed by the *OED* to Norbert Wiener, a precursor of Marshal McCluhan in the field of media studies.[2]

The root word seems to be 'cybernetics' which, literally, denotes a feed-back mechanism, in which information is not inertly stored but dynamically used to reassemble what is already known. 'Cyber' has since flown free, to attach itself parasitically to any number of host words and concepts. All over the capital cities of the world, for example, 'Cyber-cafés' are to the 1990s what coffee bars were in the 1950s and discos were in the 1970s.

The use of 'cyberspace' is applied specifically to the 'Net' and the 'Web'. Cyberspace is that notional (or 'virtual') information 'ether', in which huge quanta of information circulate in random but immediately accessible and re-arrangeable form. The Internet was not, of course, invented for the civilian population who now 'surf' it. It was invented as a military communication system to enable America to win a nuclear war. 'ARPA-net', father of Internet, was assembled in the early 1970s by the American Defense Department as a network which would still function if large sections (even the Pentagon) were knocked out by a sneaky Soviet missile attack.

Much US military research is done on American cam-puses, and out of ARPA-net and its derivatives sprang university 'Local Area Networks', connected by ethernet, or telnet programs, using UNIX, a complicated operating system, capable of communicating, via hub-computers, with other universities. In the early 1990s, 'email'—electronic correspondence via these UNIX-based networks—spread like wildfire among the academic community. An 'email address' was, at this period, for professors what the cellular phone was for their students: a sign that they were ahead of the curve.

The World Wide Web, son of Internet, was another purpose-built and essentially non-commercial system. It was origi-nated at CERN, the European Particle Physics Laboratory, in the early 1990s and was initially intended to allow the world-wide community of scientists to work collaboratively and creatively on big-science problems. Whereas the Internet could conveniently carry only words and text—typically in stripped 'Ascii' form—the Web used 'hypertext' to incorporate imagery, icons and 'browsing', or lateral links. The Web introduced a new, non-linear architecture. Duck did not have to collocate with green peas, it could also go alongside cricket, eider-filled duvets and any number of other links. Lateral jumps could be made at instantaneous speed simply by clicking on a pictorial icon, or using a 'search engine', such as Yahoo, Lycos, Alta-Vista or InfoSeek.

Everyone agrees that the future of the Net and the Web are vast and central. They began as military and academic systems. Now they are infrastructural elements in the modern cultural environment. There are, as I write, some 40 million on-line users. Five per cent of British households are 'Web households'. The figure is large, but what is more significant is the phenomenal rate of expansion. It is expected that, as with radio and television, the whole population will, within a few years, come on-line.

There is a problem in this smooth pattern of growth. Children are the most avid users of computer systems. Conditioned by arcade and video games, they graduate seamlessly into keyboard-operating adults. But the problem with children as customers for computers is that: (1) they have little or no money and (2) computers are extremely expensive. Computer literacy comes at a much higher cost than print literacy. The current start-up outlay is about £1,200 for apparatus and peripherals, and several hundred a year for operating costs, with expensive upgrades every couple of years. Pocket money won't do it.

The generation who can afford the equipment grew up, like Alvin Toffler, in a computerless environment. They are electronic illiterates. How can you get them to buy, to make the necessary financial investment to become 'Web households'? To lay out, that is to say, as much on a computer as they might pay for a second-hand car. High-pressure advertising is the answer, and the selling of the Web—to a generation of thirty-something computer illiterates—has been an extraordinary triumph for modern capitalism.

It is, of course, no use trying to explain the software mysteries of hypertext, or even expecting middle-aged users (especially males, who tend to be richer) to have keyboard skills (something they associate with lowly secretaries). Hence 'icons'—one-finger keyboarding—and a kind of computer baby-talk, glossed as 'user-friendliness'.

The selling of the Internet/Web has been facilitated, made

possible one might say, by—of all things—a novel and the school of fiction ('Cyberpunk') spun off from it. In 1984 (ominous year) William Gibson published his sf fantasy, *Neuromancer*. By a nice symmetry, Gibson was born in 1948—the year in which Orwell wrote his futurological novel.

As Gibson's title suggests, his novel is a 'new romance', crossed with the new neuromancy—computer magic. In technique it draws heavily on *noir* hardboiled crime fiction of the 1950s, crossed—provocatively—with 1980s arcade-game slam-bang violence. The novel is set in the twenty-first century after a devastating nuclear war. Japan, through its dominance in electronics, is now the global superpower. There is no 'natural environment', as such. The animal kingdom has largely been wiped out in postwar pandemics and humanity lives in huge, continental-sized geodesic domes. Planet earth has been paved over and plastic-wrapped.

Gibson's hero, Case, is a 'console cowboy', or electronic 'rustler' (a 'hacker', as the genus would later be called; hackers worship Gibson). Case lives by stealing proprietary software programs on the open ranges of cyberspace. The narrative twists itself into baffling complexities. But what proved to be most influential in the novel (published, remember, in 1984: some six years before the 'Web' came into being) was William Gibson's vision of the 'Matrix' (the global totality of databases) and of 'Cyberspace'. A potted history is given by 'voice-over':

'The Matrix has its roots in primitive arcade games, in early graphics programs, and military experimentation with cranial jacks . . . *Cyberspace*. A consensual hallucination experienced daily by billions of legitimate operators, in every nation, by children being taught mathematical concepts . . . A graphic representation of data abstracted from the banks of every computer in the human system. Unthinkable complexity. Lines of light ranged in the nonspace of the mind, clusters and constellations of data. Like city lights receding . . . ' (p. 67; my italics)[3]

Gibson is, by general agreement and his own admission,

no 'techno-nerd'. What he offered in *Neuromancer* was a poet's predefinition of the technology which would arrive a few years later. What he describes in the above passage is, of course, the World Wide Web *avant la lettre*. With some grandiose over-statement it is, I think, an uncannily accurate prediction of what the Web would be—or, at least, what we *think* it is. More to the point, Gibson passed on (free—he should have 'trademarked' the word) to the merchandisers a means of packaging and glamorising the Web, so that it could be sold to the middle-class, middle-aged masses. The merchandisers were not slow to catch on.

Literature, by its power of metaphoric concretisation, frequently serves to facilitate the absorption of technology by a scientifically sub-literate population in this way. One of the more remarkable examples is a throwaway remark of Marshal McCluhan's in *The Gutenberg Galaxy* (1962), where he grandiloquently asserts, in passing, that 'Heidegger surf-boards along on the electronic wave as triumphantly as Descartes rode the mechanical wave'.[4] *The Gutenberg Galaxy* was published in the early 1960s. These were the glory days of Californian beach culture, and their musical laureates the Beach Boys with their 'Surfin' USA' image. The image, as it was originally thrown off, was no more significant than thousands of flashy coinages in McCluhan's anthem to 'typo-graphic man'. But the notion of 'surfing the electronic wave' caught on. It was adapted, by some salesman one suspects, into the idea of 'surfing the Web'. It was as flattering an image as that of the intrepid cybernaut exploring cyberspace (which is how we see ourselves in laying out our £1,200 for a new computer). The image of 'surfing' enabled computer semi-literates to understand what they were doing. Courtesy of the image, they could represent themselves to themselves as, somehow, glamorously in charge of machineries which were, in fact, in charge of them. Who, then, invented 'cyberspace'? The scientists at CERN, or William Gibson? It all depends what you mean by 'invent'.

===

The Steinberg Effect

===

Tom Wolfe's *The Bonfire of the Vanities*, a runaway No.1 bestseller of 1987, is a novel built around an enigma. What happened on the Bruckner Boulevard in the South Bronx? Was Sherman McCoy—hopelessly lost in his Mercedes sports-car with his equally sporty mistress—about to be mugged by the two black youths ('Hunters! Predators!') approaching him? Or were they—with their neutral 'Yo! Need some help?'—good Samaritans, simply offering to help a broken-down motorist?

A panicked Sherman, and an even panickier Maria at the wheel, shot off, colliding with luckless Henry Lamb (literally a candidate for slaughter). Lamb is subsequently neglected to death by the New York hospital system, while Sherman is chewed up, and even more painfully destroyed, by the city's legal system.

Wolfe's novel picks up any number of contemporary vibes and issues of the day (Imelda Marcos, for example, makes a magnificent, if veiled, appearance). Rupert Murdoch's tabloid invasion of New York's newspaper world is a long-running target of Wolfe's satire. Hanging over the whole narrative is the running sore of the Bernie Goetz trial: was Goetz justified in shooting those black kids simply because he *thought* they were hunters, predators?

As the title suggests, *The Bonfire of the Vanities* owes much to Victorian fiction, particularly to Thackeray's *Vanity Fair* and to the Savonarola 'bonfire of the vanities' subplot in George Eliot's *Romola*. Appropriately, Wolfe adopted a Victorian publishing technique for his narrative. *The Bonfire of the Vanities* was, before appearing in volume form, serialised in the magazine *Rolling Stone*. Between serialisation and volume issue, Wolfe made a number of material changes to his plot. Notably Sherman (a writer in the serial novel) was transformed into a Wall Street investment banker. Wolfe was presumably influenced to make this change by the 'bubble' mania which preceded the cataclysmic October 1987 Wall Street 'meltdown'—in which the market fell 500 points in a day, taking down in its fall all the 'vanity' of young hotshots in red braces pulling in a million a year.

Hollywood likes films that look at Los Angeles ('Tinseltown') with a jaundiced eye. New York likes novels which look at the Big Apple in the same spiteful spirit. Both varieties of satire go together with a certain parochialism—a sense that all that matters is circumscribed within LA County, or the Five Boroughs. *The Bonfire of the Vanities* reminds one of the famous Saul Steinberg–*New Yorker* cartoon of 1976 Manhattan occupying the whole centre of a 'world' map, with unimportant places like the West Coast, Russia and Japan, clustered as tiny entities on the far side of the Hudson River and the Apple's other boundaries.

We never learn, as far as I can make out, whether Lamb and Roland Auburn had evil intent when they approached Sherman McCoy. (Roland gives a mendacious account to the police, suggesting Sherman hit Henry with his 'Merc' *before* he stopped—in fact he pulled up after hitting debris in the road, p. 402).[1] This is a enigma which, like the motives of the black teenagers in the subway car shot by Goetz, will never be known.

I want to look at a smaller enigma, inscribed in a quiet corner of the novel which is, I think, open to plausible solution. It occurs during a telephone conference at the brokerage firm, Pierce & Pierce. Sherman is frantically (everything is frantic with this 'Master of the Universe') putting together the 'Giscard deal'. If his cunning juggling with differential gold values comes off, he will make $600 million for the firm, and 10 per cent commission for himself.

The head of Pierce & Pierce, Gene Lopwitz, is currently in London 'where it was now 4:00 pm'. It is ten in New York (in fact, given the five-hour time difference, this is a small error). Lopwitz's loyal team is clustered deferentially around a 'plastic speaker . . . the size of a bedside clock radio':

An indistinct noise came out of the speaker. It might have been a voice and it might have been an airplane. Arnold Parch rose from his armchair and approached the Adam cabinet and looked at the plastic speaker and said, 'Gene, can you hear me all right?'

He looked imploringly at the plastic speaker, without taking his eyes off it, as if in fact it *were* Gene Lopwitz, transformed, the way princes are transformed into frogs in fairy tales. For a moment the plastic frog said nothing. Then it spoke.

'Yeah, I can hear you, Arnie. There was a lotta cheering going on.' Lopwitz's voice sounded as if it were coming from out of a storm drain, but you could hear it.

'Where are you, Gene?' asked Parch.

'I'm at a cricket match.' Then less clearly: 'What's the name a this place again?' He was evidently with some other people. 'Tottenham Park, Arnie. I'm on a kind of a terrace.'

'Who's playing?' Parch smiled, as if to show the plastic frog that this wasn't a serious question.

'Don't get technical on me, Arnie. A lot of very nice young gentlemen in cable-knit sweaters and white flannel pants, is the best I can tell you.'

Appreciative laughter broke out in the room, and Sherman felt his own lips bending into the somehow obligatory smile. He glanced about the room. Everyone was smiling and chuckling at the brown plastic speaker except for Rawlie, who had his eyes rolled up in the Oh Brother mode.

Then Rawlie leaned over toward Sherman and said, in a noisy whisper: 'Look at all these idiots grinning. They think the plastic box has eyes.' (pp. 66–7)

It's a funny scene. But it poses problems for English, more particularly London, readers. It is May—the cusp of the year when both soccer and cricket are played. By his own account Gene is watching a cricket match. And if he's on a 'terrace', it must at least be a county ground (and, of course, they would

be called 'stands' if it was cricket). But he's evidently not at
Lord's or the Oval. There is a Tottenham Park—but it's a
Jewish cemetery. It seems that Mr Lopwitz is at Tottenham
Hotspurs' White Hart Lane football ground. The 'Spurs', as
one of the two or three most famous British soccer teams,
might well be known to a Manhattan writer.

It could be that the wily Lopwitz is not at any match at
all. The plastic box does not have eyes—at either end. Or
could it be that he is so wholly confused by Anglo-Saxon
quaintness that he can't tell the two national games apart?
Unlikely, given the business about cable-knit sweaters and
white pants.

What seems more likely is that this is a prime example
of the 'Steinberg effect'. *The Bonfire of the Vanities* is
minutely exact about New York topography. You can stand
outside Sherman's Park Avenue co-op. If you are brave and
curious enough you can, with the aid of the Rand McNally
'Easyfinder' New York map, trace Sherman's ill-fated route.
He drifted right, not left, across the Triborough Toll Bridge
and blundered north up Bruckner Boulevard. At the 895 on-
ramp (around 'Whitlock') he had his meeting with Henry and
Roland. He shot on to the Bronx Expressway, finally making
his way south down the Deegan Expressway, which brought
him again to the Triborough Bridge, Manhattan and home.

All this is recorded with admirable precision. But, from
the Manhattanite's skewed point of view, the world outside
Manhattan is so amorphous and remote that cricket and
soccer are indistinguishable—and as unimportant to 'real
people' (i.e. New Yorkers) as whether, for example, Seattle
is in Oregon, Washington or Montana.

Why Does Patrick Bateman Wear Two Ties?

Few novels of the 1990s have excited as much fuss as *American Psycho*. It was written (and rewritten) by 'brat' author Brett Easton Ellis (born 1964), still riding high on the triumph of his first published work *Less Than Zero* (1985). His second novel, *Rules of Attraction* (1987), had not done well; *American Psycho* would be an important novel for him, career-wise. All Ellis's fiction, like that of his coeval Jay McInerney, has dealt with the so-called 'blank generation' of the 1980s—rich, well-educated, privileged kids, with nothing to do but hang out stylishly, take drugs and otherwise abuse themselves in modish ways. *Less Than Zero* and *Rules of Attraction* dealt with their college years. *American Psycho* takes the blank generation forward into their mid-twenties, the late 1980s and yuppiedom.

Less Than Zero had created considerable stir. *American Psycho*, even before publication, triggered a storm, a one-book moral panic. Simon & Schuster, having advanced $300,000 for the rights, turned the novel down at the proof stage, in late 1990. Their decision not to publish was forced by feminist outrage at violence to women in Ellis's narrative—which takes the form of an interior monologue by a sadistic psychopath recording in a cool, Holden Caulfield style his gruesome serial killings. For some years, women had been recruited into the man's world of publishing: they were now a potent presence at the senior-editorial level. Some woman whistle-blower had leaked the proofs of *American Psycho*. They were, apparently, circulating in bootlegged form among feminist groups who had mobilised to lobby against publication of this misogynistic tract.

After Simon & Schuster revoked their agreement with Ellis (how much of their advance they sacrificed is not clear) Random House took the novel over, intending to bring it out as a 'Vintage Paperback Original' (a form which had worked very well for McInerney: the theory was that young people liked soft covers). Reportedly the text was toned down. Random House declined the other publisher's film of the typeset book.

Particularly disturbing to its first, clandestine, female readers was a scene in *American Psycho* in which a woman is mutilated with a staple gun and another in which the hero's girlfriend (so called) is nailed to the floor, her tongue and nipples cut off with nail scissors, and is then forced to fellate her tormentor. In the light of such scenes, and the 'blank' manner in which they were described, the Los Angeles chapter of the National Organisation of Women demanded a national boycott of Ellis's book, under whatever imprint and with whatever revisions it might appear. The offence was already rank.

There was some mild defence of Ellis. In the *New York Times*, 10 December 1990, Richard Bernstein complained that 'a degree of hypocrisy has entered the picture . . . the company that owns Simon & Schuster is Paramount Communications, whose movie division has brought out the "Friday the 13th series" in which people are routinely beheaded or hammered to death'. Slasher movies had been around for some time, and were popular with young audiences. Freddy Kruger and Jason were probably better known than Ronald Reagan's cabinet among America's adolescents. The 'blank' generation was addicted to them.

The 'Horror Comedy' genre—something which he sees as originating with *Psycho*—was congenial to Ellis, and something he claimed to be exploring in *American Psycho*. The novel is, as the title suggests, a 'homage' to Alfred Hitchcock and there are several knowing references to *Psycho* (and the famous shower scene) in the text. Patrick Bateman, he tells us, has rented the video of Brian de Palma's homage to Hitchcock, *Body Double* (1984), thirty-seven times. Bateman particularly likes the 'drilling to death bit' (p. 112).[1] For the ingenious, the hero's name can be deciphered as an amalgam of Hitchcock's Nor*man Bates*—with 'Badman' and 'Batman' thrown in for good measure.

Patrick Bateman works (although we never see him actually *do* anything) as a broker at 'P. & P.' —a leading Wall Street firm (the same business, we must assume, as Sherman McCoy's 'Pierce and Pierce' in *The Bonfire of the Vanities*— odd colleagues they must be). Bateman is the archetypal yuppie. Someone, that is, who earns, in thousands of dollars, twice his age (in Patrick's case, 26 years old, he should be earning $52,000, and probably is). Born in 1964, Bateman is, of course, exactly the same age as his author, Brett Easton Ellis. (As Ellis has wearily insisted in interviews, the resemblance stops there.)

American Psycho takes the form of a tell-all confession, set intermittently between 1986 and 1988.[2] The narrative is broken off mid-sentence in places, which suggests a tape-recorded text. There are a number of mysteries in the journal. Patrick, for example, never mentions October 1987, and 'Black Monday', when the Wall Street market fell 500 points. How did Bateman survive this cataclysm when so many of his yuppie kind went the way of the dinosaurs? Or did he survive it?

There are other odd lacunae in the narrative. We know virtually nothing about Patrick's family, except that the Batemans are very rich. At one point a girlfriend (later a victim), Bethany, asks: 'why don't you just quit? You don't have to work.' Patrick replies, evidently embarrassed: 'Because . . . I . . . want . . . to . . . fit . . . in' (p. 237). It's a tantalising fragment of information. Is Patrick Bateman not after all a yuppie (a self-made young man of the 1980s), but a 'number one son', a 'rich kid', a 'kept man'?

It is *American Psycho*'s presiding trick that the narrative constantly decomposes into a catalogue of ultra-fashionable restaurants, designer clothes and cosmetics. Brand names come at the reader in grapeshot clusters. For whole pages the novel reads like a *GQ* advertisers' list. Fashion is not the most important thing: it's the only thing. *American Psycho* is a sumptuary novel, in which clothes do not just make the man, they create the world. Patrick is driven to kill the luckless Bethany (as noted, he impales her with nail gun, excises her nipples and tongue with nail scissors, and sodomises her mutilated head) because she 'mistook his Giorgio Armani suit for Garrick Anderson!' (p. 247).

This, and scenes like it, could be read as funny. 'Black', or 'post-black', are terms routinely applied. But there is another, more interesting possibility—is it all drug-induced fantasy? There is, for example, a critical moment early in the novel where Patrick is clearly going round the twist. He has been overdoing the cocaine. A number of characters point out to him that his nose is bleeding. Patrick describes returning to his apartment block:

I collect my mail—Polo catalog, American Express bill, June *Playboy*, invitation to an office party at a new club called Bedlam—then walk to the elevator, step in while inspecting the Ralph Lauren brochure and press the button for my floor and then the Close Door button, but someone gets in right before the doors shut and instinctively I turn to say hello. It's the actor Tom Cruise, who lives in the pent-house, and as a courtesy, without asking him, I press the PH button and he nods thank you and keeps his eyes fixed on the numbers lighting up above the door in rapid succession. He is much shorter in person and he's wearing the same pair of black Wayfarers I have on. He's dressed in blue jeans, a white T-shirt, an Armani jacket.

To break the noticeably uncomfortable silence, I clear my throat and say, 'I thought you were very fine in *Bartender*. I thought it was quite a good movie, and *Top Gun* too. I really thought that was good.'

He looks away from the numbers and then straight at me. 'It was called *Cocktail*,' he says softly. (p. 71)

One may note in passing that it is one of Patrick's endearing traits that he is very error-prone on names (particularly show-business names), compulsive as he is about accuracy.

Here he blunders over the name of Tom Cruise's 1988 film—which, as Patrick's 'quite good' implies, was not the star's best work (in career terms, Cruise was marking time, waiting for Oliver Stone's *Born on the Fourth of July*, 1989, which would be very big for him). But, we may legitimately enquire, does Tom Cruise in *fact* live in Patrick Bateman's building? Later on, when he is being interviewed by a less than sharp private detective, Patrick gives out that he lives at 'Fifty-five West Eighty-first street . . . The American Gardens Building'.

'Doesn't Tom Cruise live there?' (p. 270), asks the detective. 'Yup,' Patrick answers. This is odd. There is no such building, of course. But Tom Cruise, as various unauthorised biographies testify, did have as one of his residences at this period a New York 'studio' (not a pent-house). One of the said unauthorised biographies actually gives a (fuzzy) picture of the building. It does not resemble Patrick's swish West Side apartment block. The joke may be that, among a profession jealous of privacy, Cruise is morbidly so. His *Who's Who* entries do not even—as other stars' entries routinely do—offer the address of his agent. His home addresses are among America's best-kept secrets. Fans would pay gold for '55 West 81st. St', if it were true. (Don't raise your hopes; it's a fantasy address. If it existed it would be, I calculate, in the Impressionist Gallery of the Metropolitan Museum of Art.)

If Tom Cruise in the lift is a hallucination (and a couple of pages earlier Patrick notes that he *has* been seeing things), how can we account for the correction of the error about *Cocktail/Bartender*'s title? In a drug-induced fantasy one might well get the name of a film wrong, but would some critical *alter ego* step in to correct that mistake *within* the hallucination?

The hallucination hypothesis is none the less supported by other hints that Patrick's mind may be wrong. Immediately after the Tom Cruise encounter he goes to his apartment to prepare for that evening's date with Patricia Worrell. Details of his wardrobe are given with the usual fanatic meticulousness:

While loosening my Matisse-inspired blue silk tie from Bill Robinson I dial her number and walk across the apartment, cordless phone in hand, to flip on the air-conditioning.

She answers on the third ring. 'Hello?'

'Patricia. Hi. It's Pat Bateman.'

'Oh hi,' she says. 'Listen, I'm on the other line. Can I call you back?'

'Well . . . ,' I say.

'Look, it's my health club,' she says. 'They've screwed up my account. I'll call you back in a sec.'

'Yeah,' I say. And hang up.

I go into the bedroom and take off what I was wearing today: a herringbone wool suit with pleated trousers by Giorgio Correggiari, a cotton Oxford shirt by Ralph Lauren, a knit tie from Paul Stuart and suede shoes from Cole-Haan. I slip on a pair of sixty-dollar boxer shorts I bought at Barneys's and do some stretching exercises, holding the phone, waiting for Patricia to call back. (pp. 72–3)

How is it he is simultaneously wearing two different ties? One thing one knows about the composition of *American Psycho* is that the proofs were gone through with a fine toothcomb by two publishing houses. The detail is there, we may be sure, for a reason. But, if we credit Patrick, he is wearing around his neck at the same time a Matisse-style silk tie and a Paul Stuart wool-knit tie. Can we trust such a narrator? Would you buy a second-hand suit from this man?

There is an even more puzzling enigma about Paul Owen at the conclusion of the novel. If we credit his account, Patrick has bloodily slaughtered Paul with an axe and disposed of the body, leaving a message on his victim's 'ansaphone' that he (Paul) has gone off to London. Later, using Owen's stolen credit cards, he calls in and kills two escort girls hideously in the vacant apartment. But, when he returns some months later, Owen's apartment is being sold by a realtor and there is no evidence or record of the corpses. However dumb the private detective looking into the affair, he would hardly have missed these putrefying pieces of evidence.

Still later, a mutual acquaintance (who insists on calling Patrick 'Donaldson'—no one can get his name right), to whom he has confessed killing Owen, replies that Patrick cannot have done so. Why? 'Because . . . I had . . . dinner with Paul Owen . . . twice . . . in London . . . *just ten days ago*' (p. 388). It is very strange and ties in with other perplexing details. The escort girls would have been careful to leave the address and phone number of where they were going with their agency. Their bodies would surely have been found and reported. If Owen weren't paying his phone bills, someone would have followed up. There are any number of reasons for thinking that either Patrick is fantasising, has gone mad or is telling clumsy (but stylish) lies.

Are we, one is driven to ask, in 'Occurrence at Owl Creek Bridge' territory? In Ambrose Bierce's sharp little story, a man is hanged as a spy by Union soldiers during the Civil War. As he falls from the bridge the rope snaps, he swims to safety and makes his way back to his home. The descriptions of what he experiences in this journey home become increasingly phantasmagoric and disoriented. He finally collapses at the door to his house, and the story switches back to his corpse dangling lifeless at the end of a rope at Owl Creek Bridge. It was all in his head. Patrick Bateman, I hypothesise, lost all in the October 1987 crash: he has spiralled into a terminal drug orgy in his apartment, from which he will soon be evicted, with only his wardrobe for company. He finally overdosed, and was found, by the janitor, in early 1989. *American Psycho* is his last will and testament.

A. S. Byatt · *Possession*

═══

What Really Happened in 1868?

═══

Possession was the most critically honoured and among the most popular British novels of 1990. A. S. Byatt's novel got glowing reviews, won the Booker Prize, and headed the British bestseller list. *Possession* has retained its popularity with British and, increasingly, American readers.

Byatt's success arose in part from a canny blending of genres. Subtitled *Possession: A Romance*, the novel draws on the example of the 'Queen' of historical romance, Georgette Heyer (a novelist Byatt admires and on whom she has written perceptively), and on John Fowles's 1969 bestseller, *The French Lieutenant's Woman* (particularly influential on Byatt must have been the 1981 film version and Harold Pinter's twin-track screenplay which switched, as does *Possession*, between modern and Victorian settings).

While never surrendering its page-turning appeal *Possession* displays, as ostentatiously as any campus novel, Byatt's prodigious inwardness with Victorian poetry (and, in the long pastiche interludes, her skill in recreating it). Equally prominent is her mastery of contemporary French 'theory', that most difficult branch of literary criticism.

Possession has a strong narrative line. A post-doctoral research student, Roland Michell, works for a senior scholar, Professor Blackadder, on a collected edition of the works of the great Victorian poet, Randolph Henry Ash. Privately Roland pictures himself labouring in what he sardonically calls 'the Ash factory'—a sterile research mill. Things look up when he discovers in the London Library a letter hinting at a clandestine relationship between Ash and a woman poet, Christabel LaMotte.

Roland sets out to find out the truth of the matter. He is helped in his mission by a young feminist scholar, Maud Bailey. Maud, it transpires, is a distant descendant of LaMotte's sister, Sophia, who had a daughter May (Maud's great-great-grandmother, if I can count right). Other scholars are drawn in, all wanting in one way or another to 'possess' Ash. Heading the pack is the predatory American, Professor Mortimer Cropper. A short way behind is the wild, New York Jewish, feminist–Marxist Leonora Stern.

The truth of what went on between Ash and LaMotte is gradually uncovered—partly in historical flashback. It emerges that in 1859 the two poets indeed had a clandestine love affair; an episode which, in the way of such things, enriched his poetry and ruined her life. A misunderstanding between the lovers led to Ash's returning to his patiently devoted wife, Ellen. The keeper of his flame, she loyally stood by him until his death in 1889, dying herself seven years later.

Things turned out rather less happily for the woman poet. On learning of the affair with Ash, LaMotte's lesbian lover, Blanche Glover, drowned herself in 1861. Christabel became a recluse, turning out obscure and unread verse. She died unnoticed in 1890. All this is historical record. What was not known—until Roland and Maud discover it—is that Christabel had a child by Ash.

'Did Ash know of the possible child?' (p. 422)[1] is the question posed in the last quarter of the book, as the academic hunt closes on its prey. And what became of the child? A tantalising fragment turns up among Ash's literary remains: a letter clearly written after the affair had ended but well before his terminal illness. The letter, which may never have been sent, opens: 'I write each year, round about All Souls [i.e. 2 November] . . . I know that you will not answer.' His principal question is: 'What became of my child? Did he live?' (p. 455).

Randolph Ash, it appears, strongly suspects that their

affair has produced a child, and thinks it is probably a son. Why? All will be clear, the investigating scholars decide, if they can exhume and examine a box of letters interred with Ash. Ellen Ash, while Randolph was on his deathbed, evidently discovered the facts of the case. Christabel sent her a letter to be read by the wife and passed on to the dying poet, her husband, at Ellen's discretion. The letter begins: 'My dear—my dear—They tell me you are very ill' and goes on to inform Randolph: 'You have a daughter, who is well, and married, and the mother of a beautiful boy' (p. 499). Does Ellen in fact pass the letter on to her husband or inform him of its contents? No one knows.

The box of letters is disinterred. They reveal that Maud is, in fact, the direct descendant of Christabel's daughter May, who was adopted for secrecy's sake by Sophia. Maud now 'possesses' the Ash bequest. She is the legal inheritrix of his literary remains and copyright. The novel ends with marriage between the contemporary lovers, Roland and Maud, imminent. Romance demands such endings. But the question remains: did Ash actually know, at the time of his death, of the existence of his daughter?

Possession is an extraordinarily knowing novel, in the manner popularised by Umberto Eco's *The Name of the Rose* (1980). Byatt's narrative picks up innumerable echoes of actual literary history. Randolph Ash, man and poetry, seems to owe much to Robert Browning. The affair with LaMotte recalls Browning's relationship (only revealed in the late twentieth century) with Julia Wedgwood. As a poet, Christabel strongly recalls Christina Rossetti. And the business of the buried manuscripts recalls G. H. Lewes's love letters which George Eliot had buried with her. More morbidly, it recalls Dante Gabriel Rossetti's first burying the manuscripts of his *House of Life* sonnets with Elizabeth Siddal, then having them dug up again when he decided, after all, that the world, rather than the corpse of his lover, should have the fruits of his genius.

Byatt knows Victorian literature and all its curious little corners. Several times in her narrative, she refers to Philip Gosse's touchingly fideistic contention that a Creationist God had put the fossils into the rocks to fool the Darwinists. Did Byatt knowingly do the same thing in her novel, sowing it with deliberate mistakes? In Ellen Ash's journal (a key piece of recovered evidence) for 25 November 1889 she puts down her motives for prudent concealment. On his deathbed, Ash had instructed her to 'burn what they should not see', which she evidently did. As she explains:

He hated the new vulgarity of *contemporary* biography, the ransacking of Dickens's desk for his most trivial memoranda, Forster's unspeakable intrusions into the private pains and concealments of the Carlyles. (p. 442)

It was *not* Forster (Dickens's biographer) who carried out these intrusions into the Carlyles' married life, exposing Thomas's sexual impotence to posterity ('he should never have married', Jane observed). It was J. A. Froude (Carlyle's biographer) who betrayed these intimacies long after 1889 and some time after Ellen's death in 1896.[2] One has to assume this is a false fossil, put in to fool the unwary reader. Ellen's diary is a forgery, we may deduce. Some T. J. Wise (the famous 'Browning forger') has been at work here.

The question of what Ash knew and when he knew it is rendered even more enigmatic by the novel's 'Postscript 1868'. This is the last section of *Possession*. It is a 'hot May day' and 'This is how it was' (Hemingway's slogan), we are told:

There was a meadow full of young hay, and all the summer flowers in great abundance. Blue cornflowers, scarlet poppies, gold buttercups, a veil of speedwells, an intricate carpet of daisies where the grass was shorter, scabious, yellow snapdragons, bacon and egg plant, pale milkmaids, purple heartsease, scarlet pimpernel and white shepherd's purse, and round this field a high bordering hedge of Queen Anne's lace and foxgloves and above that dogroses, palely shining in a thorny hedge, honeysuckle all creamy and sweet-smelling, rambling threads of bryony and the dark stars of deadly nightshade. It was abundant, it seemed as though it must go on shining forever. The grasses had an enamelled gloss and were connected by diamond-threads of light. The larks sang, and the thrushes, and the blackbirds, sweet and clear, and there were butterflies everywhere, blue, sulphur, copper, and fragile white, dipping from flower to flower, from clover to vetch to larkspur, seeing their own guiding visions of invisible violet pentagrams and spiralling coils of petal-light. (p. 508)

Randolph Ash, sauntering aimlessly through this florid landscape, meets a little girl who tells him her name is Maia Thomasine—he has met Maia in May in a meadow. They fall into conversation, sitting on a 'hummock', in 'a cloud of butterflies, as he remembered it with absolutely clarity, and she remembered it more and more vaguely, as the century ran on. Beetles ran about their feet, jet and emerald' (p. 509).

'I think I know your mother', Ash says. 'You have a true look of your mother.' 'No one else says that,' the child retorts. Ash makes the little girl May a crown (she will be a 'May Queen') and quotes some appropriate lines from *Paradise Lost* about Proserpine. He then takes a lock of her hair for himself, and gives her a message for her mother: 'Tell your aunt [he means Christabel—and he is aware, apparently, that she is *not* May's aunt but her mother] that you met a poet who . . . is on his way to fresh woods and pastures new' (p. 510, another Milton echo). The novel ends: 'And on the way home, she met her brothers, and there was a rough-and-tumble, and the lovely crown was broken, and she forgot the message, which was never delivered' (p. 511).

Overhanging this coda is the crass question, 'did it happen?' or 'where did it happen?' (in Ash's head, May's head, the unidentified narrator's head?). The reader must choose between radically alternative readings of the scene. It could be a deathbed fantasy of Randolph Ash's. This—a strong probability—is supported by his semi-delirious rambling many pages earlier, where he hallucinates about Donne's 'bright hair about the bone' and incoherently babbles of Falstaff's green-fields (p. 452).

The hallucinatory reading of the scene is supported by other suspicious elements: the overload of natural ornament, for example. The 'clouds' of butterflies, 'carpets' of beetles, and profusion of wild flowers, all recall Sidney's maxim that the real world 'is brazen, the Poets only deliver a golden'. This is a golden world if there ever was one. And like other golden worlds, it defies the laws of nature. Those myriad flowers don't, most of them, bloom in May—but in the hotter months of July and August. This, we deduce from its paradisal copiousness, is a poet's vision, not an actual English meadow; something composed of dirt, flies, grass, nettles, weeds and the odd straggly wild flower.

But before jumping to conclusions we must beware the research Byatt routinely packs into her fiction. She is a scholar–novelist. If we look back at the meteorological records, we discover, perplexingly, that 1868 was—it so happens—the hottest in the nineteenth-century record books. So hot was 1868, in fact, that flowers which normally come out in the late summer months might well have appeared in that sweltering May. The heat might also create—especially in the retrospective memory—a hallucinatory nimbus.

As the critic reviewing *Possession* in the *TLS* pointed out, Byatt has contrived a 'masterly ending'. A realistic narrative finally folds into art. The main point the reader carries away is that 'research' will never know what happened between those two Victorian poets; it never can, however deep it digs or scrutinises the literary remains and historical record, whatever 'theory' it devises. In the end, only the artist—the novelist or poet—will 'know' what really happened.

=====

It's a Wise Child

=====

Any number of puzzles can be dredged up from Salman Rushdie's fiction, given the liberties magic takes with realism in his narratives. I want to investigate one which is central, I think, to *Midnight's Children* (1981), the novel that won not just the Booker Prize, but the twenty-five-year 'Booker of Bookers' prize.

The 'midnight' in the title is that of 15 August 1947: the moment at which India became independent; the moment when the English left. Correspondingly, Rushdie's dramatis personae, voluminous as it is, is almost completely lacking in ('independent of') the sub-continent's former colonial masters, the English. As far as I can discern, only a couple of white faces peer out from the mass of brown, golden and black. One is that of Brigadier R. E. Dyer—the butcher of Amritsar. He has a walk-on part in which he briskly perpetrates his massacre, exiting with: 'Good shooting. We have done a jolly good thing' (p. 36).[1]

Otherwise, the Raj is represented only by the deceitful William Methwold, whose house ('conqueror's house!') on Methwold Estate is taken over by Saleem Sinai's family after the momentous change in August 1947. The hero's birth—which occurs on the stroke of midnight, as Nehru addresses the new nation of India by radio—is the confluence of many Shandyan accidents. The nurse in the maternity ward, Mary Pereira, is in love with a radical guerilla, Joseph D'Costa. Following her crazed interpretation of the Christian Nativity (they are, after all, Mary and Joseph), and aware of her lover's desire to overthrow the class system, she changes two babies at 'the hour of their birth'. One is the newborn hero, the other a beggar's child. This furtive swap will be 'her own private revolutionary act' (p. 117).

'The crime of Mary Pereira' is discovered to the Sinai family some years later, after she has taken employment with them as a child minder ('ayah'). They generously decide that 'it made no difference' (p. 118). It is, anyway, too late to do anything about it. What Mary has done, of course, is to condemn the middle-class birth-child of the Sinais (Shiva, as he is to be known) to a vagrant upbringing. The resourceful Shiva eventually rises to high rank as a brutal army officer, doing the brutal Mrs Gandhi's dirty work. The middle-class businessman Ahmed Sinai and his wife inherit the offspring of the itinerant beggar and busker, Wee Willie Winkie. This, of course, is the narrator hero, 'I, Saleem Sinai, later variously called Snotnose, Stainface, Baldy, Sniffer, Buddha, and even Piece-of-the-Moon' (p. 8). He should, of course, be 'Shiva'.

This changeling is, almost at the moment of birth, half orphaned. While the bourgeois Mr Sinai, who has contrived to break a toe, is fussed over by the hospital doctors, the beggar's wife Vanita 'had not managed to survive her childbearing. At three minutes past midnight, while doctors fussed over the broken toe, Vanita had haemorrhaged and died' (p. 117). Sinai, his 'eyes as blue as Methwold's' (a meaningful detail), is duly taken over by his unwitting 'parents', after Mary's switch.

There are, however, further complications in this baby's parentage—hinted at by those blue eyes and early baldness. Earlier, as we are told, Methwold seduced Vanita. He sent off Wee Willie Winkie to the chemist to buy a remedy for his headache, and, while the husband was away, the wily Englishman had his way with the wife. Nine months later, to the day, Wee Willie Winkie has a 'baby to joke about' (p. 103). This baby is, of course (thanks to Mary Pereira), the narrator hero, Saleem.

As an astonished Padma (the hero's rather dim lover) puts

it, listening to Saleem's narrative and finally putting two and two together: 'An Anglo? . . . What are you telling me? You are an Anglo-Indian? Your name is not your own?' Well, yes, he is an 'Anglo-Indian'; that is precisely what Saleem is telling her. And since nationality follows the patriarchal line there is, after all, an Englishman (or at least a large part of an Englishman) centrally present in the novel. Namely Saleem Sinai.

The problem which confronts pedantic readers, however, is that there is no way Saleem can have known these 'facts' of his parentage. Nor, apart from this one allusion to Saleem's miscegenation, is it referred to again—all important as it would seem. Methwold, blue eyed and revealed at the last moment to be bald under his hairpiece, leaves India saying nothing—certainly not to the Sinais. Vanita dies, and unless she has passed her secret on to Mary Pereira, all knowledge of her adultery dies with her, at three minutes past midnight 15 August 1947. Her unwitting husband never knew he had been cuckolded. There are, of course, the blue eyes and the early baldness. But, these clues apart, one has to assume that there is more magic than realism in Saleem's knowing who his father is. He is a very wise child.

Does It Work?

The *Sunday Telegraph* of 11 January 1998 carried on page 7 a story alarmingly headlined: 'Parents Warned About Throttling Game That Kills'. There was, readers were told, a 'deadly new game' sweeping the playgrounds of Britain, a 'new craze' among primary school children. The craze had been brought to light by the death of an 11-year-old boy in Avondale. The unfortunate young victim had been found by his mother, 'with a dressing-gown cord wrapped around his neck'.

Similar tragedies, or near-tragedies, had been reported elsewhere in the country, it was stated. Evidently, children were asphyxiating themselves all over England for the oxygen 'buzz' which accompanied resuscitation from near-strangling. If misjudged, the results could be fatal and all too often were.

A spokesperson for the Confederation of Parent Teacher Associations was reported as declaring that 'as parents we should address this before it becomes an epidemic'. She added she had 'no idea' where the craze for 'peer asphyxiation' originated; but 'they are obviously copying something—they don't just dream up ideas like that at that age'.

From the school where the hanged boy had been a pupil there emerged a teasing clue as to where the asphyxiation craze originated: 'The boy's headmaster', the *Sunday Tele-graph* reported, 'has discovered since the death that a game, called "rising sun" by schoolchildren and thought to come from America, was commonplace throughout the school.' No explanation was given by the newspaper as to why children should call their dangerous game 'rising sun'. But a little recollection of recent bestselling fiction explains it.

In 1992, Michael Crichton recycled the venerable 'Yellow Peril' scenario in a novel called *Rising Sun*. It is a work about the insidious takeover of America—specifically Southern California—by predatory Japanese corporations. Crichton's fiction is legendary for its accurate prophecy. But *Rising Sun* was, in the historical event, ludicrously wide of the mark. Sony and Matsushita lost zillions by their acquisition of Hollywood studios. The Los Angeles real-estate market plummeted in the early 1990s, ruining Japanese property developers who had unwisely speculated in it. American automobiles and high-technology products became competitive and began to out-sell their Japanese and Korean rivals. And, in the late 1990s, the 'Tiger economies' of the Far East collapsed like so many dominoes. The sun was not, apparently, rising. There was, after all, no yellow peril—or at least, not at the moment.

None the less, *Rising Sun* did well as a book, making the bestseller lists. And it inspired a box-office success film, starring Sean Connery (whose ostensibly expert Japanese was found hilariously comical by Tokyo audiences) and Wesley Snipes. The film had a low '15 PG' certificate and was released in 1993 in Britain. The narrative peg on which Crichton's xenophobic vision hangs is a murder investigation. The Connery/Snipes characters are police officers, assigned to a sensitive case. A young (Caucasian) woman has been found murdered in the Nakamoto Building in LA. It emerges that she went off with someone (presumably a Japanese someone) during a party at the building. The victim was, it emerges, a high-price call girl, whose particular specialism was that—to achieve orgasm—she required near-death asphyxiation. Her client was encouraged to half strangle her while enjoying the lady's more routine services. The game has evidently gone wrong. The novel follows the fiendish ruses the Japanese use (with their amazingly advanced technology) to throw the American sleuths off the trail and cover up their deeper plans to take over corporate America and subjugate the Stars and Stripes to the Rising Sun. They are, needless to say, foiled.

Clearly English school-children had got hold of the video, or the paperback, of *Rising Sun*. It was also clear, although the *Sunday Telegraph* was too dim to make the connection (or perhaps too sensitive to the grief of the bereaved parents), that the self-asphyxiation was an accompaniment to group or solitary masturbation—for girls as well as boys. As is often the case, the book banners and book burners—while directing their fire against the films *Lolita* and *Crash* and the 'paedophile shocker', A. M. Homes's *The End of Alice*—had missed a much more immediately fatal danger to the country's youth.

The *Sunday Telegraph* tailed its story off with a speculative cross-reference to another recent self-asphyxiation *cause célèbre*:

Among adults the erotic element associated with depriving the brain of oxygen has led to numerous tragedies, although the phenomenon of auto-erotic asphyxiation, or 'scarfing', was not widely known outside police and medical circles until the body of Stephen Milligan MP was found in February 1994. He had died as the result of auto-erotic asphyxiation.

This is as badly researched as the main section of the article. Among sophisticated and adventurous metropolitan types like Milligan, the cult of auto-asphyxiation had been popularized years before, by William S. Burroughs's *Naked Lunch*. The central sections of Burroughs's novel, notably 'Hassan's Rumpus Room', are wild fantasias about hanging orgies. Young boys are hanged with red silk cords:

The Mugwump [Burroughs's code for predatory homosexual] slips the noose over the boy's head and tightens the knot caressingly behind the left ear. The boy's penis is retracted, his balls tight. He look straight ahead breathing deeply. The Mugwump sidles around the boy goosing him and caressing his genitals in hieroglyphs of mockery. He moves in behind the boy with a series of bumps and shoves his cock up the boy's ass. He stands there moving in circular gyrations.

The guests shush each other, nudge and giggle.

Suddenly the Mugwump pushes the boy forward into space, free of his cock. He steadies the boy with hands on the hip bones, reaches up with his stylized hieroglyph hands and snaps the boy's neck. A shudder passes through the boy's body. His penis rises in three great surges pulling his pelvis up, ejaculates immediately. (p. 70)[1]

As Burroughs's biographer Ted Morgan points out, when *Naked Lunch* was first published in 1959 (in Paris) and in the UK in 1961, the association of hanging with sexual excitement was seen as bizarre. Now, as Morgan points out, it is widely practised, and is part of every sexual adventurer's repertoire:

An episode that seemed revoltingly far-fetched [in 1959] was that of orgasm by hanging. But this has become a social phenomenon chronicled in articles in *The New York Times*, in a book entitled *Autoerotic Fatalities*, and on *The Oprah Winfrey Show*. It seems that there are between 500 and 1,000 such asphyxiations a year, in which thrill-seeking young men tie a noose around their necks and cut off the blood supply to the brain via the carotid arteries, to heighten the pleasure of masturbation. A little slip, a false move, and they're twisting in the wind. The product of Burroughs' fantasy in 1959 has become a documented practice a quarter century later.[2]

Morgan plausibly sees *Naked Lunch* as having popularised, and even legitimated, erotic auto-asphyxiation among gays. After its 'acquittal' and publication in the US and the UK in the early 1960s, Burroughs's novel became an instant bestseller, attracting a broad non-gay readership. 'Straights' evidently were also inspired to experiment. And even those timid souls not inclined to throttle themselves in the pursuit of good sex knew all about it. When the Australian pop singer Michael Hutchence was found hanging in his hotel room in 1997 it was widely assumed that another erotic auto-asphyxiation had gone wrong. No big deal. In fact, the coroner determined that it was a genuine suicide.

The effect of books, particularly where 'copycat' crime or self-injury is concerned, is a minefield. But there is no question that novels do serve as primers in areas where there is state-imposed ignorance, or prohibition. It is not merely sexual ignorance or prohibition. Suicide was, until very recently, a criminal offence and giving advice on means of suicide another offence. Would-be suicides were likely to find themselves in the condition of Dorothy Parker:

> Razors pain you;
> Rivers are damp;
> Acids stain you;
> And drugs cause cramp.
> Guns aren't lawful;
> Nooses give;
> Gas smells awful;
> You might as well live.

In a culture of state-enforced ignorance about 'easy ways to die', novels—or lore gleaned from them and passed on verbally—were routinely used as guide books. The fact that, if you opened the veins on your wrist, it was wise to do it in a warm bath to prevent cramps was one of the useful deductions drawn from Aldous Huxley's otherwise unmemorable short story 'Sir Hercules'.

An apparently foolproof way of deceiving the coroner (so ensuring the life-insurance company didn't withhold payment) was given by Graham Greene—a connoisseur of suicide—in *The Heart of the Matter*. Henry Scobie simulates angina and saves the Evipan tablets that his doctor prescribes until there are enough for an overdose. Of course, his medical records confirm that he was a sick man and there is no post-mortem. It was a technique that was easily adapted: you could go to your doctor with simulated insomnia, for example, and hoard barbiturates. Greene doubtless helped many unhappy readers on their way.

For decades it was believed on the basis of Dorothy Sayers's thriller *Strong Poison* that an air bubble injected into a vein with a hypodermic syringe was an infallible means of inducing heart failure and death. Derek Humphry, in his

1991 suicide manual *Final Exit*, pours cold water on this 'myth'. You would need a bicycle pump to get enough air into the circulatory system. Humphry's book, and the 'Hemlock Society' he founded, did not have much time for novels as 'how to' books for would-be suicides.

There had been, none the less, a notable leap forward in the technical reliability of descriptions of suicide methods in fiction of the postwar period. In such things, for example, as the inadvisability of shooting yourself through the temple (an error made by Goethe's Werther—it often results in a painfully lingering death. You should direct the bullet up, through the roof of the palate, as any number of thrillers made clear). A. N. Wilson's *The Healing Art* (1980) is typically sensible (for its time) in its knowing reference to the 'easiest' way to kill yourself: a bottle of whisky, a length of rubber tube to the exhaust of a car, a hole knocked in the back window to feed through the carbon monoxide, and a quiet lay-by to do it in.

Abortion, like suicide, was another area in which, until quite recently, the British population was kept in a condition of prophylactic ignorance. Like most of my generation I read Alan Sillitoe's 'angry young man' novel, *Saturday Night and Sunday Morning*, when it first came out in paperback, in 1960. I remember meeting a friend who—on the subject of the novel being raised—muttered glumly, 'It doesn't work'. Thinking he meant all the business about the motor cycles, Goose Fair and fishing in the Trent I agreed. 'No,' he said, 'the gin and hot bath doesn't work.'

Abortion was not legal in the UK until 1968. There was, before this reform, a huge demand for it, especially among the working classes. The demand was satisfied by the back-street abortionist and various more or less reliable home remedies. *Saturday Night and Sunday Morning* centres on a long description of the abortion that Arthur procures for his married mistress, Brenda, through his Aunt Ada, a kind of latter-day witch, or primitive wise woman. An abortion is urgently needed, since Brenda and her husband Jack have not had sex for months.

Brenda should, Ada advises: 'take a hot bath with hot gin. Tell her to stay there for two hours, as hot as she can bear it, and drink a pint of gin. That should bring it off. If it don't, then she'll just have to have the kid, that's all' (p. 78).[3] Most of Chapter 6 of the novel is taken up with a gruesome and detailed description of the abortion. It does, indeed, bring it off. Brenda's marriage to Jack is preserved.

The Woodfall film version *Saturday Night and Sunday Morning* was subjected to fierce and wide-ranging censorship pressures from the British Board of Film Control. Language ('bad language') was a main target. But the abortion episode was not just cut out—it was reversed. Rachel Roberts, as Brenda, is made to say: 'she [that is Ada] made me sit in a hot bath and take some gin; *it didn't work*'. She determines to have the child, and face the music. The authorities, one assumes, were alarmed that the novel's technique, if popularized by a popular film, would be imitated. The implication was that the gin and hot-bath technique was efficacious. It worked, but don't, for God's sake, let it get around.

===

Where Are the Firm's Computers?

===

John Grisham ranks as the world's top-selling novelist of the 1990s. He enjoys vast advances, in tens of millions of dollars, on the strength of his legal-thrillers. '*L.A. Law* crossed with *The Godfather*' is how one critic described the Grisham formula. He has been particularly fortunate in the success with which his narratives adapt to film treatment—creating huge 'tie-in' sales and subsidiary-rights income. Of all the 'Millionaire's Row' novelists (Stephen King, Danielle Steel, Jeffrey Archer) Grisham has proved the most consistently 'bankable' from Hollywood's point of view. Every film of his books has been a hit.

Grisham's breakthrough success came in 1991, with *The Firm* and its film version, starring Tom Cruise and Gene Hackman in 1993. Grisham was, by this period, something of a veteran with a successful non-literary career behind him. Born in 1955 he had graduated from law school in 1981, and for nine years ran his own firm. A southerner, he hailed from Arkansas and was distantly related to that state's other successful lawyer, Bill Clinton (something that did neither man any harm). Grisham served as a state legislator in the Mississippi House of Representatives, from 1984 to 1990.

His career as an author had gone less smoothly. Grisham had difficulty in getting his first novel *A Time to Kill* into print, and once published the work made little impact. It was not, to be frank, top-quality Grisham and deserved no better. But it lays out what was to be the author's invariable formula: that of an idealistic young lawyer taking on, and vanquishing, 'The System'.

The hero of *The Firm* is Mitch McDeere. A clean-living

lawyer from a disadvantaged background, Mitch has just graduated at the top of his class at Harvard. He is recruited by a mysterious law firm in Memphis. Bendini, Lambert and Locke offer vast salaries (Mitch will start at $80,000) with mouth-watering benefits (a customised BMW) and are very secretive about what they do. 'Tax' is all they will say. Mitch is duly seduced. He and his wife Abby settle in Memphis, in the luxurious house supplied, like all the other good things, by the 'Firm'.

Bendini, Lambert and Locke turn out to be a Mafia front. The discovery triggers a complicated thriller plot in which Mitch proves himself smarter than the crooks, bonds closer to his wife, and—in a thrilling climax—finds himself on the run from both the FBI and Cosa Nostra. He eludes both 'firms' to enjoy vast (if somewhat dubiously gotten) riches in the Cayman Islands.

The Firm is an efficient 'page-turner' and comes over well on film, as directed by Sydney Pollack. The final Hitchcockian chase sequence is particularly effective and the greater-than-usual length of the film (155 minutes) allows Gene Hackman to develop the supporting role of a disillusioned older ('decent but ruined', as Abby calls him) lawyer in the Firm into a show-stealer.

Pollack's *The Firm* is set plum in the present day, the early 1990s. There are innumerable little date markers in the cine-text establishing this time setting. The car which the firm gives Mitch is a 1990 model Mercedes: he has a state of the (1990) art desk-top computer in his room; he uses mobile phones, fax machines, voice-activated miniature tape recorders, computer-controlled xerox machines. On the surface, Grisham's novel also seems to be set contemporaneously, although it's not easy to be positive. Sometimes novelists will make it easy for the reader, by introducing some precise historical reference—the description of the 22 November 1963 assassination of Kennedy on the first page of Forsyth's *The Odessa File*, for instance.

In *The Firm* (the novel) we are never told what president is in the White House. And although the narrative is very precise as to months (locating such calendar days as Harvard commencement ceremonies, and 'tax day'—April 15) we are never told what year it is. We can, however, close in on it from circumstantial evidence. Since tax law is at the heart of the plot, one would expect some reference to the drastic reforms Ronald Reagan brought in, during his first administration, in the mid-1980s. There is none.

Grisham gives us a couple of clear date markers in the workings of the plot. A previous Bendini, Lambert and Locke associate 'died' (in fact he was rubbed out by the Mob for getting too curious) in 1984. The hit was made to look like suicide. It was 'years ago' Mitch is told—which would, of course, locate the action in the late 1980s, early 1990s. Somewhat later, spilling the beans to his FBI contact, Mitch talks about a front set up by the Firm in 1986 which went on to generate $80 million of illicit profit 'over the next three years' (pp. 318–19).[1] Given the fact that he knows this from stored office records, we would again hazard a narrative 'now' of around 1990. This is a 'now' not a 'then' novel.

On closer inspection, however, a number of elements in the narrative work against this contemporary setting. Mitch's starting salary of $80,000 was not something to sell your soul for in 1990. Young Wall Street lawyers in red braces with Porsche keys in their pockets would regard that as chump change (at least before the 'meltdown' of 1987). In 1986, Tom Wolfe's Sherman McCoy—only slightly older than Mitch—is finding it hard to make ends meet on a million a year. The film raises Mitch's starting salary to $96,000 with a 5 per cent guaranteed raise in the second year, to bring him to the magic 'six figures'.

The clinching dating clues are in the Firm's technology—something that was mutating by the month through the 1980s. It is striking, for example, that no one in Grisham's novel has a cellular phone. After 1985, a rising young lawyer would rather be seen in public trouserless than without his 'mobile' (the plot of the film made heavy use of mobile phones). Even more striking are the missing computers. The Firm, Mitch wonderingly notes, has a state-of-the-art library of printed legal materials. But all its computers are clustered in a 'computer room'. The room boasts 'a dozen terminals', and 'the latest, truly incredible software'. The 'latest'? Twelve computers for a firm with sixty senior associates and a hundred secretarial assistants? Where is this—Memphis or Albania?

Where, one asks, are the Pentium desk-tops, where are the $5,000 laptops, the nifty little Nokia palmtops? None of the high-flying lawyers in the novel is seen with, or anywhere near, a computer. Computers in the Firm exist only, as one gathers, for centralised 'printouts'. It seems there is just one big computer in the office (a VAX, one assumes) with its dozen 'dumb' terminals, and a clunky 'daisy-wheel' printer. Mitch, apparently, has never heard of 'personal computers'. When he studies for his bar exam (which he has to do in his first six months with the Firm), he does it all from 'notebooks' (the primitive paper-and-pen kind, not the miniaturised machines marketed by IBM after 1990). And he gets all his information from 'law books'. Has he never heard of databases? Where has Mitch been during the 1980s? Sleepy Hollow?

Not once in the novel does Mitch use a computer. The film is something else: since the late 1980s, film makers realized that films were terrific subliminal advertising. You could raise valuable collateral revenue by giving manufacturers 'space' in your movies. With fashion-driven accessories like cars and computers, it was a space to fight for. In the film of The Firm, Mitch is seen poring over a brand-marked IBM to investigate the mysterious deaths of Hodge and Kozinski. One up to Big Blue. Apple-Macintosh won the computer contract for Tom Cruise's subsequent great hit, Mission Impossible (1996; the central scene has Cruise hovering, suspended by wire, over a 'Mac' at the CIA head-quarters

in Langley; he does everything but make love to it); Nokia
got the contract for the Val Kilmer-starring *The Saint* (1997)
and the little palmtop makes so many appearances it really
should have had co-star billing.

The novel of *The Firm* is, by contrast, a computer waste-
land. Mitch's secretary mentions using one—but, we assume,
she goes to the 'Computer Room' to do so. Other secretaries
are described using IBM Selectric typewriters—Flintstone
era technology in 1990 (pp. 118–19, 159). When he finally
shops the firm to the FBI, Mitch employs the incredibly
antique technique of taking 10,000 files out of metal filing
cabinets and copying them on a 'state of the art' 8580 Canon
xerox copier (another centralised and single piece of office
equipment; by 1990 there would be copiers all over the place
in any go-ahead law firm). This clunky piece of plot machinery
was streamlined out in the film, where Mitch invents a short
cut via a mail-fraud gimmick which, frankly, I have difficulty
understanding.

Not to labour the point, the novel's computerless, mobile
phoneless environment points firmly in one direction. Backwards. Grisham has reconstructed for his 1990s novel the
period when he was Mitch's age, in 1981. If *The Firm* were
set in the present, as the spurious chronology spread thinly
on the narrative would have us believe—Mitch would have a
mobile pressed against his ear, a Compaq laptop on his knee,
and a palmtop in his breast pocket. He would be using the
Internet and the 'Web' (neither is mentioned in the novel) for
his research. Inside the glossy, up-to-the-minute narrative of
The Firm, one concludes, there is a more nostalgic novel of
the early 1980s struggling to get out.[2]

When Exactly Does Rents Read Kierkegaard?

One of the most heartening events in the British book trade over recent years has been the recruitment of a new group of young readers of fiction—readers who it was thought were lost forever to TV, record stores and dance clubs. Two writers—Nick Hornby and Irvine Welsh—have been particularly effective in attracting these new customers into book stores. And one novel stands out, Welsh's *Trainspotting*, boosted as it was by Channel Four's prize-winning film, directed by Danny Boyle.

Trainspotting is set mainly in Edinburgh—particularly the traditionally working-class Leith area of the city. The novel takes the form of a number of disconnected brief episodes featuring a quintet of young, nihilistic, work-shy Scots who live for drugs, rock and roll, brawling and selfish sex (unprotected, of course; AIDS will wipe out most of them in a year or two if the heroin and violence doesn't). The precise historical dating is never clearly given, but from external references to such things as films, songs and various internal references the stories would seem to cover a period of about eighteen months over 1988–9.

The main characters in *Trainspotting* are (1) 'Sick Boy', half-Italian, reasonably well educated, a ruthless sexual predator on under-age girls, whom he later prostitutes; (2) 'Second Prize', who never made it as a junior footballer, and is now a hopeless addict; (3) 'Spud', the nicest of the group, an incorrigible petty thief; (4) 'Franco', a psychopathic sadist and drug dealer, who likes to punch his pregnant girlfriend in the stomach by way of domestic discipline; (5) 'Rents', or, as he is more formally known, Mark Renton.

Rents is the central character, and by far the most interesting. *Trainspotting* opens with an episode showing him scoring heroin and ends with an episode in which he absconds to Amsterdam (where Welsh himself went to live after writing the novel) with the group's drug money—they will kick him to death if he ever shows his face again in Leith. Franco might well come up with something worse than simple kicking. Mysteriously, however, we are told that Rents buys a 'return ticket . . . only intending to go one way' (p. 342).[1] What does this mean?

Mark, as well as being the central character, is the only one of the group whom we can conceive writing a novel like *Trainspotting*. From incidental comments, we can put together much of his background. He is twenty-five. His parents are Catholic working class, originally from Glasgow. Some time ago his disabled younger brother, Davie, died. This profoundly disturbed him. He has an elder brother whom he does not like (Billy is later killed as a soldier in Ulster; Rents seduces—for want of a better word—his brother's very pregnant girlfriend, Sharon, in a conveniently unengaged lavatory at the funeral). At sixteen Rents was apprenticed as a joiner. But he later went to sixth-form college and got a place at Aberdeen University. He was kicked out after a year for drugs, stealing books, and sex with non-students.

On the face of it, Rents is as grossly philistine as his friends. His experiences are given in the obscenity-spattered, broad-Scots dialect of the streets. The only 'cultural' pursuits mentioned in the text are an addiction to Jean-Claude van Damme movies and the music of David Bowie. But, like Bowie (aka Ziggy Stardust), we may suspect that Rents is something of a poseur. Literary touches keep breaking in on his brutal street talk; at one point, for instance, he describes the shivers that accompany heroin withdrawal as being like 'a thin layer ay autumn frost oun a car roof' (p. 16). He routinely uses ten-dollar words like 'psychic vandalism'. In order to pick up some girls on a train down to London (he's hoping for some more sex in the lavatory), he discourses learnedly about Bertolt Brecht—something that makes Franco dangerously suspicious. Most impressively, when he and Spud are arrested for stealing from a bookshop Rents explains to the magistrate, in very technical English, the essence of Kierkegaard's philosophy. 'I'm interested', he informs the court:

'in his concepts of subjectivity and truth, and particularly his ideas concerning change; the notion that genuine choice is made out of doubt and uncertainty, and without recourse to the experience or advice of others.' (pp. 165–6)

He gets off; the inarticulate Spud goes to jail for ten months.

Rents, we may deduce, has a secret vice—an addictive habit which he doesn't want anyone to know about but can't keep entirely hidden. It's not heroin; no secret about that. It's reading. He likes to read books (and, we assume, he may even write them in Amsterdam). Of course, he can't come out with it to his friends. To suggest that there is any more pleasure in life than drinking, drugging, screwing, kung-fu videos and dancing yourself senseless at raves would be to invite guffaws or worse. But when there's no one around Rents, we assume, takes out his prized volumes from their hiding place for some furtive pleasure.

For all its crudity of language, *Trainspotting* is a subtle novel. Subliminally it sends the message 'Tough guys *do* read; books *are* a turn-on.' And this, I suspect, is part of the novel's otherwise puzzling appeal to a section of the public traditionally contemptuous of reading matter. In its consciously offensive way, *Trainspotting* may have done more to repair the ravages of adolescent illiteracy than all the GCSE boards and 'lifelong learning programmes' put together.

Why do P. D. James's Murderers Wait?

There is a telling moment in *Original Sin* where Adam
Dalgliesh, P. D. James's well-read detective (and published
poet) with special responsibility for 'sensitive' cases, surveys
the study of a deceased and old-fashioned spinster detective
novelist. She has been driven to desperate measures by
changes in popular taste. No one likes Esmé Carling's kind
of fiction any more. Her bookshelves, Dalgliesh notes (with
an uneasy sense of his own superannuation), are dominated
by 'women writers of the Golden Age':

Surveying the titles so reminiscent of the 1930s, of village policemen
cycling to the scene of the crime, tugging their forelocks to the
gentry, of autopsies undertaken by eccentric general practitioners
after evening surgery and unlikely denouements in the library, he
took them down and glanced at them at random. *Death by Dancing*,
apparently set in the world of formation ballroom competitions,
Cruising to Murder, *Death by Drowning*, *The Mistletoe Murders*.
He replaced them carefully, feeling no condescension. (p. 445)[1]

Two writers of the modern day who have most effectively
continued the tradition of 'women writers of the Golden Age'
are Ruth Rendell and Baroness James herself. Particular
praise attaches to *Original Sin* (1994), which—appropriately
enough—Ruth Rendell hails as 'the *Middlemarch* of crime
novels'.

Original Sin has, indeed, the meaty story and rich thematic
brew that nineteenth-century readers relished. A dynastic
narrative, it centres on the oldest independent publishing
house in London, Peverell Press, founded in 1792. (The
actual oldest press is Longmans, founded in 1724; James
mischievously introduces her own publisher Faber's—an

upstart firm founded in the 1920s—into the narrative of *Original Sin*: Matthew Evans, Faber's managing director, phones up during Dalgliesh's investigations and has to be fobbed off.)

Peverell Press is literally a 'publishing house'—embodied as it is in an ornate Venetian *palazzo* on the Thames, 'Innocent House'. One of the subplots in the text is whether the firm should leave town for a green-field, glass-and-chrome site as have other venerable London publishers (last time I looked there was not a single publisher left in Bedford Square: *sic transit*).

In the postwar period, Peverell has been run by a partnership between the founding line of Peverells and new-blood directors from France: namely the resistance hero Jean-Philippe Etienne and his very new-broom son, Gerard. The setting of the novel is the early 1990s (there are no prominent dating markers, but a reference on page 336 to a video of Martin Scorsese's film of *Cape Fear*, 1991, is significant).

The narrative exposition is given through the somewhat cheeky impressions of a new 'temp', Mandy, at Innocent House. The firm, we learn, is facing the most profound crisis in its long history. Peverell Press must modernise or die. Gerard Etienne is, by temperament, a ruthless moderniser—heads will roll. Employees may go to the wall, the firm will not. His father, Jean-Philippe, is retired and lives as a recluse in a deserted house on the Essex coast. He plays no part.

The plot of *Original Sin* is triggered by the murder of Gerard. It takes the form of the classic 'locked-room mystery'. His corpse is found in the archive room at Innocent House, surrounded by the firm's records. He has been asphyxiated. A draught-excluder in the shape of a long woolly snake has been strung around his neck (the Genesis allusion, tied in with the Edenic 'Innocent House', is lightly stressed).

P. D. James favours multiple-suspect plots. Many of her novels invite, at their most complicated, Agatha Christie's facile denouement in *Murder on the Orient Express*, in which a dozen likely murderers turn out to have conspired in a homicidal team effort. I should, however, issue a warning at this point: if you haven't yet read, or finished, *Original Sin*, stop here!

In the case of Gerard Etienne's murder, the culprit could plausibly be an about-to-be-made-redundant secretary, 'Blackie'. It could be an about-to-be-dropped-from-the-list author, Esmé Carling. It could be an-about-to-be-chopped rival within the firm. It could even be Gerard's hard-hearted bitch of a sister, Claudia Etienne before she, too, is murdered ('then there were nine').

It turns out (to the reader's utter surprise, of course) to be the mild, superannuated editor of the poetry list, Gabriel Dauntsey. He was, it emerges, an RAF bomber pilot during the war. In this capacity he took part in the dreadful Dresden raid of February 1945 (dropping high explosive on Kurt Vonnegut Jr, if we want to be curious about it). Dauntsey, it further emerges, had a Jewish wife and child in occupied France. They were sent to death in a concentration camp by none other than the resistance hero, Jean-Philippe Etienne. It was *Realpolitik*; the Frenchman was no Nazi and had nothing against Jews. But he needed to find some way to make the Gestapo trust him the better to foil them in the long run. It was a case of omelettes and broken eggs. If Dauntsey's loved ones were a price that had to be paid to advance the resistance cause, so be it.

James's narrative ends with a whipping series of twists and a final confrontation at Etienne's house on the Essex coast. The villain is unmasked. But, in a final twist, it emerges that Etienne's children were not after all 'his'. They were adopted Dresden-bombing orphans. Who dropped the bombs that killed their parents? The same man who killed them. Collapse of vengeful Dauntsey who rushes off to drown himself. (The watching Dalgliesh and his assistant, the 'bad Jew' Daniel Aron, permit this euthanasia.) As a final twist of twists, a confession turns up in the documents buried in the archive room. The eighteenth-century founder of the firm, Francis Peverell, murdered his wife 'because I needed her money to finish the work on Innocent House'. What, then, is the 'original sin'? Everyone's hands are clean; everyone's hands are bloody.

Original Sin is a superbly rich novel, a 'great baggy monster' with whole chapters devoted to Dalgliesh's metaphysical speculations, leisurely riverscapes, and digressive subplots about the little comedies of office life. But there is a central mystery which—for all the many denouements—remains unclear. Namely, why does Gabriel Dauntsey wait so long to execute his revenge?

He joined the firm in 1962, we learn. It was some eight years later that he came across clinching documentary proof of Jean-Philippe Etienne's villainy. His explanation for keeping his revenge twenty more years until it is such a cold morsel is, I think, unconvincing: 'You killed my children; I have killed yours. I have no posterity; you will have none,' Gerald tells Etienne *père*. 'It has taken me nearly fifty years but I have made my justice.' Etienne very sensibly retorts, 'It would have been more effective if you had acted sooner' (p. 544). What has time to do with justice? Dauntsey fires back.

Quite a lot, any prisoner who has 'done his time' might point out. No judge says to a murderer, 'I am sentencing you to a month's imprisonment, rather than a life sentence, because time has nothing to do with justice. Take the prisoner down.' Gabriel Dauntsey is now seventy-six years old, and Jean-Philippe Etienne slightly older (P. D. James, their creator, was seventy-four at the time of publishing *Original Sin*.) Common sense suggests that justice deferred so long runs the risk that one of the parties will die before it can be delivered. Worse still, Dauntsey may be so weak that he will not be able to carry out the physical task involved in strangling victims to death (the odds, for example, would be on the younger man, Gerard, in any struggle with the woolly snake). Murder is not an old man's line of work.

Significantly, P. D. James's next novel—the 1997 bestseller *A Certain Justice*—has exactly the same gimmick. **Stop here!** if you haven't read *A Certain Justice*. There are again any number of suspects (seven as I calculate) for the murder of the rising young woman lawyer in this latest whodunnit. But it turns out to be the oldest barrister in her chambers, a man in his mid-seventies. avenging a wrong of some thirty years ago. Another remote 'original sin' is purged by a veteran (and, again, the crime is solved by Dalgliesh who, as in *Original Sin*, waives arrest in view of the murderer's advanced years).

These lengthy perspectives are very P. D. Jamesian. None the less, the decades-long delayed crime in her novels creates snagging implausibilities. One might rationalise the practice biographically. After a successful professional career in the Civil Service James began writing crimes stories in 1962 (aged forty-two) with *Cover Her Face* (the first Adam Dalgliesh novel—which means that in the contemporarily-set *Original Sin* and *A Certain Justice* the detective should himself have been drawing his old-age-pension for ten years).

There is another explanation. Beneath the whodunnit-plots, and the long evolution of Adam Dalgliesh's interest-ingly deviant mentality, P. D. James's novels are obsessed (the word is not too strong) with the generational conflict between young and old professional classes and what one might call 'the pathos of modernisation'. Her readership, one suspects, is substantially composed of middle-aged and older men and women of the middle and professional classes. A group, that is, which 'efficiency' (i.e. involuntary redundancy), 'natural wastage' (i.e. enforced early retirement) and 'downsizing' (i.e. 'fire everyone over forty- five') have hit hardest. Like that odd, but revealing, film hit *The Revenge of the Nerds* James's latest fiction embodies a kind of wish-fulfilment of the down-trodden—'The Revenge of the Downsized'.

═══

Clue: Absolute Final Conclusion (9 Letters)

═══

Following the Carlton/Central televising of Colin Dexter's series starring John Thaw and Kevin Whately (as Sergeant Lewis) Inspector Morse has become Britain's best-loved policeman since Dixon of Dock Green. Colin Dexter's series-hero was introduced in the book *Last Bus to Woodstock* and has concluded (the novelist is insistent on this) with *Death Is Now My Neighbour* (1996). Morse, diabetic and snowy-haired, enters a long-deferred retirement. The shape he's in, it won't be a long retirement.

The lineaments of Morse's earlier career are well enough known. He was born in the Midlands, in the early 1930s. His mother was a devout Quaker; his father a scapegrace. None the less, his son loved him. A clever boy, he won his place at grammar school. He did his National Service in the Royal Corps of Signals (as did Dexter) before taking up an Exhibition in Classics at St John's College, Oxford (Dexter got his BA in classics from Christ's College, Cambridge). Morse left college without a degree as the result of a disastrous love affair (which has an even more disastrous sequel when the lovers meet up in later life). He joined the Thames Valley Police (based in Oxford) and worked his way up the ranks.

Inspector Morse is, by nature, donnish and misanthropic. His favourite authors are the gloomy A. E. Housman, Thomas Hardy and Philip Larkin. A *bon viveur*, he drinks 'real ale' and malt whisky, and smokes to excess. Hedonism and self-destruction mingle in his complex and introverted personality. In music, he is devoted to the operas of Wagner. He drives a 'classic' English car, a Lancia (in the TV version, a 1960s Jaguar). His 'Watson' is the philistine, but amiable, Sergeant Lewis.

Dexter is a many-time winner of national crossword competitions. He loves the 'puzzle' element in detective stories—especially verbal puzzles. In a sense, the crossword puzzle is (to use Matthew Arnold's term) Dexter's, and Morse's, 'criticism of life'. There is a telling recollection in *Death Is Now My Neighbour* of how Morse:

had been discouraged when as a young grammar-school boy he had asked his Divinity master who it was, if God had created the Universe, who in turn had created God. And after receiving no satisfactory answer from his Physics master about what sort of thing could possibly exist out there at the end of the world, when space had run out, Morse had been compelled to lower his sights a little, thereafter satisfying his intellectual craving for answers by finding the values of 'x' and 'y' in (ever more complicated) algebraic equations, and by deciphering the meaning of (ever more complicated) chunks of choruses from the Greek tragedies.

Later, from his mid-twenties onwards, his need to *know* had transferred itself to the field of crossword puzzles, where he had so often awaited with almost paranoiac impatience the following day's answer to any clue he'd been unable to solve the day before. (pp. 274)[1]

Dexter's plots are vehicles for dizzying mazes of literary allusion and encoded clues well beyond the powers of all but the sharpest reader (among whom I do not count myself). Detective and crossword fanatic alike live by the clue. And overhanging the Morse series as a whole are large enigmas and running mysteries. Where precisely in north Oxford, for example, does Morse live? (somewhere close to Colin Dexter, we apprehend, but cannot be sure). And what is Morse's first (Christian?) name. We only know the initial, 'E'. One, but not the other, of these will be concurrently solved (with the obligatory murder) in *Death Is Now My Neighbour*.

The narrative begins with Morse pondering, as he does every morning, *The Times* crossword. The last clue impedes him momentarily: 'Stand for Soldiers (5–4)'. It is, of course, 'toast-rack'. Crossword solved, on to crime. The mystery at the centre of the novel recalls those classics of university fiction, C. P. Snow's melodrama about the 'corridors of power', *The Masters* (1951), and Michael Innes's ultra-donnish murder mystery, *Death at the President's Lodging* (1936). There is also a whiff of Christie's *ABC Murders* (1935).

There are two candidates and ferocious competition for the mastership of Lonsdale College (Morse's pseudonymous Oxford institution). Murder enters the election. The unravelling of the crime involves a dazzling series of puzzles and solutions. One is particularly neat: an old-spelling extract of Rochester's verse is decoded through its irregular (and, as Morse's shrewd eye realises, textually incorrect) capitalisation, to be a ciphered message: ('Wednesday: 10:15 train'). It leads to the uncovering of a sordid sexual imbroglio, the underbelly of Oxonian, high-table, collegiate gentility.

The novel is well up to Dexter's high standard. It ends, however, with the end of Morse. The detective retires having fallen in love with, and married, the hospital nurse who has seen him through his latest and most worrying bout of diabetes. Janet McQueen has discovered what the 'E' stands for from the hospital computer records. The information is withheld from the reader, however, until the very last sentence, in the *Envoi*, on the very last page. There are some premonitory hints. Early on, we are told that Morse really should have paid more attention to geography at school, especially Captain Cook's voyages. As we come to the climactic revelation, he reminisces about his father:

He drank and gambled far too much . . . but I loved him, yes. He knew nothing really—except two things: he could recite all of Macaulay's *Lays of Ancient Rome* by heart; and he'd read everything ever written about his greatest hero in life, Captain Cook—'Captain James Cook, 1728 to 1779', as he always used to call him. (p. 410)

Finally, in a last-page postcard to Lewis, all is revealed:

Did I ever get the chance to thank you for the few(!) contributions you made to our last case together? If I didn't, let me thank you

now—let me thank you for everything, my dear old friend.
    Yours aye,
                        Endeavour (Morse)

As the solution to the clues sown throughout the series,
'Endeavour' is satisfying. It was the name of Cook's vessel
on his great exploratory voyage. Quakers, such as Morse's
mother, like to use abstract moral virtues as Christian
names ('Purity', 'Cleanth', 'Patience', etc.). There must be
some Macaulayan significance which eludes me. And, for a
policeman, 'Endeavour' has a peculiar professional appropriateness. It derives from the French *en devoir*—'in the line of
duty'.

There is, however, another significance in the name, if we
approach it—as Dexter–Morse would surely want us to—in
the spirit of crossword puzzlers. Why has Morse suppressed
it all these years? The reason, I think, is that it has been
held back for maximum effectiveness and for its most exact
appropriateness. The moment when, in short, it would serve
most effectively as the solution to a long-running series of
tantalising clues.

'Endeavour' should be taken in connection with a recurrent
note of finality in this last novel: allusions, for instance, to the
line from T S. Eliot's *Four Quartets*, 'In my beginning is my
end,' which Morse—knowingly we must suppose—misquotes:
' "In our beginning is our end" somebody said—Eliot wasn't it?
Or is it, "In our end is our beginning?" ' (p. 313). By which he
means, one supposes, something along the lines of 'the name
given at our birth is the clue to our final act'. Among its other
plurivalences, 'Endeavour' can be heard as the acoustic pun
'end ever'. If one glosses the last words along these lines, what
one ends up with is 'Yours aye, [the] end [for] ever, Morse'.
Morse is not, of course, Scottish. The Scottism 'aye' means, as
the *OED* tells us, 'ever'; thus we can gloss further as 'yours
ever, end ever, Morse'.

Dexter has been very firm that there will be no Sherlock
Holmes-like resurrections for Morse (the novelist was quite

insistent on the point in his 1997 *Desert Island Discs* appearance, for instance, where he mysteriously chose as his 'one luxury' a pair of nail- scissors).[2] This is the end for ever, fate's final snip of the shears. There is, of course, only one moment at which his name would have all its meanings fulfilled, the last line of the last novel. The question remains, did Dexter know all along? Or did he, puzzle-master that he is, devise it during the last novel to wrap up the last novel?

Almasy's Strange War

===

Board-sweeping success at the 1997 Oscars' ceremony propelled Michael Ondaatje's ultra-literary novel *The English Patient* into overnight bestsellerdom, five years after its first publication (to good reviews, joint victory in the Booker awards, and modest sales) in 1992. The *Spectator* had the bright idea of sending a less than ultra-literary novelist, Frederick Forsyth, to review the film (the book had, evidently, not come his way; nor, it was clear, would it ever).

Forsyth's piece (29 March 1997) began promisingly: 'Having read the simperingly reverential reviews of *The English Patient*, I was persuaded this was a "must".' Forsyth then, as best he could, put together the narrative which director (and screenwriter) Anthony Minghella had put together from Ondaatje's original text. It was, as a long-suffering Forsyth pedantically assembled it,

The story of a blighted and finally mortal love affair between the Hungarian Count [Ladislaus de] Almasy and the wife [Katharine Clifton] of a British colleague [Geoffrey Clifton]. It is told in (I think I counted aright) 27 flashbacks and jump-forwards between the prewar Egyptian Western desert starting around 1937 and VE Day in May 1945 in northern Tuscany . . . We start (according to a flash-up on the screen) in October 1942 with a young man taking off somewhere in the howling wilderness of desert. Amazingly he is flying an uncamouflaged, silver-painted Tiger Moth trainer with the registration number of a British flying club . . . A glamorous blonde seems to be asleep in the front seat. Within minutes he flies over the world's most isolated German machine-gun nest, a small foxhole without any life support system, stuck in a sea of sand miles from anywhere. But these Krauts are real aces; though they can never have seen a Tiger Moth, they recognise it at once

and open up with heavy machine guns. In mid-air the bullets turn
into cannon shells, leaving clusters of black flak over the blue sky.
Disdaining to take evasive action, our hero is shot down. Of the
blonde we see no more (yet), but the flier is burned to a human crisp.
The Germans are pretty *blasé*, since they decline to investigate the
wreck, but some inspiringly compassionate Bedouin wrap him in
blankets and take him by camel to the nearest British RAMC post,
a tented dressing-station. Here he gets first aid before being taken
by lorry to (presumably) Cairo for intensive care.

It would be nice to quote the whole, hilariously cross-grained
review; but copyright law forbids. Forsyth goes on to query
how the 'crisp' (as he calls the burned Almasy, alias 'the
English patient') ends up the only patient in a surplus-to-
requirements Italian field hospital, in the charge of a shell-
shocked nurse, Hana.

Forsyth, as I say, forbore to read Ondaatje's book. Had
he done so, he would have realised that—if anything—
Minghella ironed out many of the apparent anomalies in
the source narrative—although so oblique is the novelist's
technique that one cannot always be sure that they are in
fact anomalies. In so far as one can connect it from the
flashbacks, jump-forwards and many indirections Almasy's
story runs thus. He and a group of others were, in the 1930s,
an international band of explorers mapping out the Libyan
desert. One of the explorers, Geoffrey Clifton, returns to the
desert in 1936 with a beautiful young wife, Katharine (p.
142).[1] Geoffrey also brings with him a new plane, a Tiger
Moth, nicknamed 'Rupert Bear'. Another member of the
team, Madox, has an 'old plane', which is now unnecessary
(he has taught Almasy to fly in it).

When Clifton's plane—*Rupert*—flew into our midst, the ageing plane
of Madox's was left where it was, covered with a tarpaulin pegged
down in one of the northeast alcoves of Umweinat. Sand collected
over it gradually for the next few years. None of us thought we would
see it again. It was another victim of the desert. Within a few months
we would pass the northeast gully and see no contour of it. By now
Clifton's plane, ten years younger, had flown into our story. (p. 168)

Over the next three years, Katharine and Almasy have a torrid affair. In September 1939, on the eve of war, Clifton finally becomes suspicious and sets up his suicide and their murder. He intends to crash 'Rupert' (with Katharine in the second cockpit) into Almasy—standing conveniently in the desert at Gilf Kebir ('Latitude 23.30 on the map, longitude 25.15', p. 256). Clifton is crazed with jealousy and not thinking clearly. Almasy *is* thinking clearly and jumps safely out of the way. Clifton is incinerated in the blazing wreckage of his Tiger Moth. Katharine is badly injured—but not fatally so.

Almasy carries Katharine to a nearby shelter, the Cave of Swimmers, and wraps her in parachute silk. He then goes off to get help. But he is arrested by English troops and, protesting furiously, is taken off for interrogation to Cairo ('I was just another possible second-rate spy. Just another international bastard'). For some reason (presumably because of German occupation) he cannot get back to the cave.

In resentment, Almasy turns spy for the Germans, guiding their men across the desert to Cairo—notably 'Eppler' (the hero of Ken Follett's *The Key to Rebecca*—not that he is company Ondaatje would want his English patient to keep).[2] Why Almasy can't make an excursion to the Cave of Swimmers is mysterious. None the less, in late August 1942, with Alamein imminent, he finally makes it back to the cave and the miraculously preserved body of Katharine. Three years have passed.[3]

Almasy has with him a can of petrol, and apparently a naphtha lamp. Loaded down with corpse, can and lamp, he marches towards Madox's buried plane, 'Rupert Bear', near the Kufra oasis, 'carrying her body as if it were the armour of a knight'. The journey is not far (judging by the latitude and longitude measurements), but three yards so burdened would be a Herculean labour. Almasy recalls the exploit, for the benefit of an enigmatic visitor to his hospital, David Caravaggio:

At longitude 25, latitude 23, I dug down towards the tarpaulin, and
Madox's old plane gradually emerged. It was night and even in the
cold air I was sweating. I carried the naphtha lantern over to her
and sat for a while . . . The plane came out of the sand. There had
been no food and I was weak[!]. The tarp was so heavy I couldn't dig
it out but had simply to cut it away.

In the morning, after two hours' sleep, I carried her into the
cockpit. I started the motor and it rolled into life. We moved and
then slipped, years too late, into the sky. (p. 174)

The film-makers perceived the problem in that easy phrase 'I
started the motor and it rolled into life.' Minghella had a little
montage shot of German airmen servicing and fuelling the
plane for Almasy, who then *flies* it to the Cave of Swimmers.

Exactly what Almasy intends to do once airborne is not
clear. A can of petrol will not get him very far. Perhaps he
intends to finish off what Clifton started—a Viking funeral
or a Wagnerian *Liebestod*. Who knows? Anyway, there is
a short-circuit spark which ignites leaking engine oil. The
plane catches fire and crashes. Katharine's corpse (which
must be dry as tinder) is cremated. Almasy is burned beyond
recognition. He is dragged from the wreck and looked after *for
two years* by Bedouin, who apparently use his tactile ability
to recognise captured weapons by simply running his fingers
over them. But this is very obscure, and I could be wrong
here.[4]

Almasy is eventually handed over to the victorious British
at Siwa 'in 1944'. They assume he is an English casualty
who has lost his memory. 'He was moved in the midnight
ambulance train from the Western Desert to Tunis, then
shipped to Italy' (p. 95). For mysterious reasons, this very
sick man is transported to the front line, and finds himself
in a booby-trapped field-hospital, Villa San Girolamo, which
is where it all starts before the flashing back and jumping
forward.

Minghella rationalised the time line and the details. To
quote Forsyth again, shortly after being arrested by the

British armed forces (in September 1939 in the book, mid-1942 in the film), Almasy escapes 'from durance vile' and:

discovers the village where his colleague parked the trusty Tiger
Moth. Incredibly (most things abandoned in an Arab village become
gutted skeletons in ten minutes) it is in perfect nick, fully fuelled
and starts at the first kick. Anyway, he flies back to the cave but too
late. Not surprising; he has been missing for several weeks.

But, of course, in the novel it is 156 weeks. In the film, he loads Katharine's body into the forward cockpit and flies away, only to be shot down by the German machine guns, or cannon, about which Forsyth is so contemptuous. He is immediately handed over by the Bedouin to the British.

What Minghella does is to blur over the chronological improbabilities in the novel, notably: (1) the three years that intervene before Almasy returns to the body of his lover. When he does return, the body has to be as fresh as it was during the days of their passionate love affair—no maggots, please; (2) he blurs the two years that (in the novel) Almasy, burned to a crisp, spends as a guest of the Bedouin nomads. Minghella also does what he can with Madox's moth-balled Tiger Moth. Not enough to mollify Forsyth, but just enough to slip it past film-goers who don't happen to be ex-RAF fighter pilots.

According to the novel's timescale, the plane must have been drying out under its tarpaulin in the desert for eight years (1936–42). It is entirely covered with sand. Almasy 'digs' it out: with what? Has he been carrying a shovel in addition to can, lamp and corpse? Having shifted tons of sand one may wonder how ('weak' as he is) he moves, single handed, the plane out on to the level, so it can take off. How, single-handed, does he 'swing the prop' (old biplanes don't have self-starters)? With a Land-Rover, winch and half-a-dozen trained mechanics he might just do it. Apart from anything else, sand would have penetrated moving parts of the machinery and would have to be meticulously dusted out. But in the novel Almasy merely pours in his can of petrol—

and the engine starts! Well done, De Havilland. Frankly, all this is most improbable.

So delicate is Ondaatje's story-telling technique that the reader lets all this pass. But, as Forsyth points out, it does not stand up to sceptical examination. Did Ondaatje intend it to be implausible? After all, the English patient is alternatively delirious from pain and drugged to the eyeballs with morphine. His mind may be weaving fantasies, cutting corners, *rambling*. I tend to think it is.

═══

Why Hasn't Mr Stevens Heard of the Suez Crisis?

═══

Kazuo Ishiguro's *The Remains of the Day* won the Booker Prize in 1989, and as a Merchant–Ivory film (starring Anthony Hopkins) went on to win a clutch of Oscars in 1993. At first sight, it is an unlikely prize-winner. The narrative takes the form of reminiscences by an ancient butler—a trusty, but somewhat tongue-tied, retainer of Darlington Hall. Stevens is given a holiday, and permission to use the hall's venerable Ford, by Darlington's new American proprietor, Mr Farraday. He resolves to make an 'expedition' to the West Country. There he will meet another former employee of the hall, Miss Kenton, a housekeeper who left twenty years earlier.

There was a possibility that the two of them may have been in love. But they fell out over a below-stairs disagreement about who was responsible for what. Their respective professional susceptibilities were mortally affronted. They have not met since she left. Stevens has recently begun to detect in himself 'small errors' in the performance of his duties. He hopes that Miss Kenton (now Mrs Benn) can be persuaded to return to the Hall. With her help, he may be able to hold on a few years more. A letter from her, reporting marital unhappiness, gives him grounds for hope that, even at this belated stage, a reconciliation is possible.

The novel takes the form of six days' *journal de voyage*. The meeting with Miss Kenton in Weymouth is a disappointment. Her marriage is indeed unhappy. She has frequently walked out on her husband. But she will not return to the Hall. Duty forbids:

'But that doesn't mean to say, of course, there aren't occasions now and then—extremely desolate occasions—when you think to yourself: "What a terrible mistake I've made with my life." And you get to thinking about a different life, a *better* life you might have had. For instance, I get to thinking about a life I might have had with you, Mr Stevens. And I suppose that's when I get angry over some trivial little thing and leave. But each time I do so, I realize before long—my rightful place is with my husband. After all, there's no turning back the clock now. One can't be forever dwelling on what might have been. One should realize one has as good as most, perhaps better, and be grateful.' (p. 239)[1]

'My heart was broken,' Stevens writes. But he gives no sign of it. Butlers do not show feeling. His rightful place, he decides, is at the Hall, where he will serve out his time. He takes strength from a chance encounter with a stranger he meets, walking along the sea-front. Stevens confesses his misery ('I've given what I had to give. I gave it all to Lord Darlington,' p. 243). His new friend bucks him up: 'You've got to enjoy yourself. The evening's the best part of the day. You've done your day's work. Now you can put your feet up and enjoy it' (p. 244). Duly bucked up, Stevens resolves to return to Mr Farraday's service in a new spirit—what he thinks of as a 'bantering spirit'.

It is gallant, but, as we apprehend, doomed. Stevens can no more banter than he can fly in the air. Ishiguro's narrative mixes pathos and unconscious comedy marvellously. Over the six days' confessions, we gradually put together a portrait of the dignified, breaking-down, noble 'upper servant'—his little snobberies, intense professional pride and essential goodness.

From indirect comments and parenthetic recollections, we build up a picture of Lord Darlington, to whom Stevens has, as he says, given his all. Traumatised by the carnage of the First World War, Darlington laboured to build Anglo-German *entente* in the interwar years. Never a fascist (Oswald Mosley visited Darlington not more than three times, Stevens recollects), he may have been anti-Semitic (Stevens rather glosses over an episode in which he was obliged, at his employer's instruction, to dismiss a Jewish maid).

Darlington seems to have occupied the grey area between British Fascism and Chamberlain's Appeasement. He was not, apparently, interned during World War Two. But he was savagely attacked in the press. After the war he sued for libel. As Stevens recalls (to Mrs Benn, or 'Miss Kenton' as he insists on thinking of her):

'His lordship sincerely believed he would get justice. Instead, of course, the newspaper simply increased its circulation. And his lordship's good name was destroyed for ever . . . afterwards, well, his lordship was virtually an invalid. And the house became so quiet. I would take him tea in the drawing room and, well . . . It really was most tragic to see.' (p. 235)

We can work out that, shattered by the humiliation, Darlington died in 1946 and the Hall passed to its new, alien owner—who does not really understand about butlers.

A comic climax occurs on 'Day Three—Evening; Moscombe, near Tavistock, Devon'. In the 'bed and breakfast' where he is staying, Stevens gets drawn into a political discussion. He drops the names of visitors to Darlington Hall in its glory days: Mr Churchill and Mr Eden. His listeners—although he does not intend to deceive—take him for a great man, or possibly a poseur (the local doctor, who drops by, is particularly suspicious). Drawn out—and heated by the beer he has drunk— Stevens makes the injudiciously boastful statement (apropos his meeting 'Mr Churchill'), 'I tended to concern myself with international affairs more than domestic ones. Foreign policy, that is to say' (p. 187).

This points to the major vacancy in the narrative—a vacancy so glaring that it must be intended. We can work out the date of Stevens's expedition exactly from the subtitle to the opening section, 'Prologue: July 1956, Darlington Hall', and the information which Stevens gives us in his first paragraph: 'Mr Farraday took the opportunity to inform me that he had just that moment finalized plans to return to the

United States for a period of five weeks between August and September' (p. 3). At the end of the narrative, we learn that 'Mr Farraday will not himself be back for a further week' (p. 245). Stevens's six days, therefore, are at the end of August or the beginning of September 1956.

Ominous dates. Consider the following timetable of the big events of 1956: July 26, in Egypt, President Nasser announces nationalisation of the Suez Canal (owned partly by France and Britain); 31 July, Britain, France and the USA retaliate with economic sanctions; 16 August, international conference on the Suez crisis in London comes up with the 'Dulles Plan'; 9 September, Nasser rejects the Dulles Plan for international control of the Suez Canal; 19 September, a second London Conference on Suez; 29 October, after prolonged secret negotiation with Britain and France, Israel invades Egypt; 30 October, Britain and France present an ultimatum to Egypt, and start bombing next day. Public outcry over the Suez war (and American pressure) leads to Anthony Eden's resignation, 9 January 1957.

Kazuo Ishiguro was two years old and living in Nagasaki in 1956. But from July to September the Suez crisis dominated British current affairs.[2] Nowhere, however, is it mentioned in *Remains of the Day*. And none the less Stevens boasts, 'I tended to concern myself with foreign affairs.' Not only is this the biggest foreign affair since September 1939, it means the end of Stevens's world. If there is a watershed in British postwar history—a moment when the old order finally collapsed—it is September 1956. Why this blind spot in the novel?

It is there, one may be sure, for an artful purpose. With typical indirection, Ishiguro hints the major points that his novel is making. Stevens is not returning to a golden evening (the remains of his day at Darlington Hall). He is walking off the end of a plank. He does not know it, but there are no remains—except in the sense of 'corpse'. Secondly, Ishiguro delicately points an irony. Eden was driven in his mad Suez adventure by the demons of Munich—the sense that there must be no 'appeasement'. His favourite rallying call was that Nasser was Hitler all over again. But, unlike 1938, this was an occasion on which diplomacy, international co-operation—'appeasement', if you like—was exactly the right policy to have adopted. Lord Darlington's policies of discussion and *détente*, so tragically wrong in the 1920s and 1930s, would have been precisely right in autumn 1956. Who knows, if Eden had followed them, the world of Darlington Hall might have survived a decade or two longer.

How Old Is Beloved?

For students of English, there are few texts as baffling in seminar discussion as Toni Morrison's 1987 novel, *Beloved*. Powerful as the narrative is, there are details which slip infuriatingly away from the reader. If one were a registrar of births and deaths, the question in the title would be easy. The child, later to be called Beloved (after the epithet on her gravestone), is born to the slave, Sethe, in 1854.[1] While still a 'crawling baby' Beloved's throat was cut by her mother, to preserve her from the worse fate—slavery. According to the actuarial record, Beloved died at one year old.

The novel opens in Ohio in 1873, after the Civil War and Emancipation, nineteen years after Beloved's birth. Sethe is living at 124 Bluestone Road, with her daughter Denver and her lover (once a fellow slave at 'Sweet Home'), Paul D. The house at 124 has been haunted by a 'baby's venom'—the poltergeist Beloved.

The main action of the novel, in so far as it can be reconstructed, involves two exorcisms of Beloved. She seems to be banished after the arrival of Paul D., his reunion with Sethe and the sexual relations which follow. But then, after an idyllic day at a carnival, when Sethe, Denver and Paul D. return to 124 Bluestone, Beloved is discovered sitting at their gate. Finally, she is exorcised by the wise black women (white witches) of the suburb.

The problem is, the revenant Beloved seems to veer from being a little girl to being a full-blown, sexual woman. In the following episode, for example, between Denver and Beloved the ghost—by her antics and in her size ('half' as big as Denver, her elder sister)—is clearly a child:

Upstairs Beloved was dancing. A little two-step, two-step, make-a-new-step, slide, slide and strut on down.

Denver sat on the bed smiling and providing the music.

She had never seen Beloved this happy. She had seen her pouty lips open wide with the pleasure of sugar or some piece of news Denver gave her. She had felt warm satisfaction radiating from Beloved's skin when she listened to her mother talk about the old days. But gaiety she had never seen. Not ten minutes had passed since Beloved had fallen backward to the floor, pop-eyed, thrashing and holding her throat. Now, after a few seconds lying in Denver's bed, she was up and dancing.

'Where'd you learn to dance?' Denver asked her.

'Nowhere. Look at me do this.' Beloved put her fists on her hips and commenced to skip on bare feet. Denver laughed.

'Now you. Come on,' said Beloved. 'You may as well just come on.' Her black skirt swayed from side to side.

Denver grew ice-cold as she rose from the bed. She knew she was twice Beloved's size, but she floated up, cold and light as a snowflake. (p. 74)[2]

And yet the Beloved who is encountered on the family's return from the carnival is just as clearly an eighteen-year-old: sexually mature and full of a grown woman's 'venom'. A solution can be found in Morrison's dazzling last section in which Beloved's existence is remembered and forgotten and merged into the mass ('sixty million and more', as Morrison's dedication reminds us) who have been lost to memory. The novel ends with a striking image: 'Down by the stream in back of 124 her footprints come and go, come and go. They are so familiar. Should a child, an adult place his feet in them, they will fit. Take them out and they disappear again as though nobody ever walked there' (p. 275).

As I understand this, this fleeing footprint is both large and small. A child and adult foot will fit it equally snugly. So too, Beloved is baby, girl and woman. It's a fine effect, but it places an unusual strain (that of creating a 'moving image') on the reader. What does Beloved look like? It depends where you are.[3]

Is Jeanette's Mother Gay?

The following is a very small puzzle, and for many readers it may be crystal clear and no puzzle at all. It relates to one of the moments in Jeanette Winterson's *Oranges Are Not the Only Fruit* in which the little heroine is, momentarily, intimately close to her mother. They are reviewing Jeanette's mother's photograph album, specifically 'the two pages called "Old Flames" in the index':

'Why didn't you marry that one, or that one?' I asked, curious.

'They were all wayward men,' she sighed. 'I had a bad time enough finding one that was only a gambler.'

'Why isn't he a gambler now?' I wanted to know, trying to imagine my meek father looking like all the men I'd seen on films.

'He married me and he found the Lord.' Then she sighed and told me the story of each one of the Old Flames; Mad Percy, who drove an open-topped car and asked her to live with him in Brighton; Eddy with the tortoiseshell glasses who kept bees . . . right at the bottom of the page was a yellowy picture of a pretty woman holding a cat.

'Who's that?' I pointed.

'That? Oh just Eddy's sister. I don't know why I put it there,' and she turned the page. Next time we looked, it had gone. (pp. 35–6)[1]

We can guess why she put it there, and why she removed it. As Miss Jewsbury later tells Jeanette: 'that mother of yours [is] a woman of the world, even though she'd never admit it to me. She knows about feelings, especially women's feelings.' This, Jeanette decides, 'wasn't something I wanted to go into' (p. 104).

Miss Jewsbury, of course, turns out to be lesbian. So, as it happens, does every woman or girl Jeanette gets close to: Melanie, Katie, even—incredibly—'Testifying Elsie' (Norris). The difference is that some (like Jeanette, eventually) admit it. Others, like Melanie and (we may infer) Jeanette's mother deny it. All women are lesbians, and those that deny it are lying. It's an aggressive assertion, in terms of its sexual politics; almost as aggressive as Jeanette's mother's assertions about the exclusivity of worthwhile fruit. But, like everything in this delightful book, it's done so tactfully and with such delicate comic touches that even the most male-chauvinist reader acquiesces.

Authors (and Other Experts) Respond

Henry James is not available for comment. Claire Tomalin did the original screenplay for the 1997 film of *The Wings of the Dove* (the script was eventually credited to Hossein Amini). Tomalin was responsible for relocating the action from James's 1901 to high-Edwardian 1910—a setting reflected faithfully in the fashions and technological décor of the film dramatisation. Tomalin was not, apparently, motivated by post-1909 opiate legislation in proposing this significant change of date. The period following Queen Victoria's death in 1901 was drab in terms of British dress; 1910, by contrast, was a phase of peacock-brilliance in British fashion. Tomalin thinks the 'drug-fiend' characterisation of Lionel Croy, later adopted by the film-makers, is 'absurd'. Her hunch is that his 'unspeakable offence' is financial, rather than sexual. 'I'm glad you don't see Mr Croy as another Oscar,' she writes: 'I do admire OW, but the recent canonisation strikes me as absurd . . . My only reservation about your essay is that the Metropolitan Line opened in— I think—1864. Modern young women were taking it *long* before Kate Croy and Merton.'

Patrick Brantlinger, whom I quote extensively in the chapter on *Heart of Darkness*, observes wryly: 'Perhaps Conrad should have named his tale *Heart of Vagueness* . . . My French isn't fluent enough to know just how *l'horreur! l'horreur!* would sound or seem, but in English it *does* sound simultaneously odd, awkward, and somehow absolutely appropriate and profound.' Professor Brantlinger also wonders 'how *Belgian* French differs from standard, and if Conrad—had he chosen to—would or could have utilized that difference'. I have enquired of a Belgian-French speaking colleague, Professor Oscar Mandel, who informs me that Parisians very often do pick up a tincture of Flemish in

his accent—and guess, without being told, that he's Belgian
by origin. But the phonetic variation is small. He also thinks
the ejaculation *'L'horreur!'* would be unnatural in French.
'Horrible!', or the weaker *'Quel horreur!'* would trip off
the Gallic tongue more readily. But the melodramatic 'The
horror!' in either language suits Conrad's portentousness.

My favourite quotation about *Apocalypse Now*, the film
adaptation of *Heart of Darkness*, is from Francis Ford
Coppola, speaking as an award-winner at the 1979 Cannes
Film Festival: 'we were in the jungle, there were too many of
us, we had access to too much money, too much equipment,
and, little by little, we went insane'. Stanislavski would
approve.

On the other Conrad puzzle—the Professor's 'stuff' in
The Secret Agent—I made some enquiries of Christopher
Hampton, who adapted the novel for the 1997 film. He
replied:

Our researches into the matter were nothing like as detailed or far-
reaching as yours. We followed Conrad's indications and I remember
saying I supposed the explosive was some cousin of the nitro-
glycerine that went sloshing over the mountains in *The Wages of
Fear*. I've never heard of picric acid . . . Another puzzle for you is
this: what nationality is Verloc? He's not French (though he can
speak French after five years in a French jail) and in the end we
didn't see why we shouldn't make him English (though the name is
so foreign).

Michael Shelden, Graham Greene's biographer, made a
number of friendly comments about the 'Godfathers' chapter,
observing charitably:

I'm not entirely sure that Puzo, whom I interviewed last year, would
agree that Greene influenced him, but I don't think that matters.
You have a good idea and you argue your case beautifully, so that's
a rare joy in itself as far as I'm concerned. And who can say for
certain whether, in some remote part of his imagination, Puzo was
not absorbing a little inspiration from some half-remembered bit of
Brighton Rock.

Susan Hill, who was authorised by the du Maurier estate to write a sequel to *Rebecca* (*Mrs de Winter*, 1993), commented amusingly on my chapter:

Yes, the problem of the shooting and the boat and all that . . . I was very careful not to get mixed up in it! Mind, I didn't set out to solve the mystery or change anything that had gone before in retrospect, even as you note, down to Mrs de Winter's anonymity. But it doesn't hold water—good analogy in the context—and I think you're right to take it on . . . I don't really think Mrs de Winter's not having a Christian name counts as a puzzle, but makes a useful lead-in. Daphne always said she just couldn't think of the right one, but I daresay there was more to it than that because she had to go through some hoops to avoid anyone naming her. I didn't find it a problem, curiously.

The fire—well, I always assume it was Mrs Danvers and meant to be. Then she scarpered. Conveniently for me later. If she had died in the fire, as one assumes she did in the film, I couldn't have written the sequel because she's such a key character—one would have missed a lot of fun too! The ghost of Rebecca putting a light to the house. Perhaps they did it together—she egging Danny on. Mesmerizing her—'Go on Danny . . . set the torch to it . . . look how it burns! Look how bright! Listen to the flames now! Manderley can never be hers!' You've quite got me back into the swing of it . . . By the by, you might like to take a look at my own ghost story, *The Woman in Black*, some time. There are several puzzles for you in there—only just don't ask me to solve them for you! The time-scheme, the family relationships, the geography, even the railway timetable, might repay investigation!

The alternative ending to *Lucky Jim* was told me by Frank Kermode, who was a colleague of John Wain's (a close friend of Amis and Larkin) at Reading University in the 1950s (this phase of his early career is recalled in Sir Frank's memoirs, *Not Entitled*, 1995). The remark about 'would you like to be the next person to use the phone?' was a Kermode witticism which, as such things do, has stuck in my mind for twenty-five years. I have asked the editor of the forthcoming *Selected Letters of Kingsley Amis*, Zachary Leader, if he has come across this alternative ending to *Lucky Jim* in the author's correspondence. He says no.

On Piggy's vexed spectacles: I am told by a friend at the *TLS* that Charles Monteith, Golding's editor at Faber's (who were brave enough to accept and publish *Lord of the Flies*, although they insisted on changes), pointed the lens problem out to the novelist. But Golding refused to make any correction. Unfortunately, neither Monteith nor Golding is alive to corroborate this story. If true, it would support Christopher Ricks's allegations about 'hubris and overbearing' in the novelist, even at the beginning of his published career.

Julian Barnes was kind enough to comment on the Golding chapter, and to say that 'it strikes me as authoritative':

> The chapter 'E.B.'s Eyes' first appeared in *Vanity Fair*. Their fact-chroniclers bugged the hell out of me. On about the fourth or fifth call, I said, exasperatedly, 'Are you sure you haven't anything else to check?' The reply was, 'No, because we've checked your account of the lecture with Professor Ricks. Actually, we found an error which we communicated to him!' The error in his lecture, as far as I recall, had to do with Hiroshima and Nagasaki, something to do with a John Wain poem.

I asked Jeremy Irons, who plays Humbert Humbert in the latest (Adrian Lyne) film version of *Lolita*, if—as someone who knows Nabokov's character from the inside—he had any comment on the *Lolita* chapter. Mr Irons politely and inscrutably replied that he had read it 'with interest'. A historian of science colleague, Professor Alison Winter, was more forthcoming about what I suggest is Humbert's 'first crime' (frottage) and directed me to the following example from Krafft-Ebing's *Psychopathia Sexualis* (London, 1899).

> Case 180. A *frotteur*. Z., born in 1850, of blameless life previously; of good family; private official. He is well to do financially; untainted. After a short married life he became a widower, in 1873. For some time he had attracted attention in churches, because he crowded up behind women both old and young indifferently, and toyed with their

'bustles'. He was watched, and one day he was arrested in the act. Z. was terribly frightened, and in despair about his situation; and in making a full confession, he begged for pardon, for nothing but suicide remained to him. (p. 32)

Krafft-Ebing concludes: 'The simplest explanation seems to be that *"frottage"* is a masturbatorial act of a hypersexual individual who is uncertain about his virility *in corpore feminae*. This would also explain the motive of the assault being made not *ad anteriora* but *ad posteriora*.' The *modus operandi*, the physical posture and even the Nabokovian redundancy of phrase all fit Humbert snugly. The question as to whether frottage is a 'crime' if committed in private, and without the 'victim' noticing, is still open, I think.

On the 'When is Gilbert Pinfold's Ordeal?' question, Martin Stannard (Waugh's biographer) agreed that 'you have certainly pinpointed major continuity mistakes in *Ordeal*'. But Professor Stannard inclines to the opinion that they are 'mistakes', not, as I would sneakingly like to think, conscious trickery on the novelist's part: 'Surely Waugh just got in a muddle.' Professor Stannard has recently been embroiled in controversy over Muriel Spark's parentage (he is currently writing that author's biography). 'If you want another literary puzzle,' he says, 'have a look at Spark's *The Girls of Slender Means* which appears to have specific dating re: VE and VJ Days, with the general election in between (1945) but which makes (I think) a "continuity mistake".'

J. G. Ballard responded enlighteningly to a version of 'James Ballard's Auto-Erotics' which was published earlier in the *Guardian*, about the time that the movie version of *Crash* was running into its London censorship battles. 'As always,' Mr Ballard writes, with a somewhat two-edged compliment, 'you are full of witty insights that had never occurred to me':

Can I disagree with you on one point? I feel you're a little unfair in saying that Cronenberg had 'bottled out' on the subject of Elizabeth Taylor—this certainly wasn't due to any lack of courage on Cronenberg's part . . . He and I talked through the Taylor problem before he began his script, and he pointed out that Taylor herself is no longer the magnetic presence that so obsessed Vaughan 25 years ago. But finding a replacement would be virtually impossible—no actress in today's climate would be prepared to play herself in a film in which she is stalked by a psychopath eager to die in a car crash with her. The only option would be to introduce an invented film star, but this would defuse the magic that an established star generates. The invented star would also be competing with real film stars in the persons of Holly Hunter and Rosanna Arquette. I think Cronenberg more than made up for the deficit with his James Dean death-drive recreation, which expresses in a short scene the obsession with celebrity that is an important strand in the book—in any case, the film is so pure and hard-edged that it transcends the Taylor absence—I think of it as the first 21st century film.

Yes, Cape were amazingly unworried and had only just published my *Atrocity Exhibition*—a potential lawyers' field day. The ellipses were mine. You were absolutely right about Western Avenue, though in fact I do like motorways, along with U.S. cars in general.

On 'Poirot's Double-Death' the Belgian detective's 'biographer', Ann Hart, responded sympathetically and expertly. She also discovered a 'whodunnit' within the 'whodunnit':

I'm intrigued with your idea that someone erased (most of) time from *Curtain*. But who? It's well known that Christie resisted editing, even copy editing, but by the time of *Curtain's* publication she was really getting out of touch with affairs. An amanuensis? I suspect it was her son-in-law, Anthony Hicks, who she trusted greatly and is just the sort of person, from my brief acquaintance, who would happily settle down to such a task (as I recall, Agatha Christie in her autobiography wrote that Anthony reminded her of Uncle Davy in *Love in a Cold Climate* and I could see why). In view of your thesis, it would be very interesting to see the original manuscript of *Curtain*.

You know, *Curtain* is such an odd book. Ironically it has an air of senility about it and yet it was written at the height of Christie's powers. I remember now how that bothered me.

Malcolm Bradbury, David Lodge, and Martin Amis were courteous enough to comment on and correct details in the 'Hitchcock Hallmark' chapter. Professor Bradbury wrote:

I greatly enjoyed 'The Hitchcock Hallmark'. It's a very fair and accurate account of *The History Man* and the reasons for the self-presence. 'I' have to sacrifice the plot of fiction to the plot of history, so there *is* fatality. One place this comes from—though obliged to different premises—is Diderot's *Jacques the Fatalist*, and I'm writing on Diderot at this moment. There is (as in *Therapy*) another allusion, or a twist, in my preface or author's note; which takes a more sanguine view, I now notice. Of course you get your five pounds, I hope from Weidenfeld . . . Who first attempted the trick? Yes, Hitchcock's nice, but [it was] Diderot in *Jacques the Fatalist*.

Professor Bradbury points out another witty self-insertion in his *Doctor Criminale* and politely reminds me that 'I wrote an article on this, "The Novelist as Impresario", in *No, Not Bloomsbury*. Could it have been in your mind?'

It should have been. David Lodge observes in his letter that he earlier pointed out in print the irruption of the self-portrait in *The History Man* in 'The Novel Now', reprinted in *After Bakhtin* (p. 19) and in the next essay, 'Mimesis and Diegesis in Modern Fiction' (p. 43). There goes my five pounds. Professor Lodge makes the point that, as regards the self-irruption in *Therapy*, 'it might be worth mentioning that I wrote and presented a TV documentary film about the pilgrimage, *The Way of St James*, for the BBC, shown in 1993. Produced and directed by David Willcock.'

'Where did the device come from?'—David Lodge notes, 'I touch on this question in the two essays mentioned above. There are near precedents in Sterne, but the earliest clear example in modern fiction I know is in Nabokov's *King, Queen, Knave*.' He concludes:

By the way, have you overlooked the appearance of Malcolm [Bradbury] and myself in *Small World* at the MLA cocktail party (pp. 331–2 of the Penguin Edition), dividing up the academic world between us? I don't know if this has been noted in print—reviewers certainly didn't. We did actually attend together the 1978 MLA convention mentioned in the epigraph.

Martin Amis, on the subject of his self-presentation in *Money*, wrote to offer 'many thanks . . . I look forward to reading [your remarks] when I have a moment'. Interestingly, Zachary Leader points out that Kingsley Amis wrote a novel in 1948–9 called 'The Legacy' which was rejected by some fourteen publishers, has never been put into print, and has a hero called 'Kingsley Amis'.

Frederick Forsyth wrote most informatively about *The Odessa File*. His recollections add considerably to one's respect for the perceptiveness of that novel and its efficacy in bringing an egregious evil-doer to justice:

I actually researched considerably more than was printed, but Hutchinson asked me to excise some 20,000 words from the original text, most of it in the form of sidebar anecdotes thrown up by the research. Nowadays I might get away with insisting, but not then. The cut-out material would, they felt, slow up the thrust of the main narrative which, of course, was the hunting down of Roschmann.

Roschmann really existed and did all he was alleged to have done. He was eventually exposed in Argentina by a neighbour who had read the book [*The Odessa File*] in Spanish in 1978. He fled north to the safe haven of Paraguay but the strain was too much and he died of a massive heart attack on the ferry across the Rio Paraguay. Two inspectors from Vienna went over to confirm identification with finger-prints, dental impressions and my own description of the two missing toes due to frostbite. A most satisfying episode.

Anyway, some more stuff about the missing Nazi gold was in the material excised in spring 1972 which, with hindsight, was a pity.

I know about Goldhagen but he does not make me change my view. Ironically it was the Jewish Nazi-hunter Simon Wiesenthal who persuaded me that the *Gesamtschuld* (collective guilt) myth was just that—a myth.

David Morrell replied at length (and with some welcome factual corrections) on 'The Curious Career of Rambo's Knife'. 'It's very interesting,' Dr Morrell noted:

The issue of the knives is a complex one. When Pauline Kael reviewed the second movie, she was given a press kit that included my novelization. She quoted my perhaps overstated comment about the knives being works of art and quipped that she could hardly wait for her set to arrive. When I was a kid, I remember seeing an

Alan Ladd movie called *The Iron Mistress*, a very loose version of the life of American frontierist, Jim Bowie. Basically, the climax of the movie involved the invention and manufacture of the famous Bowie knife. As an adult, I would see the many so-called authentic Bowie knives, but they always looked cheap and clumsy compared to the idealized version that had appeared in the movie. Anyhow, in 1984, when I was shown the knife that was to be used in the second Rambo movie (and also shown at the same time the knife from the first movie) I had a reaction a little like what I had when I watched *The Iron Mistress*. The knives in each movie got bigger, of course, and one could joke that if there was a fourth movie, Rambo would be wielding a sword, but in spite of the ungainliness of the third one (which won an award for the best designed new knife of 1988), I continue to feel that if looked at abstractedly as utilitarian objects given an artistic design, they are all remarkable. Jimmy Lile and Gil Hibbens each gave me presentation copies and the tension between purpose and design is remarkable—almost Dadaesque. Given the events that you mention that occurred since then and given the smothering politically correct environment in which anything off-center is condemned, I'm not sure I'd make the same issue about the knives now as I did then. But I'm glad I own the knives.

'Serious knife collectors', he insists, 'are *not* gun nuts.'

Dr Morrell makes a number of other relevant and interesting points. He notes, for example, 'that an alternate ending [to *First Blood*] was filmed, tested, and rejected in which Rambo kills himself'. On the two, post-*First Blood*, novelisations which I suggest might be ghost-written, Morrell writes:

It's a complex issue. The screenplays were so paper thin in terms of texture that I did the novelizations to add a measure of characterization to something that had none at all. I was hampered by the plots, but some individual scenes work well, I think, especially the first of each book.

On the *Gravity's Rainbow* chapter I had no response from Thomas Pynchon and, as I say, a signed photograph—enigmatically unaccompanied by any other communication—from Mickey Rooney.

On *The Sea, The Sea*, Murdoch's biographer, Peter Conradi,

informs me that the novelist and her husband often holidayed with friends in the West Country, but that his (Conradi's) geographer colleague—surveying the internal evidence of the novel—came up with 'NE, and SE; but your point about sunset completes the compass and adds the W. too!' In an article on 'Iris Murdoch and the Sea' (published in the *Revue de la Société d'Etudes Anglaises Contemporaines*, June 1994) Professor Conradi expresses, much more eloquently than I can, the fascination of the sea for Murdoch:

The sea is the ideal concrete metaphor for Murdoch's own *ozeanisches Gefühl*, the zone of contingency, the mother of forms, a figure for the sublime, pointing alike to the changeability and to the beauty of the world which we share, but which we do not, in her view, in our confusion and anxiety, always accurately apprehend.

During a standing-room-only lecture which she gave to students at UCL in January 1998, I asked A. S. Byatt about the 'horticulturally overloaded' coda to *Possession* and whether it should be conceived as occurring in Ash's mind. She said that her Danish translator had made the point to her that all these flowers did not bloom either in May, or at the same time. According to Byatt what she intended at this moment in the novel was to construct the 'omniscient narrator of Victorian fiction'—the godlike George Eliot persona, for example. The same 'Victorian' narrator presides in the young lovers' Yorkshire idyll. The novel ends wrapped in the earlier period's aesthetics, as confident and ornate as William Morris floral wall-paper.

In an earlier conference, in 1997, at the Open University, I asked Alan Sillitoe about the efficacy of gin-and-hot-bath abortion. When he wrote *Saturday Night and Sunday Morning*, did *he* think it was a sovereign remedy. 'I thought it was,' he replied, with an ironic stress on 'thought'.

I showed the *Trainspotting* chapter ('When exactly does Rents read Kierkegaard?') to a colleague, Kasia Boddy, who specialises in modern Scottish writing. She made the striking point that references to Kierkegaard abound in contemporary

Scottish fiction. She cited examples of heroes immersing themselves in the gloomy Scandinavian sage in James Kelman's *A Disaffection* (1989) and William McIlvanney's *Laidlaw* (1977). In the last, the hero has a locked drawer in his desk 'where he kept Kierkegaard, Camus and Unamuno, like *caches* of alcohol'. She directed me to this charming little poem by Scottish poet Tom Leonard:

I Said

I said 'I'm fed up with funny things'
I said Listen. Heh beautiful.
Listen

The concept of irony   Right?
Kierkegaard.   Right? Aye
Well then.
Don't say I didn't tell you.

I wrote to Irvine Welsh, bringing Dr Boddy's observation to his attention and suggesting that perhaps this preoccupation with Kierkegaard owed something to the obligatory 'moral philosophy' element in the Scottish 'Ordinary' MA degree. I received the politely negative reply from Mr Welsh: 'Dear John: Many thanks for your letter. In answer to your colleague's inquiry, I had no idea there was moral philosophy in the Scottish MA. It must be Caledonian existentialist tendencies. Best Wishes, Irvine'. He's probably right. I must get an English PhD student to work on it.

Equally terse, and piquant was a postcard from Jeanette Winterson, decorated with oranges, in reply to my chapter ('Is Jeanette's Mother Gay?'): 'Dear John Sutherland, Who knows? Best Wishes, J.W.'

Notes

The Joy of Puzzles

1. Brian Boyd, *Vladimir Nabokov: the American Years* (New York, 1991), p. 174.
2. See John Sutherland, *Is Heathcliff a Murderer?* (Oxford, 1996).
3. See William Boyd, *On the Yankee Station* (London, 1981).
4. Julian Barnes, *Flaubert's Parrot* (1984, repr. London 1985).

The Wings of the Dove

1. My belief is that Milly dies of a weak heart. The clue is Kate's pointing to Merton's watch (his 'ticker'), in his left-hand waistcoat pocket, when explaining what Milly's mysterious ailment is.
2. References are to *The Wings of the Dove* (London, 'Everyman Edition', 1997), ed. Cheryl B. Torsney.
3. See, for example, Virginia Berridge and Griffith Edwards, *Opium and the People* (London, 1981).
4. Eve Kosovsky Sedgwick, *Tendencies* (London, 1994), p. 75.
5. For the 'outing' of the master himself see Sheldon M. Novick, *Henry James: the Young Master* (New York 1996); John R. Bradley, 'Henry James's Permanent Adolescence', *Essays in Criticism*, October 1997, pp. 287–314.
6. 'Henry James: the Master and the "queer affair" in "The Pupil"', *Henry James: the Shorter Fiction, Reassessments*, ed. N. H. Reeve, p. 120.
7. Richard Ellmann, *Oscar Wilde* (1984, repr. New York, 1988), p. 390.

Heart of Darkness

1. Page references are to *Heart of Darkness* (1899, 'Casebook Edition', repr. New York, 1989), ed. Ross C. Murfin.
2. Patrick Brantlinger, *The Rule of Darkness* (Ithaca and London, 1988), p. 257.
3. See Norman Sherry, *Conrad's Eastern World* (London, 1966).

4. Margaret Lane, *Edgar Wallace: the Biography of a Phenomenon* (1938, repr. London 1964), pp. 179–80.

5. Ironically *Heart of Darkness* has recently been branded as itself a 'racist text' by Chinua Achebe. See Brantlinger, pp. 255, 274.

6. Fitzgerald's discussion of the 1976 film (with screenplay by Francis Ford Coppola and John Milius) is included in *Past Imperfect: History According to the Movies*, ed. Mark C. Carnes (New York, 1979). See pp. 285–7.

The Four Just Men

1. References are to *The Four Just Men*, ed. David Glover (1905, repr. 'Oxford Popular Classics', Oxford, 1995).

2. The 'locked-room mystery' goes back to Edgar Allan Poe's 'Murders in the Rue Morgue'. See Julian Symons, *Bloody Murder* (1972, repr. London, 1985), p. 87.

3. The first immigration-control measures were introduced into the UK in 1905 with the Aliens Act.

The Secret Agent

1. Norman Sherry, *Conrad's Western World* (London, 1971).

2. References are to *The Secret Agent*, ed. Roger Tennant (1907, repr. 'World's Classics Edition', Oxford, 1983).

3. The date on Winnie's wedding ring is '1879' (see p. 309) and, as we discover, the Verlocs have been married for seven years. This gives a narrative time setting of 1886.

4. Quoted in Arthur Marshall, *Explosives* (London, 1917), II, 342.

5. See Frederick Forsyth, *The Fourth Protocol* (London, 1984).

Women in Love

1. References are to *Women in Love* (1920, 'Everyman Edition', repr. London, 1990), ed. Linda Ruth Williams.

2. Kurt Vonnegut Jr, *Slaughterhouse Five* (1968, repr. New York, 1984), p. 1.

3. Reed's remarks sparked off a lively exchange of letters about the date of the action of *Women in Love* in the *TLS*, in late 1969 and early 1970.

4. This possible line of communication is suggested by George Ford in a letter to the *TLS*, 12 Feb. 1970.

Ulysses

1. Hugh Kenner, 'Molly's Masterstroke', *James Joyce Quarterly* (Fall 1972), repr. *Ulysses: Fifty Years of Criticism*, ed. Thomas F. Staley (Indiana, 1974), pp. 19–28.
2. References are to *Ulysses* (1922, 'Penguin Edition', repr. London, 1968).
3. Margaret Honton, 'Molly's Mistressstroke', *James Joyce Quarterly* (Fall 1976), pp. 25–6.

To the Lighthouse

1. References are to *To the Lighthouse* (1927, 'Penguin Edition', repr. London, 1964).
2. George Eliot, *Middlemarch* (1872, repr. Oxford, 1988), p. 682.

Whose Body?

1. References are to *Whose Body?* (1923, repr. London, 1968).
2. See Janet Hitchman, *Such a Strange Lady* (London, 1975), p. 62; Janet Brabazon, *Dorothy L. Sayers* (London, 1981), p. 87.

The Big Sleep

1. Faulkner later won the Nobel Prize for Literature; Brackett was unusual in screenwriting in being a woman. She is best known as a writer of science fiction.
2. Tom Hiney, *Raymond Chandler: a Biography* (London, 1997), p. 163. Other biographies have the less dramatic reply, 'I don't know.'
3. References are to *The Big Sleep* (1938, repr. London, 1983).

Rebecca

1. See Hitchcock, in *Hitchcock* by F. Truffaut with the collaboration of H. G. Scott (New York, 1967), p. 178: 'Of course, there's a terrible flaw in the story which our friends, the plausibles, never picked up. On the night when the boat with Rebecca's body in it is found, a rather unlikely coincidence is revealed: on the very evening she is supposed to have drowned, another woman's body is picked up two miles down the beach. And this enables the hero to identify that second body as his wife's. Why wasn't there an inquest

at the time the unknown woman's body was discovered?'
Hitchcock cut du Maurier's 'two months' to the same day;
but the 'flaw' pre-exists in the novel.

2. References are to *Rebecca* (1938, repr. London, 1982).
3. The novelist's own lesbianism was revealed to posterity
   in Margaret Forster's biography, *Daphne du Maurier*
   (London, 1993).
4. See *Rebecca*, pp. 293, 312.

Brighton Rock

1. References are to *Brighton Rock* (1938, repr. London, 1980).
2. Greene's emendations to the text of *Brighton Rock* are
   detailed by Leon Higden, in ' "I try to be accurate": the Text
   of Greene's *Brighton Rock*', in *Essays in Graham Greene*,
   ed. Peter Wolfe (Florida, 1987), pp. 169–86.
3. *Brighton Rock* (1938, repr. London, 1970), p. xi.

Lucky Jim

1. David Lodge, *The Language of Fiction* (1966, revised and
   repr. London 1984), p. 255.
2. References are to *Lucky Jim* (1954, repr. London, 1985).
3. See, for instance, Bertrand's references to the Labour
   Government and the Mossadeq-inspired Persian oil crisis
   (p. 50). This is clearly some time before the Attlee administration lost power in 1951.

Lord of the Flies

1. References are to *Lord of the Flies* (1954, repr. London,
   1960).
2. R. M. Ballantyne, *The Coral Island* (1858, repr. Oxford,
   1990), ed. J. S. Bratton, p. 29.
3. Christopher Ricks, *Essays in Appreciation* (Oxford, 1997),
   p. 307.
4. Julian Barnes, *Flaubert's Parrot* (1984, repr. London,
   1985), p. 76.
5. *The Coral Island*, p. 340.
6. This observation is made by C. B. Cox in the opening of his
   discussion of *Lord of the Flies* in the 'Macmillan Casebook'
   on the novel, ed. Norman Page (London, 1985).

7. See page 22. A description of the early draft of *Lord of the Flies* is given in *The Reader's Companion to the Twentieth-Century Novel*, ed. Peter Parker (London, 1994), reporting a publisher who rejected Golding's manuscript with the dismissive comment: 'Absurd and uninteresting fantasy about the explosion of an atomic bomb on the colonies and a group of children who land in jungle country near New Guinea'.

8. William Golding served in the Royal Navy during World War II, in cruisers and minesweepers.

The Old Man and the Sea

1. References are to *The Old Man and the Sea* (1952, repr. New York, 1987).

2. Joseph was the eighth of nine children (and the fourth of five sons) of Joseph Paul DiMaggio, a crab fisherman in Martinez, California.

3. DiMaggio retired soon after helping his team to victory in 1949.

Lolita

1. References are to *Lolita* (1959, repr. London, 1995), ed. Alfred Appel Jr.

The Ordeal of Gilbert Pinfold

1. References are to *The Ordeal of Gilbert Pinfold* (1957, repr. London, 1962).

2. Martin Stannard, *Evelyn Waugh (1939–1966): No Abiding City* (London, 1992), p. 348. In Stannard's analysis, Waugh's breakdown was precipitated less by bromide poisoning than incipient schizophrenia.

A Clockwork Orange

1. Anthony Burgess, *You've Had Your Time* (London, 1990), p. 7.

2. Anthony Burgess, *Little Wilson and Big God* (London, 1986), p. 301.

3. *You've Had Your Time*, p. 21.

4. In Burgess's complex amalgam of Catholic belief, Augustinian conviction of original sin is in perpetual conflict with

more benign Pelagian belief in human goodness. See *You've Had Your Time*, pp. 32–3.

5. *You've Had Your Time*, p. 27.

6. See ibid, pp. 244–6.

7. A good question. Burgess claims to have overheard a cockney call something 'as queer as a clockwork orange', meaning 'as unnatural as a three-dollar bill'. There is no sexual overtone.

8. References are to *A Clockwork Orange* (1962, repr. London, 1974).

Crash

1. References are to *Crash* (1973, repr. London, 1975). David Cronenberg's screenplay was published by Faber (London, 1997).

Curtain

1. Anne Hart, *Agatha Christie's Hercule Poirot* (London, 1991), pp. 3–4.

2. The *New York Times* accorded Poirot a front-page 'obituary', 6 Aug. 1975.

3. Agatha Christie, *The ABC Murders* (London, 1935), p. 1.

4. Hart, p. 3.

5. References are to *Curtain: Poirot's Last Case* (1975, repr. London 1993).

The History Man

1. References are to *The History Man* (London, 1975).

2. See Malcolm Bradbury, *Unsent Letters* (London, 1988), pp. 154–8.

3. References are to *Therapy* (1995, repr. London, 1995).

4. References are to *Money* (1984, repr. London, 1985).

5. References are to *Slaughterhouse Five* (1968, repr. New York, 1984).

The Odessa File

1. Ted Morgan, *William Burroughs: Literary Outlaw* (New York, 1988), p. 353.

2. References are to the edition of *The Odessa File* (1972) reprinted in *Frederick Forsyth: the Four Novels* (London, 1982).

First Blood

1. References are to *First Blood* (1972, repr. New York, 1973).
2. References are to David Morrell, *Rambo: First Blood Part II* (based on a screenplay by Sylvester Stallone and James Cameron, New York, 1985).
3. References are to David Morrell, *Rambo III* (based on a screenplay by Sylvester Stallone and Sheldon Lettich, New York, 1988).

Gravity's Rainbow

1. References are to *Gravity's Rainbow* (New York, 1973).
2. See Malcolm X, with the assistance of Alex Haley, *The Autobiography of Malcolm X* (1965, repr. London, 1968), chapters 3 and 4, pp. 121–40.
3. See Mee, p. 41.
4. Mickey Rooney, *I.E.: An Autobiography* (New York, 1965), p. 158.
5. Ibid, p. 149.

The Sea, The Sea

1. References are to *The Sea, The Sea* (1978, repr. London, 1984.)

Neuromancer

1. Alvin Toffler, *Future Shock* (1970, repr. New York, 1971), p. 434.
2. See Norbert Wiener, *Cybernetics: or, Control and Communication in the Animal and the Machine* (New York, 1948).
3. References are to *Neuromancer* (1984, repr. London, 1995).
4. Marshall McCluhan, *The Gutenberg Galaxy* (1962, repr. New York, 1969), p. 295.

The Bonfire of the Vanities

1. References are to *The Bonfire of the Vanities* (New York, 1987).

American Psycho

1. References are to *American Psycho* (London, 1991).
2. See Patrick's reference (p. 6) to the Challenger space shuttle disaster, which occurred on 28 Jan. 1986.

Possession

1. References are to *Possession* (1990, repr. London, 1991).
2. See Thomas Carlyle, *Reminiscences*, ed. K. J. Fielding and Ian Campbell (Oxford, 1997), p. x.

Midnight's Children

1. References are to *Midnight's Children* (1981, repr. London, 1982).

Rising Sun

1. References are to *Naked Lunch* (1959, repr. London, 1993).
2. Ted Morgan, *William Burroughs: Literary Outlaw* (New York, 1988), p. 355.
3. References are to *Saturday Night and Sunday Morning* (1958, repr. London, 1994).

The Firm

1. References are to *The Firm* (1991, repr. London, 1993).
2. I suspect that Grisham was a long time writing his novel.

Trainspotting

1. References are to *Trainspotting* (1993, repr. London, 1994).

Original Sin

1. References are to *Original Sin* (1994, repr. London, 1996).

Death Is Now My Neighbour

1. References are to *Death Is Now My Neighbour* (1996, repr. London, 1997).
2. Rumours in newspapers in March 1998 that Morse was to be revived, as a married man, provoked mock-rage; see Allison Pearson, *Evening Standard*, 18 March: 'There should be a law against it.'

The English Patient

1. References are to *The English Patient* (1992, repr. London, 1993).
2. As Ondaatje explains (see p. 164), du Maurier's novel *Rebecca* was used as a code-book by the German spy Eppler, the hero of Follett's novel.
3. The film dates this episode on the eve of the battle of Alamein, 23 Oct.–4 Nov. 1942.
4. In the film Minghella blurs over the period Almasy spends with the Bedouin, making it plausible that Forsyth can infer that it comprises only 'weeks'.

The Remains of the Day

1. References are to *The Remains of the Day* (1989, repr. London, 1990).
2. As an eighteen-year-old schoolboy I recall a general fever of public discussion about the Suez crisis, from August onwards.

Beloved

1. In *The Voices of Toni Morrison* (Ohio, 1991), Barbara Hill Rigney points out that we never know Beloved's birth-name: 'Beloved has no identity other than that merged with the "sixty million and more" of the dedication' (p. 41).
2. References are to *Beloved* (1987, repr. London, 1988).
3. There are reports of a film in production, sponsored by Oprah Winfrey and W. Goldberg. It will be interesting to see how they handle Beloved's age and appearance.

Oranges Are Not the Only Fruit

1. References are to *Oranges Are Not the Only Fruit* (1985, repr. London, 1986).